MICHAEL WIESE PRODUCTIONS
www.mwp.com

Since 1981, Michael Wiese Productions has been dedicated to providing novice and seasoned filmmakers with vital information on all aspects of filmmaking and videomaking. We have published more than 50 books, used in over 500 film schools worldwide.

Our authors are successful industry professionals — they believe that the more knowledge and experience they share with others, the more high-quality films will be made. That's why they spend countless hours writing about the hard stuff: budgeting, financing, directing, marketing, and distribution. Many of our authors, including myself, are often invited to conduct filmmaking seminars around the world.

We truly hope that our publications, seminars, and consulting services will empower you to create enduring films that will last for generations to come.

We're here to help. Let us hear from you.

Sincerely,

Michael Wiese
Publisher, Filmmaker

MARTIN ROTH

the

WRITER'S
PARTNER

for
Fiction,
Television,
and
Screen

Third Edition

The Writer's Partner Roth

Published by Michael Wiese Productions
11288 Ventura Blvd., Suite 821
Studio City CA 91604
818.379.8799   fax: 818.986.3408
mw@mwp.com
www.mwp.com

Cover design: Art Hotel

Printed by McNaughton & Gunn, Inc., Saline, Michigan
Manufactured in the United States of America

ISBN: 0-941188-32-9

Library of Congress Cataloging-in-Publication Data

Roth, Martin, 1924–2000
    The writer's partner / by Martin Roth
        p. cm.
    Originally published: The writer's partner for fiction, television, and screen.
    2nd ed. San Diego, CA. Index Publishing Group. 1997.
    Includes bibliographical references.
    ISBN: 0-941188-32-9
    1. Fiction—Authorship. 2. Fiction—Technique. 3. Television authorship.
    4. Motion picture authorship. I. Roth, Martin. 1924–2000. The writer's partner for
    fiction, television, and screen. II. Title. III. The fiction writer's silent partner.

PN3355 R68 2001
808.3—dc21

Dedication

This Third Edition, published posthumously,
is dedicated with honor to my late husband Marty Roth
who inspired so many to accomplish so much.

Marjorie Roth

Contents

Foreword 18

Prologue (Martin Roth's original introduction to the Second Edition) 19

Introduction to the Third Edition 20

Putting Your Writer's Partner to Work for You 21

1. The Story First 23

    Backstory, Links, Arcs, the Clock, and Subplots 24

2. Characters and Development 26

    Let's Talk People 26

    Getting the Protagonist Up and Down the Tree 27

    Who's Throwing the Rocks? 28

    Not all Protagonists and Antagonists are Human! 28

    Does the Situation Decide the Characters or Do the Characters Initiate the Situation? Which Comes First, the Chicken or the Egg? 29

    Character Background 32

        Place of Origin 32

        Parents 32

        Childhood 33

        Family Members 33

        Education 33

        Behavior 33

        Hobbies, Special Skills, or Knowledge 34

        Bad Habits 35

    General Characteristics 35

        Mental and Physical Characteristics 37

        General Physical Characteristics 38

        Facial Characteristics 38

        Skin and Complexion 39

        Hair 39

Overall Appearance 39
Moral Characteristics 40
Relationships 40
Marital Status 40
Current Lifestyle 41
Home or Dwelling 41
Vehicles 41
Professions and Jobs 42
Male Characters—Dominant 44
Female Characters—Dominant 45
Names 45
Most Common Names 45
Female Names—General 45
Male Names—General 47
Nicknames—Male and Female 49
Female Names in Five Languages 50
Male Names in Five Languages 51

3. Storytelling and Plotting   **53**
Storyteller, You Are God! 53
The Theme 54
Primary Purpose, Secondary Actions, and Counteractions 56
Primary Goals 57
Deliberate Involvement 58
Nondeliberate Involvement 60
Secondary Actions and Counteractions 61
Conflict 61
Examples of Conflicts 62
Secondary Story—The Subplot 63
Using the Subplot List 63
Suggested Subplot Themes 64
The Clock is Ticking 65
The Rocky Road—The Obstacles Along the Way 66

Suspense 67
Crisis, Surprise—A Twist Is On the Rise 68
The Beginning of the End—Crises and Climaxes 71
Resolutions and Solutions 72

4. Switching   **74**
Switch Another Story to Generate a New, Fresh One! 74

5. Action and Adventure   **77**
Disasters 77
Characters in Action/Adventure Stories 78
Story Lines 78

6. Cops and Robbers (and Other Villains)   **80**
The Cops 83
The Private Eye 85
Law and the Courtroom 86

7. The Firefighters   **88**
Summary of Operations 88
Units 88
Personnel 89
Emergency Medical Services 89
Dispatches 89
Information Regarding Emergency Operations 89
Emergency Command 90
    Initial Assignment 90
    First Alarm Assignment 90
    Greater Alarm Incident 91
    Major Emergency Assignment 91
    Major Emergency (Expanded) 91
Glossary of Terms 91

8. Science Fiction, Sci-Fi Fact   96

Sci-Fi That Is Out of This World   98
Science Fiction Stories   99

9. Horror and the Occult   100

Horror Story Elements   100
Horror Story Locations   101
Horror Story Means and Devices   102
Some Horror Story Ideas   102
Characters Associated With the Occult   103
Elements in Occult Stories   103
Seen and Unseen forces   104

10. The Love Story   105

Love Story Premises   106
Breathing Life Into the Basics   107
Problems Affecting Romantic Involvements   110
Types of Attractions, Involvements, and Relationships   110
Types of Love   111
Where and How Lovers Meet   111
Things People Do to Overcome Romantic Problems
    and Barriers   111
Most Romantic and Unromantic Roles and Qualities   112
    Most Romantic Male Roles   112
    Most Romantic Male Qualities and Characteristics   112
    Most Unromantic Male Qualities and Characteristics   112
    Most Romantic Female Roles   113
    Most Romantic Female Qualities and Characteristics   113
    Most Unromantic Female Qualities and Characteristics   113
Story Elements Associated With Romance   113
Usual Romantic Locations   114
Unusual Romantic Locations   115

II. Marriage and the Family — 116

Problems Associated with Separation and Divorce   118
Problems Associated with Becoming Widowed   118
Marital Problems   118
Family Problems   119
Problems Affecting Family Members   119
     Parents   119
     Offspring   120
     Grandparents   120
Problems Associated with Marriage   121
Problems Associated with Family   121
Problems Associated with Childhood   121
Teenage Problems   122
     School   122
     Parental   122
     Appearance   122
Young Singles' Problems   123
Senior Citizens Problems   123

12. Comedy — 125

Basic Comedy Situations   127
Embarrassing Situations   128
The Fish-Out-of-Water   130
Comedic Problems of the Elderly   130
Comedic Problems of Youth and Teenagers   131
Comedic Problems of Families   131
Comedic Problems of Young Singles   132
Odd-Couple Relationships   132

13. Sports   133

The Sporting Life   133
Amateur and Spectator Sports   134
Private Clubs and Sports Facilities   134
Sports Story Themes   135
Team Sports—Competitive   136
Single Sports—Competitive   136
Sports Not Necessarily Competitive   137
Animal Sports   137
Football   138
  National Conference Teams   138
  American Conference Teams   138
  National Football League Team Addresses   139
  College Football Bowls   142
  Football Stadiums   141
  Fields and Equipment   142
  Players' Equipment   142
  Objectives of the Game   142
  Officials   142
  Teams   143
  Scrimmage Positions   143
Baseball   144
  National League   144
  American League   144
  Major League Baseball Team Addresses   144
  Diamonds and Equipment   146
  Officials   146
  Dress   147
Basketball   147
  The National Basketball Association   147
  National Basketball Association Team Addresses   148
  Courts and Equipment   149
  Dress   150
  Officials   150

    Objectives of the Game   150
    Game Time   151
    Ball Holding Time   151
    Time-outs   151
    Scoring   151
    Penalties   151
Ice Hockey   151
    National Hockey League   151, 347
    Hockey Rink and Equipment   152
    Players   153
    Dress and Equipment   153
    Game Time   153
    Objectives of the Game   153
    Penalties and Penalty Shots   154
Boxing   154
    Time   154
    Rules   155
    Rings and Equipment   155
    Officials   155
    Dress and Equipment   155
    Scoring the Fight   155
    Maximum Weights for Professional Boxing   156
    Maximum Weights for Amateur Boxing   156
Soccer   156
    The Game   156
    Objectives of the Game   157
    The Field   157
    Playing Time   157
    Playing the Ball   157
    Kicks   157
    Penalties and Infringements   158
    Fouls and Misconduct   158
    Officials   158
    Substitutions   158
    A Few Words to the Wise   158

Horse Racing   159
Glossary   160
Horse Racing Tracks   163
Auto Racing   165
*Abbreviations for Countries of Manufacturers of
Automobiles*   167
Auto Racing Tracks   168

14. Medicine   **172**

The Writer in the Medical Arena   172
From Typewriter to Stethoscope   173
How to Use This Medical Section   174
Doctors, Dentists, and Other Specialists   174
First Aid Equipment and Procedures   175
Medical/Surgical Supplies   176
Treatments for Chemical Poisoning   177
Manias, Obsessions, and Phobias   177
Causes of Death   178
Diseases of Childhood   178
Communicable Diseases   179
Afflictions, Illnesses, and Diseases   179
Major Hospital/Medical Center Departments   181
Clinics   188
Cardiology   188
Chief Residents   189
The ER (Emergency Room)   189
Cases Often Seen in Emergency Rooms   190
Medicolegal Terms   191
Medical Story Ideas   202

15. Crime   204

Crime Pays   204
Crimes and Criminal Activities   205
Motives for Crime   205
Acts Associated with Crime   205
Protagonists' Motives for Becoming Involved in the
    Crime Story   206
Methods of Murder   206
Murderers   206
Homicide and Murder   207
Forensic Science   207
Crime Scene Investigation   208
Plot Premises   209
Let's Play "What if?"   212

16. Espionage   215

For Your Spies Only!   215
Intelligence and Counterintelligence   216
U.S. Central Intelligence Agency   217
Training of Intelligence Personnel   217
Recruitment and Turning of Agents and Spies   218
Intelligence Agencies Around the World, Past and Present   218
Gadgets, Devices, and Tools of the Spy Trade   219
Spy Story Premises   220
    Possible Nondeliberate Involvements   220
    Possible Deliberate Involvements   221
Spy Speak Glossary   222

17. The Military   226

United States Army   227
    Command Personnel   227
    Commissioned Officers and Insignia   227

Warrant Officer Grades and Insignia 228
Noncommissioned Officers and Insignia 228
U.S. Army Units 228
Major Army Commands 228
U.S. Army Unit Organizational List 229
Combat Units 230
Army Weapons Used in Vietnam 231
Infantry Radios 232
Combat Vehicles 232
Cargo and Transportation Vehicles 233
Engineer Vehicles 233
U.S. Army Vessels 234
Problems Associated with Military Life 234
Locations 234
Problems Uniforms and Equipment 235
Problems Associated with Combat 235
Problems Associated with the Military 237
Military Law and Law Enforcement 237
Means of Attack 237
Means of Defense 238
United States Navy 238
Officers Descending in Rank 238
Enlisted Ranks 238
U.S. Navy Insignia 239
Sections of the Navy 239
Naval Aircraft 240
Naval Vessels and Warships 240
Unites States Marine Corps 241
The United States Air Force 241
Its Heritage 241
Mission 241
Organization 242
Strategic Air Command 242
Air Training Command 243
Air Force Systems Command 243

Air Force Communications Command   243
Air University   243
Alaskan Air Command   243
Electronic Security Command   244
Pacific Air Forces   244
United States Air Forces in Europe   244
Air Force Organizational Units   244
Commissioned Officers   244
Noncommissioned Officers   245
Enlisted Personnel   245
U.S. Air Force—Major Air Commands   245
Major Air Force Squadrons   245
Types of Aircraft   246
Air Force Programs   246
Fixed Wing Aircraft in Vietnam   246
Helicopters   246
Abbreviations and Acronyms   247
Air Force Academy   248
Themes for Military Stories   248
Military Story Premises   249
Problems and Conflicts Relating to the Military   250

18. Vehicles   **253**
Street Vehicles   253
Off-Road   253
On Tracks   254
Air Vehicles   254
Snow and Ice Vehicles   254
Country Vehicles   254
Sea Vehicles   254
Heavy Equipment   255

19. The Old West 256

The Code of the Old West 257
Life Out West 257
Characters of the Old West 258
Names Associated with the Old West 258
Places Associated with the Old West 259
Interior 259
Exterior 259
Modes of Transportation in the Old West 259
Problems Associated with the Old West 260
Problems Associated with Cowboys 260
Weapons of the Old West 260
American Indian Tribes of the Old West 261
Indian Warriors and Medicine Men 262
Glossary of Old West Lingo 262
Basic Premises for Old West Stories 264
Getting a Fresh Start 265

20. Religion 267

Terms Associated with Religions and Sects 267
Hinduism 267
Brahmanism 269
Yoga 269
Bhakti 269
Popular Hinduism 269
Buddhism 270
Zen 270
Taoism 270
Confucianism 271
Shintoism 271
Islam 272
Judaism 272
Christianity 273
Mysticism 273

Religious Leaders   274
Others Associated with Religion   274
Religious Articles, Rituals, and Facilities   274

21. Language   277

Action Verbs   278
One From Column A, One From Column B   282
Americanisms   283
Briticisms   292
Common Expressions   294
Phrases, Idioms, and Colloquialisms   295
Short-Order Cook Slang   297
Slanguage   297
Recent Common Expressions   302
Down-Home Talk   303
Southern Words and Sayings   305
How to Speak Southern   306

22. Locations   309

Unusual Locations   309
Locations Associated with the Elderly   310
Locations Associated with Youth   310
Foreign Beaches   311
Archaeological Areas   311
Areas, Centers, Parks, and Suburbs in the U.S.   312
Foreign Areas, Centers, Parks, and Suburbs   313
Amusement Areas   314
Locations—General   316
Film Commissions   318
   State Offices   318
   Indian   323
   International   323

23. Reference and Research **326**

Dictionaries, Encyclopedias, and Guide Books   328

Capitalization   330

Abbreviations   332

Numbers   333

Names and Titles   334

Newsman's Dictionary   335

24. Putting It All Together **338**

Appendix **342**

Web Wordage   342

National Hockey League Teams   347

Additonal Sports League Offical Offices   349

Foreword

I knew Marty for forty years as a client and then as a friend. His knowledge and approach to writing and show business was always something I admired. I just recently re-read *The Writer's Partner,* and it reminded me that there is not a writer young or old who shouldn't refer to this book daily. If you've seen what's on television or in the movies, you realize that they are not making Marty Roths today . . . he will be sorely missed. But he left us with this great reference book on writing that will be with us forever.

—Bernie Brillstein
Founder of Brillstein & Gray

Prologue

Martin Roth's original Introduction to the Second Edition

We all make mistakes. The first edition of this book had an inadequate and probably misleading title.

Although the book garnered widespread plaudits, great reviews, and substantial sales, the original publisher chose to title the book *The Fiction Writer's Silent Partner,* despite the fact that the book was intended to be for *all* writers, including those working in television and film media.

The people here at Index Publishing Group, mainly its publisher, Linton M. Vandiver, immediately saw the limitations in that title and asked me to revise the contents of the original book, change its title to what it should be called, and, in addition to updating the book (names and addresses have changed over the years), I was told to liberally expand the book, adding new chapters and a substantial amount of additional material that was not in the first edition. This I have done with much enjoyment, as evidenced by the Table of Contents. Now the book carries the title it rightfully deserves, one that accurately reflects its value as a day-to-day working tool: *The Writer's Partner for Fiction, Television, and Screen.*

This second edition is now truly a working partner for every writer who needs help in generating ideas, in getting facts and information he or she would not ordinarily find—at least, not all in one place. It's a book loaded with lots of "what ifs" and "hows abouts," and it's sure to get your creative juices flowing.

This is a thought-provoking book that is meant to provoke *your* thinking. And best of all, you don't have to share any of your royalties or residuals with *this* partner.

Introduction to the Third Edition

White empty space. . . . Frustration and anguish . . . all of a sudden your head starts hurting from too many cups of coffee and an empty stomach. Does this ring a bell?

There isn't a writer out there who isn't familiar with the torture of a blank white page on a writer's block day.

This white page stares at us. And what do we do? We stare back!

We stare at it in silence, or accompanied by our favorite tunes in the hope that maybe an inspiration will come with music. Inspiration—the magic word. Desired by so many, easily achievable by only a few.

And what about the rest of us mortals?

We look for ways to find it—in books, in the movies, in life. We spend days and nights in pain. We walk the earth listening to other people's conversations, trying to make sense of what it is we want to say, searching for a perfect story that will put us over the top.

Sound familiar?

Well, what if I told you that there's a remedy? And a cure for many other writer's ailments—including the search for a theme, a subject, a character, a plot direction, an interesting location in which to play out your story or a special scene—even that certain word that hangs on the tip of your tongue but refuses to jump onto the page.

All you need is *The Writer's Partner!*

Sure, there are many resources available today—the Internet, CD-ROMs, and electronic dictionaries. But none of them will offer you the benefits of *The Writer's Partner*—it's a thorough convenience and the ultimate timesaver.

Just check the Table of Contents and see how everything is categorized. Need to know all about firefighters, the teams in the NBA, or the makeup and organization of a hospital? It's all there.

The Writer's Partner is always ready to serve you and your story!

Oh, and by the way, it won't even ask for food or water. It won't ask for a cut of that big advance check or a share of the royalties.

Now that's what we call an ideal partner!

Putting Your Writer's Partner to Work for You

Are you looking for a theme? A dramatic or comedic situation? A way out of a dilemma? The means of getting a character involved in your story?

Do you need a fresh location? Do you need a new perspective? Have you overlooked an obvious element, or do you need to broaden your focus?

Whatever your problem, the answer is probably between the covers of this book. *The Writer's Partner* can assist you in a number of ways:

It can suggest themes and areas for stories.

It can help you create and fully develop a character.

It can suggest ways to involve your characters.

It can help you create and fully develop a plot.

It can help you put a character into a dramatic or comedic situation.

It can help you develop a scene or a chapter.

It can suggest normal or odd locations in which to place a scene, a chapter, or an entire story.

It can suggest themes, conflicts, crises, climaxes, problems and obstacles to overcome, solutions, relationships, activities, crimes, and events.

It can aid you in language and slang.

It can suggest areas of research.

It can suggest character's names in five languages.

It can provide information regarding religion, sports, the military, medicine, espionage, horror, the occult, and even the Old West.

It can suggest alternatives to consider in character, plot, action, and locations.

It can do all of these things and more.

What this book can't do is determine what you require from it.
The book is not necessarily to be used in sequential order. You
decide how best to use your Writer's Partner. If you just need one
suggestion to act as a catalyst, simply turn to the section that can
best fulfill that need.

For instance, the character section can help create entire characters or provide you with some addition to round out a character for
you.

If you want your Writer's Partner to help you build an entire plot
from theme to solution, the final chapter, *Putting It All Together,* will
show you how best to accomplish just that.

1

The Story First

Naturally, a writer must have a story in mind before sitting down at the typewriter or the computer or even to a pad and pencil. The question is, will the story have all the ingredients necessary to make for a book, film, television episode, or movie made for television?

First off, does your story have a HOOK? The GRABBER that immediately attracts the reader or audience's attention and interest? If professional readers, producers, and story editors who read umteen stories, books, and scripts a week don't get involved in the first 20 pages, you can pretty much bet your story or screenplay will be put on the "pass pile." And the same goes for the common folk who just love to read. They'll pick up a book in a bookstore, glance at the first few pages and either it grabs them or back on the shelf it goes. So make sure you have a good hook to your story.

Every story MUST HAVE an INCITING INCIDENT, the first event that gets your story going, gets your characters involved, and begins propelling them towards their eventual goals. Remember the cliché, "Boy meets girl, Boy loses girl, Boy gets girl back." Well, your inciting incident must be prepared to take the characters and the story all the way through to the crisis, climax, and the final resolution. Inciting incidents can be brought about by deliberate involvement or by non-deliberate involvement. In other words, a PRINCIPAL CHARACTER can set out on a particular mission or something can draw that character into the INCITING INCIDENT merely by chance.

The PROTAGONIST and the ANTAGONIST must each have a PLAN, although one may begin with a plan that is contradictory to the other, causing the latter to develop a counterplan. The plans of course must be those of the Protagonist and the Antagonist and be fraught with obstacles, usually created by the OPPOSING PRINCIPAL CHARACTER. Plans, or at least one initial plan, should be brought into the story as earlyas possible.

CONFLICT! Without conflict, there can be no drama. There must be conflict between opposing forces. It is the root of dramaturgy. The sooner conflict is introduced, the sooner drama becomes present. Opposing forces can exist between two humans, two animals, a human and an animal, a human against the forces of nature...

Along the way, each story must have story or "PLOT" POINTS with the first plot point showing up by the conclusion of the first act or, in the case of a book, by chapter two or three at the latest. The main objective of establishing that first plot point is to create an initial problem for the protagonist of the piece, In a three-act screenplay structure, plot points B and C would occur in Act Two, threatening the protagonist's chances of achieving his or her goal, with plot point C presenting the ultimate obstacle or complication for the protagonist. In essence, plot points are actually "crises" along the way leading to the CLIMAX; they create suspense, action, failures, and a sense of irresolution whether the protagonist's goal will be achieved.

Then comes THE MOMENT OF TRUTH, that moment when the protagonist appears to be finished and ready to give up or surrender but for one thing that must happen to bring your protagonist face to face with himself or herself and to rise above fear or the appearance of defeat and go on, possibly with a change of tactic. The climax should bring it all to a head, ending in a satisfactory resolution. In reaching this climax, it is best you remember your theme, that your character remains true to his or her traits and gains a secondary moment of greater strength. To put it succinctly, the hook should grab the reader and from there on the story must build, even when your protagonist faces a momentary setback, and the story must continue to build until it reaches its climax.

The RESOLUTION is the final element, the outcome of your story. It can result in your protagonist having accomplished his or her goal or your protagonist has grown so that he or she has found the original goal to be lacking and has changed to something more worthy.

BACKSTORY, LINKS, ARCS, THE CLOCK, AND SUBPLOTS

All of these elements are necessary to both the plot and the characters. The BACKSTORY consists of all that had gone before, things that happened that, although they may be in the past, have some definite effect upon the character(s), the plot, or both.

The backstory should be revealed in bits and pieces, hopefully in a creative way rather than in an expository scene where the character sits down and talks about it.

LINKS are part of the chain of events that keep your story connected. They help bring about the forward progress of the story by linking one scene to another to provide unity and, at times, they can hint at upcoming events or situations.

ARCS are the phases the characters and the plot go through. They are the internal change points in the character(s) in the story, and deal with the character's sense of commitment and possibly, obsession. As the story unfolds, the level of the character's awareness increases. New information, altered situations, changes in action can cause the internal change in the character to become an external change when we actually see the arc completed, the character now reacting on a different and probably higher level.

The CLOCK plays an extremely important role in a story. It is what adds intensity and the sense of urgency to the story. More often, it means or signifies a *time limit*—that something devastating will happen if the protagonist does not prevent it in time. The clock is usually introduced half to three quarters of the way through the story and increases as the clock ticks louder and louder, the hands of the clock (the story action) getting closer and closer to the appointed time when something will happen that will destroy the protagonist or at least, surely, the protagonist's goal.

The SUBPLOT: There are basically two types of subplots of 'B' stories. One is often referred to as "railroad tracks." Railroad track subplots never have any real effect upon the main story. For example, it might be something as simple as an friend or someone associated with the protagonist has a problem or is trying to attain a goal that has nothing to do with that of the protagonist. It has its own conflict, crisis, climax, and resolution. These railroad track 'B' stories have a much shorter life span and many times are used as humorous relief.

The crossover track's subplot, on the other hand, often can play a vital role in the main plot. Although it may start off seemingly having no connection to the main plot, at some point it crosses into the main plot and by doing so, brings about a radical change in the main plot, in many cases causing a major crisis or obstruction to the protagonist. It can bring about an emotional change in the protagonist or it can bring a major setback to whatever advancements the protagonist has made towards achieving his or her goal.

So... structure is critical and the story's architecture **must** come first.

2

Characters and Development

LET'S TALK PEOPLE

People!

That's the name of the game.

No matter how clever, exciting, funny or dramatic your plot may be, the characters that people it are not only indispensable elements of your story, but they are also the most important element in any story.

They are crucial to the theme and the plot.

People care about people, not just about things or happenings. The more interesting and fascinating the characters you draw, the better your story will become and the more the reader or viewer will care about what happens to them.

A good writer will let his characters tell him where they will go, how they will behave, and what they will do to accomplish their aims and goals.

A character with a college education will think and behave differently than a high school dropout. Someone who has always known wealth will think and behave differently than someone who has always been poor. A character who has grown up in a happy household will think and behave differently than someone who was abused as a child.

The protagonist in a story should always be someone the reader or viewer likes and cares about. This is not to say that your protagonist must start off as a goody two-shoes. But the spark must be there to make the reader/viewer want to see change occur in that character along the way.

No matter how harsh or seemingly uncaring your protagonist may appear at the beginning, there must be some redeeming feature that you will ignite at some point. Usually that point is the protagonist's "moment of truth," when he or she decides what the right thing to do is and then does it.

In many stories, there is a second protagonist, usually the first protagonist's love interest or a character with another relationship to the primary protagonist.

This character, like other major characters, should be fully drawn for change and growth to take place. At some point in the story, something important happens to further the relationship with the protagonist or conclude it for better or for worse.

The protagonist in your story is, naturally, the hero of your piece.

That does not mean he or she is Superman or Superwoman. The protagonist(s) should have weaknesses and most important, an Achilles' heel. The protagonist must be vulnerable. He or she must be able to lose, be hurt, or even die, depending on the story.

GETTING THE PROTAGONIST UP AND DOWN THE TREE

The three basic elements of storytelling are to get your protagonist up a tree, throw rocks at him or her, and then get your protagonist safely down the tree.

In other words, get your protagonist into some kind of problem either directly or indirectly (see pages 59-61 on deliberate and nondeliberate involvement), putting him or her in conflict with an antagonist. Place obstacles in the way of the protagonist as he or she attempts to resolve the problem, and then get your protagonist to resolve the problem, achieving his or her original goal.

Protagonists must have a purpose or goal to attain, whether they set out to accomplish it or it is thrust upon them.

Examples of purposes might be to live, to love, to be happy, to prosper, to recover, to discover, to reach a goal, for the protagonist or another.

In developing your protagonist, bear in mind your protagonist's purpose. Who that protagonist will be dictates how that protagonist will accept the challenge, deal with obstacles, and how he or she will manage to overcome those obstacles to reach a satisfactory conclusion. For example, a character with a college education or someone with some specific skill or knowledge would function differently than a character not possessing that education, skill, or knowledge.

Suppose the protagonist is someone who loved the great outdoors and had camped, hunted, hiked, etc. Wouldn't that individual have a better chance of surviving in the wilderness than a character born and bred in the city, and whose closest encounter with a tree was in a local park?

Now reverse the situation.

Wouldn't an urban, street-wise individual survive the city jungle better than a character who was pretty much a country bumpkin?

WHO'S THROWING THE ROCKS?

Now let's talk about the antagonist in your story.

In order to create conflict (which every story must have), there must be someone or something working against your protagonist, and that antagonist should always be a worthy adversary.

The competition and conflict should not be easy to overcome for the protagonist.

Another thing... although we often refer to our protagonist as the one in the "white hat," and the antagonist as the one in the "black hat," the more human the antagonist is, the more real that antagonist becomes.

But . . .

NOT ALL PROTAGONISTS AND ANTAGONISTS ARE HUMAN!

Although most writers think of protagonists and antagonists as humans, protagonists in recent stories included Flipper, Lassie, Gentle Ben, Clarence the Cross-Eyed Lion, Judy the Chimp, Rin Tin Tin, and most recently, The Lion King.

Although many times the elements are considered obstacles in the path of the protagonist, there are stories where such obstacles are the antagonists.

Hemingway's *The Old Man and the Sea* is an example. The old fisherman's duel was with the sea and not with a human being.

In Hitchcock's *The Birds*, the antagonist was the birds, as was the shark in *Jaws* and the bees in *The Swarm*.

Still another consideration is the will to overcome a handicap which again is not the typical human antagonist. Although a handicap could be considered an obstacle, it might be the antagonist of the piece. Some of the following nonhumans or elements might be considered as protagonists or antagonists:

A curse	Killing coldwave
A domestic pet	Killing heatwave
Acid rain	Monster
Air pollution	Physical handicap
Aliens from outer space	Race or ethnicity
An intellectual handicap	Radioactivity
Birds	Reptile
Blazing light	Robot
Contagious disease	Rodent
Darkness	Sand storm
Drought	Sea creature
Dust storm	Spirit from another world
Earthquake	Storm
Famine	The sea
Farm animal	Tidal wave
Fears and phobias	Tornado
Fire	Typhoon
Flood	Volcanic eruption
Hurricane	Wild animal
Insect	Wild but caring animal

Excluding the elements, of course, you should develop a character bio for nonhuman protagonists and antagonists to have better insight into their behavior and motivation.

DOES THE SITUATION DECIDE THE CHARACTERS OR DO THE CHARACTERS INITIATE THE SITUATION? WHICH COMES FIRST, THE CHICKEN OR THE EGG?

That depends on you.

Sometimes the writer comes up with a great, fully-developed character and then goes searching for a situation or a plot in which to place that character.

Then again, and more often than not, the writer comes up with a situation and then seeks to "people" it. The type of character you choose to put into that situation will determine how the plot must be structured and how that character will handle the situation.

For example, if your protagonist is a police officer assigned to a murder case, that character will face the problem as a police officer, though he or she may take certain liberties that real-life police officers would not take.

However, if the protagonist you choose to involve in the murder case happens to be a used-car salesman with no investigative experience, naturally the approach that character will take will be worlds apart from the way the law enforcement protagonist would take.

The choice is yours as to what you start with, the plot or the character.

Whichever the case, the character you eventually choose must be fully developed. The following list can aid you in developing the characters in your story.

Where was the character born and raised?

Who were the parents?

What was the character's childhood like?

What members of a family does the character have?

What education did the character have?

What kind of student was the character?

What special skills or knowledge does the character possess?

What hobbies did or does the character have?

What are the bad habits of the character?

What are some of the traits of the character—emotional, mental, and physical?

With what kind of job or profession is the character occupied, past and present?

And finally, what are some of the character's past and present relationships?

If you use the next lists (pages 32-52), your characters can easily become people that you and the reader or viewer can come to know and understand.

Armed with the knowledge of who a character is, let the character help you decide the course he or she will take in your story and what changes in that character will be brought about as the plot develops.

For example, let us say our protagonist is a young man by the name of Joe Smith.

Who is Joe Smith?

Select one or more items from the list titled PLACE OF ORIGIN. For example, Joe was born in a factory town in the northern U.S. From PARENTS, select one or more items. For example, his parents were poor, working, religious, strict, but loving parents.

From CHILDHOOD, select one or more items. Joe was an only child but came from a close, very happy family.

From FAMILY MEMBERS, select one or more items. Joe's family consisted of his mother, father, paternal grandfather, and his uncle.

From EDUCATION, select one or more items. Joe attended public elementary school, public high school, a state college. He also served in the army and received MILITARY TRAINING.

From EDUCATION BEHAVIOR, select one or more items. Joe was a classroom cut-up but also a good student.

From SPECIAL SKILLS select one or more items. Over the years, Joe has taken up sky diving, become a sports enthusiast, become a good hunter, learned how to fly in the service, has handled weapons (service), become expert in survival (service), is mechanically inclined, is a good pool player.

From HOBBIES, select one or more items. Joe began collecting baseball cards when he was a kid and still collects them. He's into camping, fishing, sports, and weekly card playing with some close friends.

From BAD HABITS, select one or more items. Joe doesn't have many bad habits, but he is impatient or short tempered, and he is not the neatest person in his housekeeping.

From GENERAL CHARACTERISTICS, select one or more items. Joe is honest, a romanticist, humorous, a sometimes drinker, happy-go-lucky, a nonsmoker, at times impractical, a sensitive man, often curious, and usually optimistic. He's a loyal friend, is danger-loving, can be charming in his own way, is not a quitter.

From MENTAL AND PHYSICAL CHARACTERISTICS, select one or more items. He is mature, tall and gangly, wears contact lenses in preference to eyeglasses, has prematurely graying hair, suffers from a fear of heights, is his own man, strong-willed and downright stubborn at times.

From PROFESSIONS and JOBS, select one or more items. He worked his way through school as a short-order cook and as a part-time security guard. He played pro football but was injured early in his career. He then worked as a salesman but decided to get into law enforcement.

From RELATIONSHIPS and MARITAL STATUS, select one or more items. Joe is divorced after one marriage. He has one small child he sees as often as he can. He has a number of friends through professional and social contacts. He has no steady girlfriend at present.

From CURRENT LIFESTYLE, select one or more items. Joe is a bachelor and enjoys doing his own thing, shies away from commitment to another marriage, dates attractive single women, lives a fairly low-key lifestyle.

From HOME, or DWELLING and VEHICLES, select one or more items. Joe lives in a small, inexpensive, one bedroom rented apartment in a middle class section of the city. He drives an expensive sports car, the one luxury he affords himself.

We have now developed the skeletal outline of Joe Smith and put some meat on the bones.

The creativity of the writer should now come into play to further embellish the character of Joe Smith by additional suggestions from the lists or any other ideas the writer can come up with.

A quick suggestion: to get a good physical description of a character, you might refer to photographs of friends or from magazines.

CHARACTER BACKGROUND

Place of Origin

At sea	Northern U.S.
Big city	On the road (migrant)
Desert	Orphanage
Eastern U.S	Prison
Factory town	Ranch
Farm	Reservation
Foreign country	Resort
Foster home	River or lake front
Great Plains	Seacoast
Island	Slums
Lower-class neighborhood	Small town
Middle-class neighborhood	Southern U.S.
Midwest	Swamps
Military post	Wealthy neighborhood
Mountains	Western U.S

Parents

Abusive	One-parent household
Bigoted	Poor
Conservative	Professional
Deceased	Religious
Divorced	Retired
Easy-going	Rich
Educated	Separated
Famous	Sick
Foreign-born	Strict
Handicapped	Talented
Liberal	U.S.-born
Loving	Uneducated
Middle class	Unknown
Neurotic	Unskilled

Childhood

Abused
Broken home
Close family
Juvenile delinquent
Large family
Loner
Normal
Only child

Raised by relative
Religious upbringing
Sickly
Spoiled
Two sets of parents
Unhappy
Very happy
Withdrawn

Family Members

Aunt
Brother
Brother-in-law
Cousin
Daughter
Daughter-in-law
Father
Father-in-law
Former husband
Former wife
Foster parent
Godparents
Husband
Maternal grandfather
Maternal grandmother
Mother

Mother-in-law
Nephew
Niece
Paternal grandfather
Paternal grandmother
Paternal son, daughter
Sister
Sister-in-law
Son
Son-in-law
Stepbrother
Stepfather
Stepmother
Stepsister
Uncle
Wife

Education

Art school
Boarding school
Business college
Dance school
Educated at home
Junior college
Language school
Law school
Medical school
Military school
Military training
No schooling
Parochial or religious school

Post graduate
Prep school
Preschool
Private elementary
Public high school
Reform school
School dropout
School for the handicapped
Self-educated
Special school
Trade school
University
War college

Education Behavior

Average student	Poor student
Classroom cut-up	Problem student
Excellent student	Teacher's Pet
Good student	Truant

Hobbies, Special Skills, or Knowledge

Acting	Foreign affairs
Ancient history	Gambling
Animals	Gardening
Archery	Geography
Art	Gourmet cooking
Astrology	Ham radio
Astronomy	Handicrafts
Ballet	Hiking
Bird watching	History
Boating	Horseback riding
Boxing	Hunting
Bridge	Hypnosis
Building	Investigation
Business	Investing
Camping	Languages
Card playing	Laser technology
Carpentry	Literature
Carving	Lovemaking
Ceramics	Martial arts
Checkers	Mathematics
Chess	Mechanics
Collecting	Medicine
Computers	Metal working
Cooking	Military experience
Criminal activities	Mind reading
Dancing	Model construction
Designing	Mountain climbing
Directing (film, theater)	Music
Driving	Musical instruments
Economics	Mythology
Explosives	Nature studies
Farming	Nursing
Fencing	Opera
Fine wines	Painting
First aid	People watching
Fishing	Pets
Flying	Photography

Physical fitness
Politics
Pool, billiards
Psychology
Public speaking
Puzzles
Racing
Reading
Rebuilding
Running
Science
Scuba diving
Selling
Shortwave radio

Singing
Skeet shooting
Sky diving
Sports
Sports fan
Survival
Teaching
The occult
Traveling
Typing
Weapons
Weight lifting
Woodworking
Writing

Bad Habits

Antisocial behavior
Being impolite
Belching in public
Cursing
Discourtesy
Disregard for others' property
Disrespects others
Drug use
Ear pulling
Excessive drinking
Fingerpointing
Frowning
Gossiping
Impatience
Inconsideration
Insensitivity
Interrupting
Jumping to conclusions
Knuckle-cracking
Lateness
Loudness
Messy

Nail biting
Nose picking
Nosiness
Obnoxious
Ostentation
Picking at food
Poor table manners
Preoccupation
Profane
Quarrelsome
Scratching
Selfishness
Smoking
Spreading rumors
Squinting
Stooping over
Stubbornness
Suspiciousness
Unkempt appearance
Vulgarity
Whining

GENERAL CHARACTERISTICS

Abrupt
Agnostic
Alert
Aloof
Ambitious

Aristocratic
Artistic
Atheistic
Blowhard
Brash

Bratty
Brooding
Businesslike
Busybody
Calculating
Careless
Charming
Cheap
Cheerful
Chronic liar
Clockwatcher
Clownish
Compassionate
Complainer
Complex
Conformist
Crabby
Cranky
Crass
Creative
Curious
Danger-loving
Defensive
Demonstrative
Dizzy
Domineering
Downer
Dreamer
Drinker
Earthy
Effeminate
Efficient
Extroverted
Fall guy
Feminine
Fickle
Flirtatious
Frail
Frigid
Gentle
Generous
Go-getter
Golddigger
Gossip
Gracious
Greedy

Grim
Gullible
Happy-go-lucky
Heroic
Hip
Hotheaded
Humorless
Humorous
Hustler
Hypocritical
Imaginative
Impractical
Indifferent
Indulgent
Inhibited
Intelligent
Introverted
Jealous
Lazy
Leech
Literate
Loser
Loudmouth
Lover
Loyal
Lucky
Lustful
Masculine
Miserly
Nagging
Ne'er-do-well
Neat
Never-say-die
Nonconformist
Nonsmoker
Nosy
Not a quitter
Obsessive
Old-fashioned
Optimistic
Orderly
Overprotective
Pessimistic
Polite
Pompous
Power seeker

Proud
Pushover
Pushy
Quick-tempered
Quitter
Raucous
Realist
Redneck
Reserved
Romanticist
Screwball
Self-indulgent
Sensitive
Sharp
Show-off
Shrewd
Shy
Sickly
Simpleminded
Sloppy

Smug
Sneaky
Snob
Soft-spoken
Spendthrift
Square
Stubborn
Studious
Sucker
Suspicious
Swindler
Teetotaler
Tense
Uninhibited
Unscrupulous
Vital
Warm
Whiner
Withdrawn

Mental and Physical Characteristics

Allergic
Asthmatic
Athletic
Bigoted
Blind
Burned
Clairvoyant
Compulsive
Contact lenses
Deaf
Deformed
Disfigured
Disturbed
Down Syndrome
Eccentric
Extroverted
Farsighted
Fear of heights
Gangly
Giant
Graying hair
Handicapped
Heavy drinker

Heavy smoker
Her own woman
His own man
Hyperactive
Hypochondriac
Illiterate
Imaginative
Infantile
Intelligent
Intense
Introverted
Intuitive
Invalid
Logical
Mature
Multiple personality
Muscular
Mute
Myopic
Nearsighted
Nervous
Neurotic
Optimistic

Paralyzed
Paraplegic
Pessimistic
Psychic
Psychotic
Retarded
Scarred
Scheming

Schizoid
Sickly
Sociopathic
Streetwise
Strong-willed
Stubborn
Telepathic
Unimaginative

General Physical Characteristics

Adam's apple
Anorexic
Barrel-chested
Bony
Bowlegged
Buxom
Curvaceous
Fat
Flabby
Flat-bellied
Flat-chested
Flat-footed
Frail
Hairy
Heavyset
Humpbacked
Knock-kneed
Large-breasted
Long-legged
Medium height
Muscular
Obese

Paunchy
Pigeon-toed
Potbellied
Round-shouldered
Rugged
Scarred
Scraggly
Scrawny
Short
Slight
Slim-hipped
Statuesque
Stocky
Swaybacked
Tall
Thick-necked
Thin
Voluptuous
Well-rounded
Wide-hipped
Wiry
Youthful

Facial Characteristics

Beady-eyed
Bearded
Bulbous nose
Bushy-browed
Clean-shaven
Deep-set eyes
Dimpled
Double chin
Droopy-eyed
Full lips
Gaunt

High cheekbones
Jutting jaw
Moustache
Pinched lips
Pug nosed
Roman nosed
Round jawed
Slant-eyed
Square jawed
Squinty-eyed
Sunken cheeks

Thin-browed
Thin-lipped

Skin and Complexion

Albino
Birthmark
Black
Brown
Fair
Flushed
Freckled
Milky white
Olive
Pale
Pasty
Pinkish
Pockmarked

Wide-eyed
Wrinkled

Red
Ruddy
Sallow
Scarred
Smooth
Sunburned
Swarthy
Tanned
Tattooed
Weather-beaten
White
Wrinkled
Yellow

Hair

Afro
Bald
Black
Bleached blonde
Blonde
Braided
Brunette
Burned
Bushy
Close-cropped
Curly
Dreadlocks
Fair
Frizzled
Gray
Graying
Hairy

High-top phase
Long
Mid-length
Redhead
Salt-and-pepper
Shaved
Short
Shoulder-length
Straight
Streaked
Sun-bleached blonde
Teased
Thin-haired
Tipped
Wavy
White
Yellow

Overall Appearance

Attractive
Baggy
Beautiful
Bookish
Conservative
Droopy
Fashion plate
Fastidious

Flashy
Glamorous
Grotesque
Handsome
Homely
Matronly
Mousy
Outrageous

Plain
Raggedy
Scholarly
Seedy
Sloppy
Smartly dressed
Stooped

Striking
Stylish
Swarthy
Ugly
Unattractive
Well-groomed
Wrinkled

Moral Characteristics

Bigoted
Charitable
Cheater
Deadbeat
Dedicated
Devoted
Dishonest
Disloyal
Fair
Godly
Honest

Liar
Loyal
Patient
Reliable
Religious
Ruthless
Sincere
Spiritual
Trusting
Truthful
Vengeful

Relationships

Acquaintance
Business acquaintance
Business competitor
Business friend
Childhood enemy
Childhood friend
Childhood sweetheart
Co-worker
Employee
Employer
Ex-husband
Ex-wife
Family member
Former employee
Former employer
Former lover
Former neighbor
Former teacher
Former teammate

Husband
In-law
Lover
Long distance relationship
Military buddy
Mistress
Neighbor
New-found friend
Offspring
Old boyfriend
Old girlfriend
Partner
Rival
Roommate
School friend
Teacher
Teammate
Wife

Marital Status

Divorced (X times)
Dating
Living with lover

Long distance relationship
Married
Never been married

Officially engaged
Presently single
Remarried (X times)
Seeing someone; not engaged

Separated
Widow
Widower

Current Lifestyle

Bachelor
Beach type
Glamorous
High on the hog
High society
Independent
Living above means
Loner

Moving in criminal circles
Moving in the fast lane
On the road
Quiet
Shy
Street life
Suburban
Typical family

Home or Dwelling

Apartment
Barracks
Basement
Bungalow
Cabin
Castle
Cave
Cellar
Chalet
Chateau
Cliffhouse
Condominium
Cottage
Hacienda
Hospital room
Hotel
House/private home

Houseboat
Loft
Mansion
Motel room
Motor home
Nursing home
Palace
Penthouse
Ranch house
Rented room
Retirement home
Shack
Tenement
Tent
Thatched hut
Trailer
Tree house

Vehicles

Airplane
Bicycle
Bus
Camper
Classic car
Company car
Expensive car
Houseboat
Mobile home
Motor boat
Motorcycle/with sidecar

New car
Old car
Power boat
Race car
Sailboat
Scooter
Sports car
Station wagon
Truck
Van
Yacht

Professions and Jobs

Accountant
Actor
Agent
Ambulance driver
Analyst
Anesthetist
Architect
Arranger
Artist
Assembly member
Athlete
Attorney
Bagger
Bail bondsman
Bailiff
Baker
Bank guard
Bank teller
Banker
Bartender
Baseball player
Basketball player
Biologist
Bishop
Breeder
Bricklayer
Broadcaster
Broker
Builder
Burglar
Bus driver
Butcher
Butler
Cabdriver
Cabinetmaker
Camera operator
Cardinal
Carpenter
Cashier
Casino employee
Chauffeur
Chef
Chemist
Chief (fire, police, Indian)

Chiropractor
Chorus boy or girl
Cigarette girl
Circus performer
City editor
Clerk
Coach
Columnist
Comedian
Composer
Con artist
Conductor
Construction worker
Cook
Copilot
Council member
Counselor
Counterfeiter
Courier
Cowboy/Cowgirl
Crew member
Crime boss
Criminologist
Cutter
Dancer
Demonstrator
Deputy
Designer
Detective
Developer
Director
Disc jockey
Dishwasher
District attorney
Diver
Doctor
Domestic servant
Doorman
Draftsman
Dressmaker
Druggist
Ecologist
Editor

Electrician	Maintenance worker
Elevator operator	Maitre d'
Engineer	Manager
Executive	Marine
Explorer	Mate
Farmer	Mechanic
Fence	Medical examiner
Fireman	Medical technician
Fisherman	Member of Congress
Flight attendant	Merchant
Football player	Messenger
Forest ranger	Meteorologist
Forger	Mind reader
Fortune teller	Minister
Gambler	Model
Garbage collector	Money lender
Gardener	Mortician
Gas station attendant	Musical conductor
Geologist	Musician
Golf pro	Navigator
Governor	Newspaper reporter, editor
Grocer	Nun
Ground crew member	Nurse
Groundskeeper	Office manager
Guide	Opera singer
Historian	Painter
Hit man	Pastor
Horseman	Pathologist
Hunter	Pharmacist
Ice skater	Photographer
Interior decorator	Pilot
Inventor	Pimp
Investor	Plumber
Janitor	Police officer
Jockey	Politician
Judge	Pool cleaner
Laboratory technician	Porter
Lifeguard	Postal employee, letter carrier
Lighthouse keeper	President
Lobbyist	Presser
London bobby	Priest
Magician	Principal

Prison guard
Private investigator
Prizefighter
Producer
Promoter
Prostitute
Psychiatrist
Psychologist
Public relations agent
Publisher
Rabbi
Radio announcer
Radio operator
Real estate agent
Referee
Reporter
Representative
Riding instructor
Riveter
Safecracker
Sailor
Salesperson
Scientist
Scrubwoman
Seamstress
Secretary
Security guard
Senator
Sheriff
Ship captain
Shipbuilder
Short-order cook
Singer
Ski instructor
Soccer player
Social worker
Society editor

Soda jerk
Soldier
Sports editor
Spy
Stagehand
Stoker
Stool pigeon
Stunt performer
Subway guard
Supervisor
Surgeon
Swimmer
Swimming instructor
Switchboard operator
Tailor
Taxi Driver
Teacher
Team manager
Telephone operator
Tennis pro
Test pilot
Thief
Ticket taker
Track runner
Trainer
Travel agent
Truck driver
Typist
Waiter/Waitress
Warden
Weathercaster
Welder
Window washer
Wrestler
Writer
X-ray technician
Zoologist

Male Characters—Dominant

Baron
Best man
Bishop

Brother
Cardinal
Chief

Count	Knight
Duke	Lord
Earl	Nephew
Father	Pope
Grandfather	Priest
Groom	Prince
Husband	Uncle
King	Widower

Female Characters—Dominant

Aunt	Mother
Baroness	Niece
Bride	Nun
Bridesmaid	Priestess
Countess	Princess
Debutante	Queen
Duchess	Sister
Grandmother	Squaw
Lady	Widow
Maid of honor	Wife
Mistress	

NAMES

Most Common Names on Nationwide Basis in Order of Frequency

Smith, Johnson, Williams, Jones, Brown, Miller, Davis, Anderson, Wilson, Thompson, Moore, Taylor, White, Thomas, Martin.

Female Names—General

Agatha	Billie	Connie
Alice	Blossom	Cora
Amy	Bonnie	Corrine
Anabelle	Candy	Debra
Anne	Cara	Dee
Arlene	Carol	Delia
Audrey	Cathy	Della
Babe	Ceil	Diane
Bea	Cheryl	Donna
Belle	Chloe	Dora
Bernice	Christine	Doris
Bertha	Cindy	Dorothy
Beth	Claire	Dotty
Beverly	Clarice	Edna

Eileen	Jessica	Muriel
Elaine	Jill	Naiome
Elizabeth	Joan	Nan
Ellen	Joanna	Nanette
Elsa	Josephine	Natalie
Emma	Judy	Nellie
Enid	Juliet	Nora
Erica	Karen	Norma
Estella	Kate	Olive
Esther	Katherine	Opal
Eunice	Kim	Patricia
Eva	Kitty	Patty
Felicia	Laura	Paula
Flora	Lauren	Pauline
Florence	Laurette	Pearl
Francine	Laverne	Peg
Francis	Lena	Peggy
Frieda	Leslie	Penny
Geraldine	Lilly	Penolope
Gina	Linda	Phyllis
Ginny	Lisa	Pina
Gloria	Lottie	Piper
Glory	Louise	Pippa
Grace	Lulu	Portia
Gretta	Mabel	Rachel
Gwenn	Mae	Rae
Harriet	Mandy	Renee
Heather	Marcia	Rhoda
Hedda	Margaret	Rita
Helen	Margie	Riva
Helene	Marie	Rochelle
Hermione	Marlene	Rosa
Hester	Marsha	Rosalinda
Ida	Mary	Rose
Ilsa	Mattie	Roweena
Ina	Maureen	Ruby
Irene	Maybelle	Sabina
Irma	Meg	Sadie
Jackie	Megan	Sally
Jacqueline	Melody	Sarah
Jamie	Micky	Selena
Jane	Mikki	Selma
Jasmine	Millie	Sharon
Jean	Mimi	Sheba
Jeanette	Missy	Shelly
Jenny	Mona	Sherry

Simone	Theresa	Vivian
Steffy	Tillie	Vonda
Stella	Tina	Wallace
Suzy	Toni	Wanda
Sydney	Tracy	Wendy
Sylvia	Una	Wilma
Tanya	Velvet	Yetta
Teddy	Vera	Yolanda
Terry	Veronica	Yvette
Tessa	Vicki	Zelda
Thelma	Vilma	Zina
Theodora	Virginia	Zoe

Male Names—General

Al	Bert	Damon
Aaron	Boris	Daniel
Abbey	Boyan	Darryl
Abe	Boze	David
Abekenezer	Brandon	Dean
Abel	Brewster	Delbert
Abraham	Brian	Dennis
Adam	Brigham	Dimitri
Addington	Brooks	Donald
Adlai	Bruce	Douglas
Adolph	Buck	Duncan
Albert	Bud	Dutch
Alex	Buford	Earl
Alexander	Buster	Ed
Alfonso	Calvin	Edmund
Alfred	Carl	Edward
Allison	Carlos	Edwin
Aloysius	Caroll	Eldred
Andrew	Casper	Elroy
Andy	Charles	Ernest
Anthony	Chester	Ernesto
Antoine	Christian	Eugene
Arnold	Clarence	Evan
Arthur	Clark	Evert
Austin	Claude	Fay
Barney	Cliff	Felix
Barton	Clifford	Ferdinand
Basil	Clive	Ferguson
Ben	Conrad	Ford
Benedict	Craig	Francis
Benjamin	Culbert	Frank
Bernard	Cy	Franklin

Fraser	Jed	Mark
Fred	Jedro	Marshall
Fredrico	Jeff	Martin
Fritz	Jefferson	Marty
Gary	Jeffrey	Marvin
George	Jerry	Matt
Gerald	Jess	Matthew
Gifford	Jesus	Maurice
Gil	Jim	Maurie
Gilbert	John	Max
Glen	Jose	Michael
Glendon	Joseph	Mike
Goodwin	Judson	Miles
Grant	Julian	Mooney
Gregory	Julius	Murray
Guido	Julson	Nat
Guinn	Junior	Nate
Gunther	Justin	Nathan
Gus	Keenan	Nathaniel
Gustave	Keith	Nelson
Guthrie	Kelly	Nicholai
Guy	Ken	Nick
Hans	Kenneth	Noah
Harland	Kenny	Nobel
Harold	Kent	Norbert
Harry	Kilgore	Norman
Harvey	Kilroy	Norvel
Henry	Laddie	Olaf
Herbert	Lambert	Ollie
Herman	Lee	Omar
Hildreth	Leo	Orville
Howard	Leon	Oscar
Hy	Leonard	Oswald
Hyman	Leroy	Otis
Ian	Leslie	Otto
Ignacio	Lester	Pancho
Ira	Lew	Pasquali
Irv	Lloyd	Paul
Irving	Loomis	Pedro
Isaac	Loren	Pepito
Isadore	Louis	Peter
Izzy	Lowell	Philbert
Jack	Luke	Phillip
James	Macio	Preston
Jasper	Mack	Pritchard
Jay	Manuel	Ralph

Randolph	Seth	Vernon
Randy	Seymour	Victor
Raphael	Sidney	Vince
Ray	Simon	Vincent
Raymond	Sol	Virgil
Richard	Stanley	Walker
Robert	Stephen	Wallace
Rod	Steve	Wally
Rodney	Sy	Walter
Roger	Tad	Webster
Roland	Tanis	Wendell
Ronald	Teddy	West
Ronny	Telford	Widen
Roy	Theodore	Wiley
Rubin	Todd	William
Russell	Tomas	Willis
Sam	Tommy	Willy
Samuel	Tony	Xavier
Sandy	Ulrich	Zachary
Sanford	Uriah	Zack
Sasha	Vasily	Zoltan
Saul	Vern	

(handwritten annotation near "Tony": "Toni — Girl name too")

Nicknames—Male and Female

Ace	Fast	Mumbles
Babyface	Fats	Noodles
Baldy	Fatso	Nosey
Bananas	Fingers	Penny
Big Boy	Flip	Pickles
Blackie	Freckles	Pimples
Blondie	Frenchy	Poopsie
Blue Eyes	Gunner	Pops
Bones	Hats	Punchy
Boss	Horse	Rabbit Ears
Bright Eyes	Hotshot	Red
Buck	Jiggles	Rocky
Buddy	Jojo	Sailor
Bull	Kiddo	Scrappy
Bunny	Kip	Shorty
Cappy	Kook	Shrimp
Corky	Kookie	Skinny
Crazy	Legs	Skip
Daddy	Liver Lips	Slappy
Dimples	Loverboy	Slim
Dopey	Mick	Sly
Duke	Monk	Snooker

Sonny	Sport	Sunny
Spider	Stoney	Tootsie
Spike	Sugar	Twinkle Toes

Female Names in Five Languages

English	French	German	Italian	Spanish
Agatha	Agathe	Agathe	Agara	Agata
Agnes	Agnes	Agnes	Agnese	Ines
Alice	Alice	Alice	Alicia	Alicia
Amelia	Amelie	Amalia	Amelia	Amelia
Ann	Anne	Anna	Anna	Ana
Blanch	Blanche	Blanca	Bianca	Blanca
Bridget	Brigitte	Brigitta	Brigida	Brigida
Caroline	Caroline	Karoline	Carolina	Carolina
Catherine	Catherine	Katherine	Caterina	Catalina
Cecilia	Cecile	Cacilia	Cecilia	Cecilia
Dorothy	Dorothee	Dorothea	Dorotea	Dorotea
Eleanor	Eleonore	Eleonore	Eleonora	Leanor
Elizabeth	Elise	Elisabeth	Elisabetta	Elisabetta
Emma	Emma	Emma	Emma	Ema
Esther	Esther	Esther	Ester	Ester
Eugenia	Eugenie	Eugenia	Eugenia	Eugenia
Florence	Florence	Florenz	Fiorenza	Florencia
Frances	Francoise	Frenziska	Francesca	Francisca
Frederica	Frederique	Friederike	Federica	Federica
Isabel	Isabelle	Isabelle	Isabella	Isabel
Joan	Jeanne	Johanna	Giovanna	Juana
Josephine	Joesphine	Josephine	Guiseppina	Josefina
Julia	Julie	Julie	Guilia	Julia
Louisa	Louise	Luise	Luisa	Luisa
Lucy	Lucie	Lucia	Lucia	Lucia
Margaret	Marguerite	Margarethe	Margherite	Margarita
Marianne	Marianne	Marianne	Marianna	Mariana
Martha	Marthe	Martha	Marta	Marta
Mary	Marie	Maria	Maria	Maria
Matilda	Mathilde	Matilde	Matilda	Matilda
Paula	Paule	Paula	Paola	Paula
Philippa	Philippine	Philippine	Filippa	Felipa
Rachel	Rachel	Rehel	Rachele	Raquel
Rebecca	Rebecca	Rebekka	Rebecca	Rebeca
Rose	Rose	Rose	Rosa	Rosa
Sophia	Sophie	Sophia	Sofia	Sofia
Susan	Susanne	Susanne	Susanna	Susana
Theresa	Therese	Therese	Teresa	Teresa
Victoria	Victoire	Victoria	Vittoria	Vitoria
Wilhelmina	Guillemette	Wilhelmina	Guglielma	Guillelmina

Male Names in Five Languages

English	French	German	Italian	Spanish
Abraham	Abraham	Abraham	Abrahamo	Abrahan
Adam	Adam	Adamo	Adano	Adan
Albert	Albert	Albrecht	Alberto	Alberto
Alexander	Alexandre	Alexander	Alessandro	Alejandro
Alfred	Alfred	Alfred	Alfredo	Alfredo
Alvin	Aluin	Alwin	Alvino	Aluino
Andrew	Andre	Andreas	Andreas	Andres
Anthony	Antoine	Anton	Antonio	Antony
Arnold	Arnaud	Arnold	Arnollo	Arnaldo
Arthur	Artus	Art(h)ur	Arturo	Artur
Bernard	Bernardin	Bernhard	Bernardo	Bernardo
Charles	Charles	Karl	Carlo	Carlos
Christopher	Christophe	Christophoro	Cristoforo	Cristiano
Conrad	Conrade	Konrad	Conrado	Conrado
Cornelius	Cornelius	Cornelius	Cornelio	Cornelius
Cyril	Cyrille	Cyrill	Cirillo	Cirilo
Daniel	Daniel	Daniel	Danillo	Daniel
Edmund	Edmond	Edmund	Edmondo	Edmondo
Edward	Eduoardo	Edward	Eduardo	Eduardo
Ernest	Ernest	Ernst	Ernesto	Ernesto
Eugene	Eugene	Eugen	Eugenio	Eugenio
Ferdinand	Ferdinand	Ferdinand	Ferdinando	Hernando
Francis	Francois	Franciscus	Francesco	Francisco
Frederick	Frederic	Friedrich	Frederico	Federico
George	Georges	Georg	Giorgio	Jorge
Gilbert	Guilbert	Gilbert	Gilberto	Gilberto
Godfrey	Godefroi	Gottfried	Goffredo	Godofredo
Gregory	Gregoire	Gregor	Gregorio	Gregorio
Henry	Henri	Heinrich	Enrico	Enrique
Herbert	Herbert	Herbert	Erberto	Heberto
Jacob	Jacob	Jakob	Jacopo	Jacobo
Jerome	Jerome	Hieronymus	Geronimo	Jeronimo
John	Jean	Johann	Giovanni	Juan
Joseph	Joseph	Joseph	Guiseppe	Jose
Julian	Julien	Julian	Guiliano	Julian
Lawrence	Laurent	Laurenz	Lorenzo	Lorenzo
Leonard	Leonard	Leonhard	Leonardo	Leonardo
Louis	Louis	Ludwig	Luigi	Luiz
Matthew	Mathieu	Matthaus	Matteo	Mateo
Maurice	Maurice	Moritz	Maurizio	Mauricio
Michael	Michel	Michael	Michele	Miguel
Nicholas	Mcole	Nikolaus	Niccolo	Nicolas
Oliver	Olivier	Olivier	Oliverio	Oliverio

Patrick	Patrice	Patrizius	Patrizio	Patricio
Paul	Paul	Paul	Paolo	Pablo
Peter	Pierre	Peter	Pietro	Pedro
Philip	Philippe	Philipp	Filippo	Felipe
Raymond	Raymond	Raimund	Raimondo	Raimundo
Richard	Richard	Richard	Riccardo	Ricardo
Robert	Robert	Robert	Roberto	Roberto
Samuel	Samuel	Samuel	Samuele	Samuel
Stephen	Etienne	Stephan	Stefano	Estefan
Theodore	Theodore	Theodor	Deodoro	Teodoro
Timothy	Timothee	Timotheus	Timoteo	Timoteor
Vincent	Vincent	Vicenz	Vincente	Vicente
Walter	Gauthier	Walther	Gualtiero	Gualtierio
William	Guillaume	Wilhelm	Gugielomo	Guillermo

3

Storytelling and Plotting

STORYTELLER, YOU ARE GOD!

That's right.

When you create a story and people it with characters you create out of your imagination, you are, for those magical moments, playing God. You and you alone decide who lives and who dies, who succeeds and who fails, who gets the girl (or guy) and who won't, who gets the funny lines and who doesn't. Playing God makes you all-powerful, but the responsibility is as awesome as it is fascinating.

You must think not only as one person but as every one of the characters you create.

You must know them inside out, for you alone have created them.

You must know what they will do, how they think, and what brains, talent, and abilities they have to live the life you have given them.

You are also fate and destiny, for you alone decide the outcome of their lives.

You know, of course, that once you give them life you must also give them purpose.

A reason for being.

A reason for doing what they do.

Each has faults as well as other qualities.

Each has goals and, as in life, the road to those goals is paved with many obstacles.

So, if you are to play God, you must know all the steps along the way.

The characters you create must be whole, must have a purpose for living, and must have goals to achieve, if only for this particular story.

Each major character must have obstacles to overcome that cause conflict, surprise turns in the road, crises to deal with, and the ability to succeed (or fail) in the situation into which they have been placed.

Good luck and may God be with you.

THE THEME

A theme suggests the arena of a story.

In the arena there is a problem to be overcome, a desire to be fulfilled, or a goal to be obtained.

The goal, desire, or problem is brought about by deliberate or nondeliberate involvement.

Involvement initiates motivation to achieve the goal, desire, or creates conflict.

An obstacle or antagonist opposing the goal, desire, or problem facing a protagonist creates conflict.

The conflict between the antagonist and the protagonist creates additional obstacles that must be overcome for the characters to achieve their goal, desire, or to resolve the primary problem.

Attempting to overcome obstacles leads to a crisis or series of crises, which in turn leads to the climax.

The climax leads to a solution that resolves the problem. The protagonist either achieves or fails to achieve the goal or desire.

Every story must have one basic element.

The theme.

A theme defines the type of story that is to be told, the general arena that defines the master plot.

The search for one's true self might be considered the theme of *The Wizard of Oz*, in which Dorothy finds that all she really wanted she had right at home. The Cowardly Lion finds his courage, the Scarecrow finds he always *had* brains, and the Tin Man finds he always *had* a heart.

In the film *Tootsie*, a male actor pretends to be a woman in order to get a role, and in this impersonation learns what it is like to be a member of the opposite sex.

The theme of *Gorillas in the Mist* was obsession.

The theme sets the arena for the development of the plot.

The following list suggests arenas in which you can build a story. For example, if you selected one of the following items, *power*, it could suggest a variety of paths.

It could suggest a story on the power of the press and the effect it has upon your protagonist.

It could become a story on the struggle for power between two giants in industry or two political candidates.

Ambition or greed was the theme of the film *Wall Street*.

The following themes are presented as suggestions. The story you tell must come from your own creativity.

However, by choosing a theme listed below, combining it with a protagonist and a worthy antagonist (see Chapter Two, Characters and Development) you can begin building a story premise.

Then, using the other chapters and sections in this book on purpose, involvement, conflict, secondary actions, crisis, turning points and surprises, the clock, obstacles, climax, and solution, you can develop a story outline upon which to base a more complete work.

Themes

Abortion	Happiness
Abuse	Hate
Addiction	History
Ambition	Homosexuality
Anger	Illness
Bigotry	Justice
Burnout	Loneliness
Capital punishment	Love
Corruption	Lust
Cover-ups	Marriage
Crime	Mercy killing
Discovery	Morality
Divorce	Nuclear power
Drugs	Obsession
Education	Old age
Environment	Passion
Failure	Police brutality
Freedom	Politics
Greed	Pornography

Possessiveness	Success
Poverty	Suicide
Power	Terrorism
Prostitution	The future
Rape	The handicapped
Religious persecution	The past
Revenge	Vivisection
Revolution	War
Rights	War veterans
Stress	Wealth

PRIMARY PURPOSE, SECONDARY ACTIONS, AND COUNTERACTIONS

Desire and purpose are the roots of goals, aims, and problems.

In order to create a story, you must give your protagonist(s) and antagonist(s) conflicting desires or purposes.

Once each has opposing desires or purposes, conflict ensues.

Primary purpose can be initiated by the protagonist or the antagonist either by deliberate or nondeliberate involvement (see page 58).

Once conflict has been established, both the protagonist and the antagonist seek to overthrow the other. During this battle, the protagonist and antagonist achieve secondary goals and maneuver to win the war.

To distinguish between primary goals and the additional moves that must be made to achieve the primary goals, let's call the additional moves secondary actions.

For example, let us say the primary goal of a protagonist (brought about by deliberate involvement) is to help a friend by proving the innocence of the friend.

And let us say the primary goal of the antagonist who actually committed the crime is to escape the law, having an innocent person pay for the crime. What might be the next action taken by the protagonist to help the friend accused of the crime?

From the list of SECONDARY ACTIONS, you might have the protagonist attempt to learn the truth.

The antagonist might counteract by seeking to implicate another, quite possibly the protagonist.

Now it's the protagonist's turn to counter, this time not only trying to accomplish his or her primary purpose but also having to prove his or her own innocence. See the COUNTERACTION list.

In between these actions, both sides would face obstacles, surprise twists, the ticking of the clock, the complications of the subplot, etc., until the story builds to a crisis, a climax, and the final resolution.

The following is a list of PRIMARY GOALS for your consideration.

Primary Goals

To prove one's own innocence
To prove the innocence of another
To achieve success
To find or locate a missing person or object
To create a work of art
To win the love of another
To aid someone in trouble
To further a cause
To bring about a better world
To learn one's true identity
To overcome a handicap
To overcome financial hardship
To save a business
To begin a profession or a career
To gain an important position
To implicate another
To commit a crime
To assume power
To run for political office
To bring about the downfall of another
To rape
To cause harm to another
To seek revenge
To escape the past
To follow in another's footsteps
To regain something lost or stolen
To win a game or contest
To get a promotion or a raise
To serve justice
To gain forgiveness
To repay a debt
To learn the truth
To alter the truth
To alter a mistake
To search for treasure
To achieve fame and fortune
To teach someone a lesson
To right a wrong
To alter the course of history

> To save a marriage
> To prevent a crime
> To get back home
> To find a witness
> To get rid of a witness

Involvement is the way you bring your protagonist and antagonist into your story to permit each to attempt to achieve his or her primary goal, which in turn precipitates conflict.

If you wish your protagonist to initiate the situation, then select DELIBERATE INVOLVEMENT.

If, on the other hand, you wish your protagonist to be drawn into the situation other than by his or her initiation, then choose NONDELIBERATE INVOLVEMENT.

Even though your protagonist is the hero or heroine of your story, the protagonist does not always initiate the situation, though he or she eventually becomes the moving force in the story.

For example, let's say your protagonist is a police officer who reacts to a crime.

The police officer doesn't cause the crime to be committed. It's the antagonist who commits the crime to which the police officer responds.

The police officer's duty is to solve crimes and bring perpetrators to justice, but the officer's involvement in this particular case would be nondeliberate.

Once involved, the police officer would become a moving force, as he or she seeks to solve the case and bring the criminal to justice.

The antagonist's or criminal's involvement would be deliberate if the crime was premeditated.

The criminal's involvement would be nondeliberate if the crime was accidental.

In a sense, this is another "chicken or egg" problem. The answer depends solely on the story you wish to tell.

Let's take a look at some of the deliberate and nondeliberate means of involvement.

Deliberate Involvement

> Setting out to help another
> Volunteering for a mission or a job
> Fulfilling a duty, responsibility, or obligation related to vocation
> Seeking revenge
> Seeking justice
> Becoming a crusader

Pursuing a hobby or avocation
Becoming involved to win a bet
Seeking to protect another
Taking a job, being in need of money
Wanting to win the woman
Wanting to win the man
Having lofty ambitions
Beginning a new life
Seeking to right a wrong
Seeking to bring about change
Wanting to prove a point
Being normally curious
Being psychologically disturbed
Planning a crime
Attempting to prevent a crime
Attempting to escape the past
Being terrorized
Seeking to relieve suspicions
Seeking to prove oneself
Seeking to prove another's innocence
Seeking to overcome an inhibition
Seeking to overcome a handicap
Searching for a missing loved one, friend, family member
Being asked to act as an intermediary
Wanting to be the best
Seeking to regain something
Wanting to get married
Wanting to remain single
Seeking excitement or adventure
Answering an advertisement
Accepting a challenge
Seeking to return something
Seeking to join
Worshiping a hero
Having a specific talent or training
Seeking reason
Seeking reward
Having a secret desire
Seeking redemption
Being dedicated to a holy mission
Attempting to fulfill a promise
Practicing one-upmanship
Needing the job
Acting out of greed
Acting out of jealousy
Enjoying competition

Being prone to violence
Being blackmailed
Seeking power
Covering up a previous crime
Pursuing a cause
Acting out of anger
Seeking to overthrow another
Seeking to destroy the competition
Paying off a debt
Repaying a debt of honor
Seeking a promotion
Attempting to even the score

Nondeliberate Involvement

Becoming a victim of mistaken identity
Befriending someone in trouble
Accidentally coming into possession of an object desired by another
Being the victim of an attempted assassination
Being at the wrong place at the wrong time
Receiving a letter or package sent to another
Receiving a phone call meant for another
Overhearing a plot
Discovering someone in hiding
Discovering a body
Being bothered by a stranger
Becoming involved with someone who is not what he or she
    pretends to be
Getting on the wrong train, plane, bus, or ship
Answering a newspaper ad that's not what it seems
Being wrongfully accused
Becoming stranded in an unfamiliar place
Coming into a sudden or strange inheritance
Suffering a loss of memory
Coming to the rescue of another
Being sent to a wrong address
Giving a hitchhiker a lift
Becoming a witness to a crime or an event
Being entrusted with the safety of an object or person
Finding an infant on the doorstep
Being forced to comply at gunpoint
Purchasing something desired by another
Being forced to commit a crime
Discovering stolen loot
Being under the influence
Committing a crime accidentally
Being abandoned

Picking up the wrong luggage
Attempting to return a lost or stolen article
Having no recourse but to fulfill an idle boast
Paying the price for assuming another's identity
Having special talents
Being kidnapped
Being dispatched on a mission that is not fully explained
Inquiring about someone
Reading one's own obituary
Inheriting something of value
Becoming a victim of a hoax
Hitching a ride
Being involved in an accident
Signing aboard a ship
Recognizing someone who doesn't want to be recognized
Answering a knock at the door
Renting a cottage for a vacation
Being a passenger on a ship or a plane
Stumbling into a mysterious meeting
Spending a night in a strange place
Discovering something was planted in clothing or luggage
Investigating a minor infraction of the law
Going on a blind date

Secondary Actions and Counteractions

To aid another to escape
To alter evidence
To alter identity
To attempt to perform an act
    with no prior experience
To become an impostor
To bluff
To borrow
To break an alibi
To bribe
To bring a villain to justice
To call attention to a fact
To call in an old debt
To call upon some special
    skill or knowledge
To cover an existing crime
To erase evidence
To destroy something
    of value
To escape

To feign illness
To file charges
To find a body
To find a replacement
To find a witness
To find help
To find the guilty party
To find the real weapon
To get back home
To get rid of a witness
To get someone to break a
    promise
To go into hiding
To hide another
To investigate
To kill
To lie
To locate the real culprit
To overcome one's own fears
To panic

To prevent another crime or
  act of violence
To prove a lie was told
To rectify a mistake
To search for evidence
To search for information
To secure an alibi
To see that the truth is told

To seek the help of the police
To spy
To stay and fight
To steal
To travel to another town,
  city, state, country
To trick someone to
  commit an act

CONFLICT

Remember the old saying "opposites attract"? That may be true, but in storytelling, opposites collide. It is essential that a story have conflict to be dramatic. To produce conflict, the protagonist's purpose (aim, goal, desire) encounters an obstacle, the obstacle being either the elements or an antagonist whose purpose is opposed to that of the protagonist. A story may begin with the purpose, aim, or goal of the protagonist or that of the antagonist for conflict to be initiated.

Examples of Conflicts

Protagonist	**Antagonist**
In love	A rival
In love	Seeks to separate lovers
Wants object	Wants same object
Seeks justice	Seeks to escape justice
Wants to succeed	Wants protagonist to fail
Wants job	Wants the same job
Seeks to achieve goal	Seeks to achieve same goal
Seeks to achieve goal	Seeks to prevent achievement
Seeks to discover something	Seeks to prevent discovery
Has one philosophy	Has opposite view
Looks to build something	Attempts to destroy it
Seeks to defend	Wants to attack
The victim	The assailant
The defender	The aggressor
The loyalist	The traitor
A competitor	A competitor
Seeks to recover object	Steals an object
Looks to reveal truth	Seeks to hide the truth
Happy	Jealous of that happiness
Possesses property	Seeks the property
Seeks to regain what is right-fully his or hers	Seeks to prevent recovery

Seeks to overcome handicap	Seeks to prevent it
On the side of good	On the side of evil
Seeks to prevent possession	Seeks to possess
Seeks to destroy power	Seeks to be all-powerful
Seeks fame	Seeks to defame

SECONDARY STORY—THE SUBPLOT

A subplot is a secondary story linked to the master plot, or it may be on its own, not directly involved in the master plot but affecting one or more of the principal characters.

A subplot may be dramatic, or it might serve as comedic relief. If the master plot is comedic, it might serve as a counter-comedic plot; that is, it's either serious or even sillier.

Subplots are often referred to as "railroad tracks" because they run parallel to the master plot. Not all stories require a subplot. You will seldom find one in short stories or in most straight-line episodic television shows.

Subplots should not be confused with the simultaneous story lines in a TV soap opera or a series such as "Hill Street Blues." These seldom have a master plot but combine a number of stories, each independent.

Let's say you are writing a story about a pair of detectives investigating a homicide. Finding the murderer is the master plot.

But one of the detectives is also having a domestic problem affecting his work and other relationships.

If the emphasis of the story is the investigation of the homicide, the detective's domestic problem is the subplot and runs parallel to the master plot. It has an emotional effect on the detective but has nothing to do with solving the murder.

If the domestic problem is the master plot, the theme being the effect a detective's personal life has on his work, you have *Detective Story*, a play by Sidney Kingsley later made into a film starring Kirk Douglas, Eleanor Parker, and Lee Grant.

In television's *The Fugitive*, each episode had the subplot of the protagonist searching for the "one-armed man" who could clear him of a crime. Each week's master plot was a plot unto itself.

Using the Subplot List

The subplot depends upon the master plot and what your protagonist is doing.

For example, an ambitious, young, married man seeks to beat the competition to land an account that could get him a promotion and a much-needed raise.

The writer might use one or more subplots, remembering that the subplot may or may not connect to the master plot.

For instance, while attempting to achieve his primary goal, the protagonist's wife, tired of being left home alone, becomes involved with another man who later is shown to be involved in the master plot. Or the protagonist's wife is close to having a baby, or she threatens him with divorce (unconnected subplots). Or perhaps he must contend with his wife's jealousy.

Or let us assume your protagonist is unmarried and he or she falls in love or suddenly discovers an illness.

A subplot might have no bearing on the master plot or eventually cross into the master plot.

For example, the protagonist falling in love might not complicate his primary goal.

That would be an unconnected subplot as it only creates an additional situation for the protagonist to deal with.

However, if later in the story the newly-found love interest is instrumental in helping the protagonist achieve his or her primary goal, that subplot would be connected to the master plot.

It is up to you as to when and how to use a subplot.

Suggested Subplot Themes

Separation, divorce (see list of DOMESTIC PROBLEMS)
Awaiting news of some medical tests
Falling in love
Continuing love affair
Another romantic or sexual involvement
Sudden inheritance
Financial problem
Searching for someone
Fighting an alcohol or drug habit
Taking care of someone
Preparing for a trip or vacation
Pursuing a hobby or avocation
Attending school, night school
Fighting an illness no one else knows about
Giving a surprise party
Trying to keep the past a secret
Getting an offer that cannot be refused
Planning a change in career, job or profession
Jealousy
Competition
Crime that eventually links to the master plot
Expecting the birth of a child

Trying to keep an appointment
Trying to fulfill a promise
Trying to contact someone
Somebody close expecting you to meet him or her
Spouse's, lover's or child's birthday
Trying to collect what is owed
Trying to find a new place to live
Having to move
Trying to lose weight
Being sued
Trying to evade or avoid another
Making and breaking dates, appointments
Trying to get somewhere on time
Trying to get to the church on time
Trying to settle a dispute
Suspecting that a mate or lover is cheating
Becoming a new parent
Trying to deal with fears or phobias
Trying to overcome a gambling habit
Seeing a psychiatrist or therapist
Living a double life

THE CLOCK IS TICKING

Although not every story demands it, to heighten drama and suspense a writer may add an element often referred to as "the clock."

This element is usually used early or midway through the story. The clock is used to increase the intensity of a situation that must be resolved within a given time. If the goal is not accomplished within the time set by the clock, all will be lost.

Time limits combined with various obstacles put additional pressure on the protagonist.

The following lists things that might happen should time run out:

The protagonist will lose a lover or loved one.
A villain will escape.
A crime will be committed.
The patient will die.
A bomb will detonate.
A storm will arrive.
A collision will occur.
A person will commit suicide.
A terrible, irreversible mistake will take place.
A secret will be revealed.
A marriage will be torn asunder.
A cave-in will occur.

Something important will be destroyed.
An identity will be revealed.
The truth will never be known.
The awful truth will become known.
The wrong instructions will be followed.
A witness will be silenced.
A wild animal will escape.
A pet will be destroyed.
The wrong person will die or suffer a terrible fate.
A donor will not be found.
The case will never be solved.
An explanation will come too late.
An animal or human will be put to death.
An innocent person will pay the ultimate price.
Someone will never know the truth.
The killer will strike again.
The bank will foreclose.
The plane, train, or ship will depart.
A warning will not be received in time.
A fortune will be lost.
A terrible wrong will never be righted.
The enemy will attack.
A war will begin.
The environment will be affected.

These are a few of the more traditional clocks. When and where to use the clock is a decision only you can make, but once the clock is running, you've unquestionably increased the suspense of your story.

THE ROCKY ROAD—THE OBSTACLES ALONG THE WAY

As it's been said, "Life isn't fair." The road to achieving your protagonist's goal cannot be clear and uncluttered. In storytelling, if the road is not filled with obstacles, the story is sure to be boring and probably not worth telling.

Remember the concept of storytelling: Get your protagonists up a tree, throw rocks at them, and then get them down.

Obstacles need not always be physical. They can often be psychological or emotional.

Some stories might require a combination of physical and non-physical obstacles.

That choice is yours.

The following list of obstacles should ignite a spark.

One's own fear must be overcome.
Bad weather forestalls a search.

Bad weather forestalls an escape.
Bad weather forestalls the execution of a plan.
Fire inhibits progress.
An earthquake occurs.
An explosion takes place.
A bridge is washed out.
The road is out.
A promise was made not to do a particular thing.
A truth cannot be told.
A vehicle breaks down.
A vehicle runs out of gas.
A hostage is taken. Innocent people are in the way.
Someone comes between.
An old lover returns.
Transportation is unavailable.
The protagonist becomes a suspect.
The protagonist is pinned down by enemy fire.
A witness is killed.
A witness disappears.
Evidence is destroyed or missing.
A weapon cannot be used.
Ammunition has run out.
Supplies have run out.

SUSPENSE

Suspense depends on the conflict between the protagonist and the antagonist. Suspense may be generated by the success or failure of someone allied with the protagonist. Suspense is acutely intensified by doubt about whether the protagonist or an ally will succeed or fail to overcome an obstacle or the antagonist.

For example, let us say that your protagonist learns something vital to achieving his or her goal and victory over the antagonist. If the protagonist immediately uses that information to achieve his or her goal, all suspense is ended.

However, if the protagonist has difficulty using the information, the suspense is intensified.

To achieve suspense, the following situations might be used:

It appears the message will not be delivered in time.
It appears the message will be intercepted by the enemy.
It appears that help will not arrive in time.
The antagonist is poised to strike again.
There is doubt that the witness will come forward.
It appears the truth will not be learned in time.
It appears the lie will not be exposed.

It appears the protagonist or an ally will not survive the obstacle.
The protagonist or ally cannot reach safety.
The person being sought is no longer alive.
The rescue attempt of the protagonist or ally is delayed
      or obstructed.
The proposed meeting place is found abandoned.
The protagonist is unaware that his or her plan has been exposed.
The protagonist or ally falls prey to a scam or a lie.
The protagonist is unaware that the antagonist's plan has already
      been executed.
The protagonist is unaware that a false motive has
      been substituted.
The protagonist is unaware that a false villain has been substituted.
The protagonist is unaware that an ally is really the enemy.
An ally suddenly or unexplainedly turns on the protagonist.
The protagonist is unaware that someone is lurking in the shadows.
The protagonist is unaware that a trap has been set.
The protagonist is unaware that the food and drink has been poisoned
      or drugged.
A phone keeps ringing but there is no one there.
Unknown hands cut telephone lines, electric wires.

CRISIS, SURPRISE—A TWIST IS ON THE RISE

To heighten the suspense in a story and to keep it as unpredictable as you can, the more twists and turns you take (within reason), the better. Especially if it's a crime story. Twists, turns, and crises in comedy, romance, or any other drama can be an advantage, too. The following list should tweak your creative imagination to help you provide a crisis or turning point.

Story twists should always come when the reader or viewer least expects them. In episodic television, they had better come at least at the end of each act just before the commercial to draw the viewer back. Twists or surprises can be obstacles for the protagonist to overcome or temporary setbacks just as it looks like everything is going well.

As examples:

Someone unexpected walks in at the wrong time.
Someone gets or delivers the wrong message.
An urgent call is made, but the person who was to receive
      the call isn't there.
An inheritance comes unexpectedly.
An unexpected discovery is made.
Something of value has disappeared.
A suspected enemy turns out to be a friend.

A trusted friend, lover, or employee is not what he or she
     appeared to be.
A person thought to be dead is found to be alive.
A person thought to be alive is found dead.
Someone suffers an unexpected change of heart.
The suspected motive is shown to be false.
Someone is kidnapped or abducted.
An unexpected body shows up.
The body is missing.
The weapon is gone.
Unexpected help arrives.
Someone is double-crossed.
The telephone line has been cut.
The road is out.
A killer waits in the shadows.
The enemy has discovered the plan.
A man turns out to be a woman.
The gun is out of bullets.
Something terrible is about to happen, but it's only a dream.
A warning sound turns out to be a cat.
The train, boat, or plane is missed.
Someone makes a wrong assumption.
Help that is urgently needed doesn't show.
The wrong person is killed.
The car is stopped, but the wrong person is behind the wheel.
Someone's dirty trick pays off.
The boat is beginning to sink.
There is no place to land the plane.
The bridge is going up.
The train is coming right at the stalled car.
A letter that can change the course of events is discovered.
An innocent person stands accused.
Lovers are separated because a lie is believed.
Moral or financial support is suddenly and
     unexplainedly withdrawn.
No one believes the truth.
The child is not waiting at the school.
There's no money left.
The wrong person shows up.
An unexpected invitation arrives.
The jackpot is hit.
The horse comes in.
A bomb is discovered.
A shot is fired by an unseen assassin.
A witness comes forth.
A husband, wife or lover is deserted.

The place has been ransacked.
An accident claims the life of someone close.
A close friend is found to be an enemy.
A traitor is present.
A baby is on the way.
Pregnancy is discovered.
A job offer arrives.
Orders come at a most inopportune time.
Just when needed, the car won't start.
A sudden opportunity presents itself.
The husband walks in, or the wife walks in.
The situation is construed to be something it isn't.
The bluff is called.
A little lie grows into a giant.
A superior prevents further involvement.
A sudden injury halts progress.
Action is delayed.
Orders from superiors conflict.
Needed equipment is unavailable.
A means to communicate is unavailable.
A code has yet to be broken.
A large amount of money is needed to continue.
Another is also in need at a precarious moment.
Wild animals prevent proceeding further.
Hostile tribes prevent proceeding further.
Diplomatic immunity prevents arrest.
A guarded border prevents escape.
Proper identification or papers are lost.
Confidentiality of church, attorney, doctor halts progress.
Sudden mental breakdown halts progress.
A character is knocked unconscious.
Proceeding places someone else in jeopardy.
Cover has been blown.
Secret information is revealed.
Parents interfere.
An old wound is opened.
The escape is blocked.
A pursuit is in progress.
Expected information does not arrive.
A legal technicality blocks the way.
Booby traps prevent advancing.
A mine field prevents advancing.
A landslide occurs.
A hiding place is or will be revealed.
An associate becomes a turncoat.
Help is refused.

Trust is withdrawn.
A loyal friend defects.
Presence is discovered.
A larger opposing force is faced.
A character is unable to gain entrance.
A character is torn between two impending disasters.
A character is unable to learn the location of a person or a thing.
An object blocks the way.
Pressure is brought to bear to prevent progress.
Difficult terrain must be crossed.
The objective is impossible to reach.
Proper means to continue the chase or escape are unavailable.
A character is unable to operate technical equipment or a vehicle.
Weapons are insufficient to overcome an opposing force.
Time is insufficient to achieve the immediate goal.
A character suddenly loses sight, hearing, motion.
A character is unable to break out of bondage or imprisonment.

THE BEGINNING OF THE END—CRISES AND CLIMAXES

The crisis of the story is that final confrontation with the last remaining obstacle. The climax of a story is where the question is decided one way or the other, when victory or defeat is established, when the outcome is determined by a solution and the protagonist achieves his or her goal. In other words, the crisis point is when the protagonist of your story:

Discovers the identity of the antagonist
Discovers the location of the antagonist
Discovers the motive of the antagonist
Learns of the final danger that still lies ahead
Discovers the mistake
Uncovers the secret
Discovers the lie
Learns the truth
Remembers something
Finds the key to the solution
Learns what is to happen
Manages to escape
Discovers the real plot
Realizes someone was falsely accused
Discovers he or she has been conned
Faces his or her moment of truth
Regains his or her senses
Learns the location of the object or person he or she seeks

The climax is the action taken by the protagonist to bring about a resolution by means of a solution.

RESOLUTIONS AND SOLUTIONS

Resolutions and solutions are simply the way you wish to resolve the problem or achieve the goal of your protagonist. As I said earlier, if your characters are well drawn, they will tell you what they will do and to what lengths they will go to achieve their goal or to resolve their problem.

Remember the Achilles' heel of each character.

What have they learned about each other, and what tools or devices will they use to achieve that ultimate goal?

Is your protagonist the kind of person who would use a weapon? Does he or she know how to use a weapon? How clever is your protagonist? What special skills or knowledge can he or she draw upon in that climactic scene?

How evil is your antagonist? Is he or she capable of violence at the showdown? Would he or she suffer the pangs of guilt or sudden remorse?

These are just some of the questions you must ask yourself and your characters before deciding on the resolution or solution.

The following list suggests ways for your protagonist to resolve the story, the details of which must come from your imagination, and from the characters created.

> The protagonist gets the antagonist to confess his or her sins or
> crime or goal.
> The protagonist causes the villain to return to the
> scene of the crime.
> The protagonist plays upon the fears of the antagonist to bring about
> his or her confession.
> The protagonist convinces the antagonist that an accomplice has
> confessed the crime or the intent.
> The protagonist tricks the antagonist into telling the truth.
> The antagonist is caught before committing another crime or
> act of violence.
> The protagonist rescues the intended victim.
> The hostage is rescued.
> The intended victim is found safe.
> All is forgiven.
> The antagonist suffers an error in judgment.
> A prayer is answered.
> The antagonist sees the error of his or her ways.
> The antagonist brings about his or her own demise.

Last minute evidence is found to clear the innocent suspect and
    prove the guilt of another.
Memory is restored.
The patient recovers.
A cure is found.
The medication is brought in time.
The lovers learn the truth and are reconciled.
A runaway comes home.
Someone sacrifices himself or herself for another.
The antagonist suffers a change of heart.
A coward becomes a hero.
The final plan is successful.
A former enemy reverses his or her role.
There is a last-minute reprieve.
A dream is finally fulfilled.
The antagonist takes his or her own life.
Someone believed dead is found alive.
An accomplice turns on the antagonist.
A bizarre accident resolves the problem.
Someone's faith is restored.
A terrible wrong is finally righted.
A reunion is brought about.
Financial aid is found.
The storm finally subsides.
The rains come.
Help arrives.
A wrong promise is rightfully broken.
A promise is kept.
A final obstacle is removed.
The man gets the woman; the woman gets the man.
The promotion is received.
Fears are finally conquered.
Opportunity is provided.
A lesson is learned and acted on.
An understanding is brought about and acted on.
Everything is back where it was before.
The battle is won.
The revolution succeeds.
The revolution fails.
Evil is dethroned.

4

Switching

Taking another writer's story or characters without legal permission is plagiarism, and it should not be condoned by any writer. However, there are just so many basic premises, and every one has been used thousands of times with different plots, characters, locations, and times in which the story takes place. Each premise became new and fresh stories.

Switching is a common practice so long as the writer uses nothing more than the basic premise, and the characters, plot development, dialogue, and locations are all new.

For example, the concept of Romeo and Juliet has been done umpteen times—two lovers caught between feuding factions. The Broadway musical and film *West Side Story*, was a variation, or switch, on Romeo and Juliet.

Television's *The Fugitive* used the premise of *Les Miserables*. How many versions have you seen of *Abie's Irish Rose* (racial or religious differences in a romance), or thieves greedily falling out with one another as in *The Treasure of the Sierra Madre*?

If you're going to switch a story, first make sure it's a story worth switching.

The classics are probably the best place to start.

Then consider changing the period that the original story took place in, the location where it took place, and the characters in it.

If the protagonist was a man, consider what would happen if "he" became a "she."

What if the ages were changed dramatically?

If the original story took place in an urban area, would the story work if it took place in a remote or rural area?

What if the story took place in the past? The present? The future? What would Romeo and Juliet be like in space, each from a different planet?

How about *The Merchant of Venice* in New York, today? Let's try *Dr. Jekyll and Mr. Hyde*. Suppose the time is the present and the good doctor is a young chemistry student who accidentally creates a formula that changes him (or her) into someone of the opposite sex rather than into a monster?

Here's a list of books that are ripe for switching:

Appointment in Samarra
Don Quixote
God's Little Acre
Count of Monte Cristo
Faust
J'Accuse
Kidnapped
The Three Musketeers
Alice's Adventures in Wonderland
Around the World in 80 Days
Captains Courageous
A Connecticut Yankee in King Arthur's Court
Elmer Gantry
Frankenstein
Gentlemen's Agreement
Innocents Abroad
Les Miserables
Lord Jim
Men Against the Sea
Monsieur Beaucaire
Murders in the Rue Morgue
The Picture of Dorian Gray
The Postman Always Rings Twice
The Prince and the Pauper
The Scarlet Pimpernel
Tarzan
The Third Man
Topper
Treasure Island
What Makes Sammy Run ?
The Devil and Daniel Webster
Here Comes Mr. Jordan

When considering switching a story, ask yourself:

Who is my new protagonist? Male? Female? A child or teenager? Who is my new antagonist? Male? Female? A child or teenager? What change of goals are there in my new story? What kind of new ending can I find? What other period of time could this premise work in? The past? The present? The future? What would be a new and fresh location in which to play the story? Rural? Urban? Foreign country?

Answer these questions creatively and it's a whole new ball game. Seek and ye shall find!

5

Action and Adventure

Right up there with crime and comedy are action/adventure stories. This genre can be historical or contemporary and includes numerous areas such as westerns, war and the military, fire fighting, search and rescue, disasters, treasure hunting, archaeological digs, big game hunting, pirates on the high sea, spy thrillers, some types of science fiction, chase stories, exploration stories,and some sports such as auto racing, boat or yacht racing, bull fighting, sky diving, and free-falling.

Historical and period stories like *Ben Hur, The Three Musketeers, Robin Hood, The Count of Monte Christo,* and *Treasure Island* are just a few that made for excellent action/adventure stories. And let's not discount the great action/adventure films that starred Sylvester Stallone and Arnold Schwartzenegger or the films of Steven Spielberg.

DISASTERS

Disasters most always make for good action/adventure stories as proven by the movies *The Towering Inferno, Black Sunday, The Titanic, The Poseidon Adventure*, and *Backdraft*. These were just a few of the big disaster films that did excellent box office business.

Here's a list of disasters that would make for excellent action/adventure stories.

Airplane crash	Flood
Avalanche	Forest fire
Blizzard	Heat wave
Building collapse	Hurricane
Cave-in	Landslide
Cold wave	Mudslide
Disease	Sinking ship
Drought	Terrorist attack
Earthquake	Tidal wave
Epidemic	Tornadoes
Explosion	Train crash
Famine	Typhoon
Fire	Volcanic eruption

CHARACTERS IN ACTION / ADVENTURE STORIES

Anti-terrorists	Paramedics
Bodyguards	Pilots
Brave individuals	Race car drivers
Coast Guardsmen	Sailors
Counterspies	Seabees
Cowboys	Search and Rescue teams
Divers	Ship captains
Doctors	Ski patrols
Drivers	Skiers
Explorers	Sky divers
Fire fighters	Soldiers
Guides	Soldiers of fortune
Hunters	Special Service forces
Lifeguards	Spies
Marines	SWAT teams
Members of the Bomb Squad	Terrorists
Mountain climbers	Test pilots
Nurses	Western & Indian scouts

STORY LINES

A plane crashes in very rugged territory in the mountains, leaving only 10 survivors, all blinded, and a storm is coming sometime within the next 24 hours. How will they survive the freezing storm and make it back to civilization?

Three convicts, who hate one another, manage to escape from prison and have to learn to trust and depend on each other if they're to succeed in their escape.

A double-agent prepares to alter his identity so that he can escape the world of espionage where he knows he is to be "taken out," but has no idea which side it is that wants him dead.

Terrorists take over a small town that is adjacent to a prison farm and the only ones who can save the town are the prisoners from the farm.

Three soldiers of fortune set out to find the one man who can save the life of the wife of one of the men they seek, who has been hired to participate in a Middle-Eastern revolution.

A new bacterial strain is being brought into this country by a courier for a scientist who is planning to use in in an experiment. However, the courier meets with an accident, the container is broken, and those aboard the plane are unwittingly contaminated, each going in different directions. Suddenly an epidemic becomes evident and those who have been exposed to the bacteria must be found before they contaminate the entire city, if not the state or country or world.

The race is on between two rival factions for a sunken treasure that lies beneath shark-infested waters.

6

Cops and Robbers
(and other villains)

Few individuals in television, film, or fiction will disagree that crime *does* pay when you're writing it for the media. More than 65 percent of TV news "breaking stories" deal with crime, and if you check your *TV Guide*, the movie section of your newspapers, or your local bookstore, just take a look at how many shows, films, and books deal with crime. There are all sorts of crimes, ranging from battering to criminal homicide, from burglary to robbery to rape. Crimes are committed by individuals, terrorist groups, organized crime, serial killers, kidnappers, street gangs, white collar criminals, by those who commit domestic crimes, and by political, computer, and blue collar criminals who steal from their place of employment.

There are minor crimes or misdemeanors, as well as felonies and criminal homicides with special circumstances that demand the death penalty.

Here are some **characters** that could appear in a crime story:

Amateur sleuth	Ex-convicts
Associates of the antagonist	Friends of the victim
Associates of the suspect(s)	Girlfriend of suspect
Business associates of victim	Girlfriend of victim
Convicts	Investigative reporter
Defense attorney	Judge

Medical Examiner
Members of the Crime
    Lab team
Members of the jury
Members of the
    victim's family
Police investigators
Prison guards
Private Investigator

Prosecutor
Snitches
Spouse of suspect
Spouse of victim
Suspect(s)
Underworld characters
Victim(s)
Warden
Witnesses

Every criminal has a **motive** and every crime story has a **theme**. In many instances, the motive is the theme or the theme suggests the motive. Here are a few possibilities:

Abuse
Addiction
Ambition
Concealing another crime
Domestic problems
Fear of discovery
Financial gain
Greed
Hate
Impulsive/compulsive

Jealousy
Love
Lust
Mental illness
Mercy killing
Passion
Power
Revenge
To be set free
To maintain a secret

There are a multitude of crimes, many of which involve more than one criminal activity. For example, an armed holdup man may be intent on committing a robbery but winds up committing murder as well. Or a kidnapper intentionally or unintentionally kills his victim.

Often one crime begets another. Example: someone who is being blackmailed is forced to kill the blackmailer, or a spouse being abused kills in self defense. Therefore we may have a variety of felonies when dealing with a *"criminal"* homicide. A homicide is the taking of a human life. A *criminal* homicide is the taking a human life that is neither excusable or justifiable. A *criminal* homicide must carry with it any of the following: premeditation, the intention to kill or commit bodily harm, the perpetrator must be engaged in a dangerous act with wanton regard for human life, or be engaged in a felony against a person as in robbery, rape, aggravated assault, hijacking, or arson. This is known as *Felony Murder.*

Among those charges involving a **homicide** are:

A murder of passion
Multiple murders
Spree killing
Manslaughter
Voluntary manslaughter

Serial killing
Special circumstances
Mass murders
Involuntary manslaughter
Driveby killings

The terms *Justifiable* and *Excusable* are explained as follows.

Excusable homicide means a homicide was committed but it was not considered criminal as it was not brought about with any criminal intent nor did the homicide occur during the commission of a felony. It could have been an accidental taking of a human life while performing a legal act, or the individual was being threatened or intimidated with a lethal weapon and was in fear the weapon would be used in taking his life.

A *Justifiable* homicide is the authorized taking of another life to prevent the commission of a felony such as in rape, robbery, or to prevent the escape of an armed perpetrator; or under authorization of proper legal authority, such as a police officer in the line of duty, a soldier during time of war, or the carrying out of a legal death sentence.

Naturally, not every crime committed is a criminal homicide. The following is a partial suggested list of other types of criminal activities:

Arson	Kidnapping
Assault	Molestation
Battery	Piracy
Blackmail	Pornography
Burglary	Prostitution
Counterfeiting	Racketeering
Drug trafficking	Rape
Embezzlement	Robbery
Extortion	Sabotage
Forgery	Shoplifting
Gambling	Smuggling
Hijacking	Terrorism

Although many crimes are committed by individuals, we must not overlook the vast amount of criminal activity committed by organized crime, which includes such criminal organizations as the Mafia, the Chinese Triads, the Japanese and Korean Yakuza, neighborhood street gangs, the Mexican Mafia, the Black Brotherhood, the Jamaican Posse, and others.

To these have been added the Israeli Mafia and the Russian Mafia. All these groups are presently operating in the United States and abroad.

Criminal homicides are committed in every conceivable way imaginable, from shooting to stoning to garroting the victim. Although pages upon pages could easily list the means of taking another life, here are but a few grisly suggestions:

Beating	Drowning
Burying alive	Freezing
Decapitating	Gassing

Hanging	Setting afire
Impaling	Starving
Over-dosing	Stomping
Poisoning	Strangling

STORY NOTIONS

A criminal with a known M.O. (*modus operandi*) is forced to find the copycat who is committing crimes all over the city and making these crimes look like they were carried out by the former. The police are sure it is he who is committing the crimes.

A innocent cop is framed for [murder] [robbery] and his brother, an underworld figure who lives on the other side of the law, has to turn private eye to come to his brother's aid.

A woman with a multiple personality disorder is unaware that one of her personalities is a killer.

An important artifact is stolen from the church where the Mafia Don and his family worship. The Don orders his lieutenants and his soldiers to find the thief and make sure the artifact is returned to the church.

An otherwise normal man finds himself suffering from a compulsive order to kill and although he cannot bring himself to turn himself in, he leaves messages at the scene of each crime, pleading for the police to find him and kill him before he kills again.

A hypno-analyst turns his patients/subjects into hitmen and hitwomen by giving them post-hypnotic suggestions that are triggered by a telephone call.

THE COPS

Most people who work for law enforcement are a breed unto themselves. Most are very dedicated people and although every so often we read or hear about a rogue cop, on the whole people in law enforcement are law-abiding citizens who "protect and serve."

I can't recall a time any police officer I know ever received a telephone call inviting him or her to a party with "civilians." The calls they "catch" always deal with the seamy side of life, the scum of the world, and the bloody remains of (more often than not) innocent men, women, and children. Although many of us writers, directors, and producers portray cops as being hardened to what they come up against, their minds are scarred with vision of what one human being can do to another. Perhaps that is one of the reasons they are a close-knit community staying within the confines and the company of others in law enforcement. In most cases their thinking is it's *"us"* against *"them."*

When we speak of **law enforcement**, we include:

Bureau of Alcohol, Tobacco and Firearms	Drug Enforcement Agency
County Sheriffs	Federal Bureau of Investigations
Federal Air Marshalls	Highway Patrol
Immigration & Naturalization	Postal Inspector
Internal Revenue Service	Secret Service
Metropolitan Police	U.S. Coast Guard
State Police	U.S. Customs
Central Intelligence Agency	U.S. Marshalls

And let's not forget all of the military services that maintain their own criminal investigative commands, along with a host of other agencies under The Department of Justice, The Department of the Interior, The Department of Defense, as well as other national organizations

When writing about law enforcement, it is essential that you, as the writer, decide at what level your law enforcement people should be— local, county, state, or federal.

You should also decide whether your locale will be fictional or an actual locale. If the latter, before you start writing about them, their jurisdiction, their ranks, and operations, you should contact the Public Relations Department of that specific locale to get the necessary information, since no two law enforcement agencies, on any level, operate the same way, have the same radio codes, carry the same kind of weapons, have the same size facilities, or must rely on outside facilities to assist them.

A sizable **police department** usually will maintain the following units (or their equivalents):

Antiterrorist Unit	Motorcycle Section
Auto Theft	Mounted and Bicycle Patrol
Bunco-Forgery	Narcotics Units
Canine Section	Organized Crime Section
Criminal Conspiracy Section	Pawn Shop Detail
Crisis Intervention Team	Pornography
Detective Support Division	Rape and Domestic Violence
Fugitive Section	Robbery/Homicide
Gaming Section	RPC (Radio Patrol Car) Section
Gang Activities Section	
Homicide Special Section	Safe and Loft
Internal Affairs	Special Weapons Assault Team (SWAT)
Juvenile	
Major Crimes Unit	Vice

Naturally, the smaller the department, the less personnel it has to maintain all of these sections. Consideration must be given to the law enforcement agency you choose and to its locale.

STORY NOTIONS

A cop suspects he helped send the wrong man to death row and the innocent prisoner is due to die within 72 hours.

A group of extremely brilliant college students majoring in criminology go on a crime spree to prove how much smarter they are than the police. Our protagonist (a very young officer) is sent in undercover to locate and infiltrate the group.

A hitman suffers a fatal heart attack after checking into a big city hotel. The police know that the man had a contract to fill but the question is who is the contract on, since another hitman is sure to follow once the person who ordered the contract learns his first selection can no longer fulfill his contract.

A homicide detective returns home one evening to spot a man behind the wheel of a car parked across the street from his house. The detective confronts him and learns the man is an ex-con the detective had sent to prison. The detective leaves the ex-con and starts back across the street when he sees a figure in the shadows raise a gun and point it at the detective. The detective draws his weapon, and orders the man in the shadows to put down his gun. He does not do so and the detective fires, hitting and killing the man in the shadows. When he gets to the body, he recognizes him as a neighbor who wouldn't hurt a fly and what's more, as neighbors and onlookers arrive, the gun the detective saw in the man's hand has disappeared. There is a hue and cry for justice for a cop killing an innocent, unarmed man. The detective knows different, but the only witness he has is the ex-con he sent to prison and who is nowhere to be found, even if he would testify for the detective.

THE PRIVATE EYE

The Private Investigator. Unfortunately, in real life, few P.I.'s ever become involved in a murder case, although there have been some occasions when families or friends of the victim do not believe the police have done all the investigative work that possibly could have proven the suspect they have in custody is innocent of the crime.

Most P.I.'s (in real life) handle domestic situations, missing persons and children, helping an individual escape from inside a cult, debugging, child recovery from a divorced parent who has absconded with their child, insurance fraud, industrial espionage and industrial theft, hitech surveillance, and protection.

STORY NOTIONS

A noted writer of "tell all" books is found drowned in his swimming pool. The police say it was an accidental drowning. His secretary says it was murder, especially since the new manuscipt he was working on is now missing. She hires a private investigator and gives him over twenty names that would have appeared in the book and who are likely suspects and wish to kill the writer and the book.

The son of a famous political figure is kidnapped, murdered, and buried in a grave in the desert. A short time later, his exact look-alike (an illegitimate brother) shows up, claiming to be the political figure's son. The father sees right through him but when he is blackmailed about having an illegitimate son, a potential disclosure that could ruin his career, he pretends to accept the interloper/killer. The one person who doesn't buy it is the dead son's girlfriend and she hires a private investigator to prove that the one posing as her sweetheart is an imposter. The P.I. meets with a fatal accident and the sweetheart now becomes the one to have to investigate and prove the hoax and the murder.

A private investigator is hired by a terminally ill man's wife. She refuses to believe her husband confessed to murdering a wealthy doctor's wife despite the evidence that her husband indeed committed the heinous crime. What the P.I. will eventually discover is that the doctor paid the blue-collar patient to write and sign the confession for a sum his wife would collect after his death to cover the murder of the doctor's wife by the doctor, himself.

LAW AND THE COURTROOM

The same careful consideration should be given to "the law" itself since laws vary from one place to another and if you are writing about a specific locale, find out what the law is in that city and that state. Check with the District Attorney's office and the prosecutor and a criminal defense attorney in that city.

You should also be aware of what court the case would eventually be tried in if you intend that your story should lead to a court trial. The public is pretty well informed today and is not easily fooled by a lot of mumbo-jumbo. Get your facts straight.

Remember that in the event of a murder, the police Homicide department reigns supreme. Law enforcement officers from Vice, Robbery, etc., do not investigate or interfere with Homicide unless, for some reason, they are invited to do so.

Jurisdiction plays a vital role in law enforcement. The question you must ask yourself is who's jurisdiction the case falls into—the local, county, state, or federal level.

Sometimes it depends on where the crime was committed. Other times it's the type of crime that will determine who catches the case or takes over the investigation. How do you determine that? By researching the practices in the locale you have selected for your story.

SUGGESTED READING

For additional information concerning crime, here is some suggested reading that can provide you with a wide variety of material for the writer of crime stories.

Richard H. Akin. *The Private Investigators Basic Manual.* Springfield, IL: Charles C Thomas.

Corvasce/Paglino. *Modus Operandi.* Cincinnati, OH: Writers Digest Books.

Barry Fisher. *The Techniques of Crime Scene Investigations.* New York, NY: Elsevier Publishing Company.

Mactire. *Malicious Intent.* Cincinnati, OH: Writers Digest Books.

Dustin D. Marks. *Cheating at Blackjack* and *Cheating at Blackjack Squared.* San Diego, CA: Index Publishing Group.

Joel Norris. *Serial Killers.* New York, NY: Dolphin/Doubleday.

Martin Roth. *The Writer's Complete Crime Reference Book.* Cincinnati, OH: Writers Digest Books.

Olaf Vancura. *Smart Casino Gambling.* San Diego, CA: Index Publishing Group.

Wingate. *Scene of the Crime.* Cincinnati, OH: Writers Digest Books.

7

The Firefighters

(Los Angeles as an example)

SUMMARY OF OPERATIONS

Emergency Responses
Fires
False Alarms
Rescue Ambulance
Structure Fires
Firefight Inspections
Fire Prevention Bureau Inspections
Firefighting Training
Firefighter Injuries
Burn Cases, Civilian (non-fatal/fatal)
Incendiary Fires

UNITS

Single Engine Stations
Task Force Stations
Rescue Ambulance Companies
Squads
Helicopters
Fireboats

PERSONNEL

Uniformed
Civilian

EMERGENCY MEDICAL SERVICES

Ambulances
EMT
Personnel

DISPATCHES

Aircraft : (Normal Standby; Alert 22; Standby 1 = minor problem).
(Full standby; Alert 33; Standby 2 = major problem).
Investigative responsibility; F.A.A. and the National
Transportation Safety Board.

Bomb: Police responsibility. F.D. will standby.

Brush : (1 Task Force, 4 Engines, 2 Helicopters, 2 Battalion Chiefs).
Not an indication as to the amount or size of fire.

Full Assignment: (3 to 6 companies). Not an indication as to the
amount or size of fire.

Grass: (2 Engines) Sometimes mistakenly called Brush Fires.

Mutual Aid: Municipality in which the incident exists is responsible
for release of information.

Non-Fire Department incidents: Many incidents the F.D. responds
to are the primary responsibility of other governmental
agencies.

Traffic: (Normally 1 Rescue Ambulance) If person is trapped, 2 fire
companies and 1 Battalion Commander.

INFORMATION REGARDING EMERGENCY OPERATIONS

The Fire Department officer in charge of an emergency is responsible for media relations during the entire emergency. The Public Information Officer (P.I.O.) at the scene of an emergency reports to the officer in charge and will provide information to the media. The P.I.O. can take reporters to points of greatest interest at the fire and assist them with names, Fire Department terminologies, and photographic possibilities. A yellow pennant with the word "PRESS" will be displayed on the P.I.O.'s vehicle. The P.I.O. vehicle will be located in an area separate from the command post vehicle to avoid congestion there.

It is illegal for Fire Department personnel to release information to unauthorized persons regarding any patient treated or transported by the Los Angeles Fire Department. All persons other than members of the District Attorney's Office, City Attorney's Office, or Police Department, seeking such information shall be referred to the Arson Unit.

California State law permits bonafide members of the news media to be on the scene of an emergency, provided they are not directly interfering with emergency operations. Under these conditions, accredited members of the media may be allowed to be on the scene upon their request and after they have been warned regarding any unsafe conditions.

At incidents where the officer in charge determines there is danger to members of the media or that their presence would seriously hamper Fire Department operations, he may restrict entry to the area.

Preserving evidence at the scene of a fire is imperative to a successful investigation. The fire scene includes not only the immediate fire area, but the complete premises. The officer in charge may restrict entry to essential fire fighting personnel and investigative agencies such as the Coroner's Office, Los Angeles Police Department, and Arson Investigators.

Investigators respond to many fires not because arson is suspected but because they are the experts in determining the cause. The cause of a fire will be immediately released when known. Fires may be listed as "under investigation," "suspicious," or incendiary."

Damage estimates are arrived at by compiling information from several different sources and may take hours to complete.

EMERGENCY COMMAND

Emergency incidents are generally categorized by the amount of resources committed. Incident commanders are assigned accordingly.

Initial Assignment

A company, task force, or combinations thereof, originally dispatched to an incident. The first arriving officer is in command until relieved by a superior.

First Alarm Assignment

1. Up to and including five companies,

or

2. All companies included in the initial assignment when the initial assignment exceeds five companies due to the inclusion of one or more task forces,

or

3. Brush dispatch—consists of one task force, four engines, two helicopters, and two Battalion Commanders.

Greater Alarm Incident

Any incident which includes more companies than a First Alarm Assignment (5) and less than a Major Emergency Assignment (16). Normally commanded by a Division Commander (Assistant Chief)

Major Emergency Assignment

When more than 15 companies are dispatched. Normally commanded by a Deputy Department Commander, with required staff assistance.

Major Emergency (Expanded)

The organization readily expands to provide for a Department Commander, with required staff assistance.

GLOSSARY OF TERMS

(Common to the Los Angeles City Fire Department)

Administrative office: The office of the Chief of Engineer and General Manager.

Alarm: A notification to respond to an emergency.

Apparatus: Any Fire Department vehicle or boat.

Apparatus operator: Engineer, apparatus driver, aerial ladder operator or anyone acting in any of these positions.

Back draft: An explosion at a hot, smoldering fire in a confined atmosphere of a structure due to an inrush of oxygen.

House line: A hose line in a building for fire fighting provided by the building. Interior standpipe hose.

Immediate family: Father, mother, brother, sister, spouse, child.

Knock down: Phase of extinguishment where fire is reduced to semi-extinguished state inhibiting its spread.

Loom-up: A column of smoke indicating the presence of a fire.

Open up: Or "Opening Up"—the process of effecting entry into a burning structure. The opening of windows, doors, and cutting of holes for ventilation.

Overhauling: The final operation at a fire. Investigating the entire premises for the main purpose of determining that no more fire exists. The moving and/or removal of involved materials for this purpose.

Platoon: One of the groups of Fire Suppression and Rescue personnel which is alternately on duty.

Quarters: Any engine house, Department building, office, storeroom, workroom, yard, shop, or place wherein members are assigned or employed.

Rig: Fire fighting apparatus.

Run: The action of a fire company responding to an alarm. Usually includes its return.

Section: A subdivision of the Department, other than Fire Suppression and Rescue, directly subordinate to a Bureau or Division. Usually commanded by a Battalion Chief or civilian administrator.

Shift: A period of 24 consecutive hours starting at 8:00 A.M.

Size-up: Verbal appraisal of conditions at scene of fire by the first-in company.

Spot fire: Usually in connection with grass and brush fires. A small fire caused by unconnected extension from another fire; usually caused by flying brands.

Strike team: Formed to meet the needs of emergency situations. May be formed by the Operations Control Division or at the direction of the officer in charge of an incident. A strike team may be any combination of manpower with or without apparatus. Strike teams larger than regular task forces are normally commanded by a Chief Officer.

Task force: Consisting of a truck company and a two-piece engine only = Light Task Force. Task forces are normally housed in and respond from the same station.

Truck company: Fire fighting vehicle which provides rescue, entry, ventilation, salvage, and basic emergency medical service support capabilities. Equipped with a hydraulic aerial ladder, ground ladders, rescue and fire fighting tools. Normal assigned staffing: 5 personnel.

Unit: A basic organizational unit of the Department, other than Fire Suppression and Rescue.

Ventilate: The operation of opening windows, doors, and cutting holes in a building for the purpose of relieving the building of pent up smoke, heat, and gases. This facilitates an improved working environment for firefighters as well as reducing smoke and fire damage to the structure.

Worker: A fire of such magnitude that a major fire-fighting effort is required for its extinguishment.

The LA city fire department uses the Incident Command System (ICS) for all brush incidents in the city. The following terms may also be used during other types of emergency incidents.

Apparatus inventory
Aerial Ladder Truck
Airport Crash Protection
Ambulance
Boat
Buses
Carryall, Station Wagon
Display Equipment
Heavy Utility

Helicopter
Hi-Pressure Wagon
Lightwater and Foam Apparatus
Mobile Laboratory
Patrol Tanker
Pickup truck, Stakebodies
Salvage
Sedans
Snorkel or Squirt
Tractor and Tractor Transport
Triple Combination Engine
Van Service Truck

Assisting agency: An agency directly contributing suppression, rescue, support, or service resources to another fire suppression agency.

Automatic aid: A system wherein two or more fire departments operate essentially as a single agency to respond routinely across jurisdictional boundaries for distances not in excess of 5 miles to render mutual assistance in combatting fire emergencies.

Base: That location at which the primary logistics functions are coordinated and administered. There is only one base per incident.

Branch: That organization level having functional/geographic responsibility for major segments of incident operations. The branch level is organizationally between Section and Division.

Camp: Provides food, water, rest, and sanitation. May be near Staging.

Command staff chief: Coordinates information, safety, and liaison.

Communications unit: A vehicle (trailer or Mobile Van) used as a communications center.

Cooperating agency: An agency supplying assistance other than direct suppression, rescue, support, or service functions to the incident control effort (e.g., California Highway Patrol—traffic management.)

Core area: A geographic portion of the firescope. Basically, the area includes Ventura County, a portion of L.A. County, the Angeles National Forest, and portions of the Los Padres and San Bernardino National Forests.

Firemodel: A computer program which, with given information, will predict an hourly rate of spread from an ignition point.

Firecast: A set of FIREMODELS run during fire season at the OCC on preselected locations to indicate possible firespread from those points for that date.

Flycrew: A handcrew of predetermined size transported to an incident via helicopter.

Forest fire meteorological research network (METNET): An experimental network of weather stations established in Southern California to study Santa Ana conditions. This network can provide certain data to augment meteorological data obtained from the National Weather Service and the AFFIRMS Systems.

General staff: The group of incident management personnel comprised of: The Incident Commander, The Suppression and Rescue Chief, The Planning Chief, The Logistics Chief

Helibase: A location within the general incident area for parking, fueling, maintenance, and loading of helicopters. May have water loading capabilities.

Helispot: A location where a helicopter can take off and land. May have water loading capabilities.

Incident action plan: The basic operational plain for the incident.

Incident command system (ICS): The combination of facilities, equipment, personnel, procedures, and communications operating within an organizational structure with responsibility for the management of assigned resources.

IR (INFRA RED): A heat detection system used for fire detection, mapping, and hot spot indentifications. **FLIR** (Forward Looking Infra Red): A portable IR scanner, usually airborne.

IR Groundlink: A capability through the use of a special mobile ground station to receive air to ground infra red imagery for interpretations.

Logistics chief: Base, camp, air support, medical supplies.

Multi-agency coordination system (MACS): The combination of facilities, equipment, personnel, procedures, and communications integrated into a common system with responsibility for coordination of assisting agency resources and support to agency emergency operations.

Mutual threat zone: An area between two or more jurisdictions into which those agencies would respond on initial attack.

NOAA mobile weather station: A weather data collection and forecasting facility provided by the National Oceanic and Atmospheric Administration.

Operations coordination center (OCC): The primary facility of the Multi- Agency Coordination System. It houses the staff and equipment necessary to perform the MACS functions.

Orthophoto maps: Aerial photographs corrected to scale.

RESTAT: An acronym for Resource Status Unit.

Planning chief: Sitstat, Restat, Communications, water, and documentation.

SITSTAT: An acronym for the Situation Status Unit. A Unit within the Planning Section.

S & R (Suppression and Rescue): Chief; Manages incident control operations, may be Assistant Chief or Deputy Chief.

Staging area: That location where incident personnel and equipment are assigned in anticipation of assignment to suppression and rescue operations.

Strike team: Specified combination of suppression and rescue resources and a leader. Usually five engines and one Battalion Chief.

Strike team numbering : Strike teams dispatched by OCD will be numbered starting with 20 (i.e., B-20, B-21, etc.). Strike teams which are formed at the scene of the emergency will be numbered starting with 50 (i.e., B-50, B-51, etc.).

Tactical team (Tac Team): A group of suppression and rescue resources with a leader temporarily assembled for a special mission and disbanded at the conclusion of the mission.

Tactical team numbering: Tactical teams of mixed resources are normally formed at the incident. They will be referred to as "TAC Teams," and will be numbered starting with 1 (i.e., TAC Team 1, TAC Team 2, etc.).

8

Science Fiction, Sci-Fi Fact

The term "Science Fiction" is a fairly narrow descriptor for this genre. Although more often than not associated with flying saucers and space travel, science fiction actually covers a much broader spectrum.

Most of the stories done on Rod Serling's *Twilight Zone* were fantasy sci-fi stories that took place right here on terra firma. Michael Crichton's *Jurassic Park* takes place right here on earth and in the present, yet it is easily classified as science fiction. The same could be applied to the *Andromeda Strain* or *Voyage to the Bottom of the Sea* or *The Time Machine.* Each deals with some science fiction application yet it does not venture into outer space like the *Star Trek* voyages where no one has gone before or *Star Wars.*

The wonderful thing about a science fiction story is that it allows the writer total creativity. The writer can be completely uninhibited when it comes to writing fantasy/fiction.

On the other hand, when the writer enters the world of science fact, he or she must be governed by the existence of some basic scientific fact that can act as the launching pad for the story. In other words, once transplanted organs became a scientific fact the writer could then use that fact to launch the transplanting of a human brain.

Another example of science fiction/science fact might be a story such as in *Jurassic Park,* although it leans more to science fiction than to science fact. Although there is no proof that an egg millions of years old could be hatched in the present, stretching the fact that it had been frozen or in some state of suspended animation might be the springboard and, coupled with biochemistry and DNA, enough groundwork could make it somewhat convincing.

What with the discovery of genetic codes, advances in molecular biology, micro-surgery, nucleic-acid engineering, synthetic blood, and so much more happening each and every day, what once might have been fantasy is rapidly becoming reality. What would have happened if a hundred years ago or more, people had been told they could fly, speak over wires, see pictures from thousands if not millions of miles away at that very second, that man would go to the moon ... Nothing is impossible IF it is based on some scientific fact. No matter how minute that fact may be today, your story would be considered sci-fi fact. For example:

A human (or animal), once deceased, is brought back to life cryogenically. Although no one who has been cryogenically sealed has returned from death, obviously there is some basis for cryogenics, so it loosely could be considered science fiction/fact if given the proper foundation.

A human accepts a body part replacement that is taken from a primate and begins to develop the body of the animal but retains the brain of a human. There have been cases where humans have received transplants of certain organs from primates and have lived normal lives. What might happen later, or in that patient's life, when a child is born of that parent is still something we know little if anything about.
But what if...?

Scientists have long sought what they consider the "living cell." Some claim they have discovered it but whether that cell can reproduce life is yet to be determined. However, there is a basic foundation upon which to build a story. For example, the living cell, taken from a human and that has been stored for many years following that human's demise, is used to recreate that same individual fifty, a hundred years later.

Then, of course, there are the non-space sci-fi stories that are pure fantasy, such as:

The world is destroyed and man is forced to live below ground and begin life anew without ever seeing daylight again. Or, hundreds of years after the surface of the earth has been destroyed, man sends forth a new version of Noah's Ark to see if humans can venture back out onto the surface again.
Alternatively, a person could be sent back to our present from many years in the future.

A man or woman is sent back into the past to alter history.
Computers that take over the world.

Here is a list of possibilities that could be used or included in a science fiction/science fiction-fact story that takes place here on earth, now, in the past, or in the future.

Acid rain destroys the world's food	Melting of the Pole
	Mutant insects
Big Brother takes over	Mutant rodents
Bomb leaves a few survivors	Nuclear war
Disfigurement	Overpopulation of the world
Drought	Pets turn on their owners
Holocaust	Plague of a new disease
Life beneath the sea	Sunlight is obliterated
Man attacked by insects	Superior intelligence
Man attacked by nature	The effects of a
Man attacked by reptiles	chemical war

SCI-FI THAT IS OUT OF THIS WORLD

Long, long, before *Star Trek* and the coming of television or Orson Welles' radio broadcast of invasion from Mars, men and women around the globe have wondered and fantasized about life on other planets.

Here is a list of characters, vehicles and other assorted items that exist in many science fiction stories dealing with outer space and interplanetary plots, wars, and travel:

Alien ships	Decoders
Aliens	Delta rays
Antimatter	Dog men
Antigravity	Earthlings
Asteroids	Energy
Battle cruisers	Energy fields
Beams	Evasive maneuvers
Black holes	Fighter planes
Blasts	Flying saucers
Blobs	Force fields
Body snatchers	Galactic wars
Capsule	Gamma rays
Cat people	Giant insects
Clones	Gravity
Colonies	Gremlins
Computers & computer banks	Guidance controls
Craters	Gyros
Creepers	Hanger decks
Death rays	Holographs

Humanoids
Incredible creatures
Intergalactic wars
Interstellar travel
Invisible men
Lasers
Life forms
Light years
Liquid people
Melting pools
Mind warps
Modules
Molecular structure
Monster robots
Mystic markings
Neutron field
Nova
Orbit
Patrol ship
Planet of vampires
Planets
Pods
Prehistoric planet
Probes
Psychokinesis
Reactors
Robots

Scanners
Scout vessels
Sea monsters
Sensors
Shuttle craft
Solar flares
Solar system
Space giants
Space legs
Space monsters
Space pirates
Space ships
Space stations
Space suits
Stars
Synthesizers
Telepathy
Teleportation
Thermonuclear missiles
Time machines
Time travelers
Time warps
Transmissions
Transporters
Undersea monsters
Video screens
Vortex

SCIENCE FICTION STORIES MIGHT DEAL WITH:

Crack in the earth
Discovery
Dream people come to life
Earth 2
Earth invaders
Escape from a planet
Falling meteors
Insect empire
Interplanetary marriages
Interplanetary wars
Invasion of the rattlers
Mind stealers
Monsters on the loose

People in altered states
Planet of superior beings
Planet of the ants
Secrets beneath the streets
Space medicine
Space stations
Space travel
The day the dogs went wild
The day the sun disappeared
The last days on Earth
The living brain
Visit to hell
Worlds colliding

Horror and
the Occult

Next to crime, comedy, and romances, the most widely read novels and most popular films are of the horror and occult genres.

There is a major difference, however, between the two.

Although both genres contain elements of terror, suspense and quite often the grotesque, the occult story deals with the supernatural, parapsychology, and metaphysics, whereas horror stories are much broader in scope to achieve terror, suspense, and violence.

The classic Edgar Allan Poe stories, the contemporary Stephen King novels, and films such as *Psycho, Texas Chain Saw Massacre, Halloween, Nightmare on Elm Street, The Creature from the Black Lagoon*, all fall into the horror genre, whereas novels and films such as *Frankenstein, Dracula, The Amityville Horror, The Exorcist, The Omen, Poltergeist,* and *Rosemary's Baby* deal more with the spiritual world, ghosts, and demons.

HORROR STORY ELEMENTS

Abominable snow man	Bats
Aliens from inner space	Beasts
Aliens from outer space	Bigfoot
Alligator people	Birds
Banshees	Black

Blobs
Body parts
Body snatchers
Cat people
Cats
Centaurs
Crab monsters
Crawling hands
Creeping flesh
Dragons
Fiends
Forces of energy
Giants
Hounds
Humanoids
Insects
Invisible man or woman
Living brain
Living dead
Mad scientists
Madmen
Madwomen
Maniacs

Monsters
Mummies
Mutations
Parasites
Phantoms
Prehistoric monsters
Psychos
Robots
Rodents
Sadists
Sea monsters
Serial killers
Serpents
Slime
Snake people
Snakes
Spiders
Vampires
Warlocks
Werewolves
Wild men
Wild women
Zombies

HORROR STORY LOCATIONS

Attic
Basement
Bathroom
Boathouse
Bottom of a lake
Burial vault
Campsite
Castle
Cemetery
Closet
Crypt
Dark staircases
Deserted beach
Deserted fun park
Deserted island
Deserted mine shaft
Deserted street
Deserted theater
Deserted warehouse
Dilapidated houses

Foggy street
Garage
Ghost boat
Ghost town
Heavily wooded area
Hidden caves
House of mirrors
Inner space
Jungle
Lagoon
Locked room
Lonely road
Monastery
Mortuary
Moving driverless vehicle
Science laboratory
Secret passageways
Secret room
Sewers
Storage room

Strange planet
Swamps
Tower
Trunk

Tunnels under the city
Under the sea
Underground tunnels
Wax museum

HORROR STORY MEANS AND DEVICES

Ax
Beheading
Boiled in oil
Buried alive
Carnivorous plants
Chain saw
Crushing
Dipped in wax
Dismembering
Eating alive
Fire
Flying monsters
Flying objects
Gouging
Hammer
Hanging
Hatchet

Hot wax
Impaling
Insects
Massacre
Reptiles
Ripping
Rodents
Sacrifices
Scalding
Skinning
Spikes
Stakes
The rack
Vampire bite
Vines
Voodoo
Wild animals

SOME HORROR STORY IDEAS

A psycho kills mother- or father-figure over and over.

A monster, wild animals, reptiles, or rodents infest a village
or town.

Part of a dismembered body refuses to die and seeks revenge.

A scientist creates life or energy that goes out of control.

An archaeologist disturbs a tomb with a curse on it.

An accident or incident causes a mutation of insects, rodents,
humans, animals, or a sea creature.

An individual badly burned or scarred hides in world of his or her
own and preys upon those believed (wrongly or rightly) to be
responsible.

A sociopathic serial killer seeks to eliminate those he or she
believes should be destroyed.

A religious fanatic tries to rid the world of sinners.

The living dead seek to regain life by taking over others' lives.

An artist uses real people for his wax or bronze life-sized sculptures.

An individual suffers a premonition of his own or
another's demise.

A scientist falls prey to his own creation or experiment.

A clairvoyant envisions a heinous crime but cannot convince
   anyone that it will happen.
A monster seeks to take a human for its mate.
A train or other vehicle departs its route and drives into Hell.
Satan seeks an heir or a bride.
A laboratory experiment goes awry causing an insect, a sea creature,
   or an animal to be crossed with a human, producing a
   monstrous mutation.
A mysterious circus lures young victims to a performance that turns
   them against their parents and other adults.
A cult seeks human sacrifices.
Parasites escape a laboratory and begin eating a town.
A person with multiple personality disorder harbors a killer within.
An alien in liquid form begins to engulf everything it encounters.
An electrical charge feeds on whatever energy it can find to grow
   stronger and more deadly.
A computer takes on a personality of its own as it taps into other
   programs. Eventually it gains control over humans.
A prisoner is executed but does not die, and it appears nothing on
   earth can kill him.
A cult believes in cannibalism to secure everlasting life.
A research experiment leads scientists into someone's dreams and
   nightmares.

CHARACTERS ASSOCIATED WITH THE OCCULT

Clairvoyants	Poltergeists
Clergy	Priests
Cultists	Psychics
Dybbuk	Satan
Exorcist	Sorcerers
Ghost hunters	Spirits
Ghosts	Spiritualists
Ghouls	Telepaths
Mediums	Warlocks
Mummies	Witch doctors
Mystics	Witches

ELEMENTS IN OCCULT STORIES

Cults	Human and animal sacrifices
Clairvoyance	Idols
Disturbed graves, crypts	Impaling
Extrasensory perception (ESP)	Incantations
Flying objects	Infestation
Hauntings	Levitation
Hell	Materialization

Messages from beyond
Mystic chants
Oppression
Ouija boards
Out-of-body experiences
Phenomena
Possession
Potions
Premonitions and prophesies
Psychokinesis (PK)
Religious objects
Seances
Signs
Skeletons
Tarot cards
Tombs
Voices from beyond

SEEN AND UNSEEN FORCES

A *seen* force, is as the word implies, a phenomenon that manifests itself or materializes into one form or another, such as:

Alteration of appearance by demonic possession
Appearance of victim from limbo
Distorted figure of a human or sub-human
Electrical discharge
Ghosts
Living dead
Mummy
Oozing matter
Visions

An *unseen* force makes its presence felt by:

Alteration of object, picture, individual, animal
Bizarre sounds, voices, laughter, screams
Disappearance of people or objects
Doors or windows opening or locking by themselves
Extinguishing of lights, candlelight
Flying objects
Levitation
Moving of objects
Objects flung around room
Strange or musty odor
Swirling winds
Unexplained taking of a human life

10

The Love Story

Whether you are writing a love story per se or a story with a romantic involvement, all love stories spring from one basic formula: "Boy meets girl, boy loses girl, boy gets girl." Every love story that doesn't follow that line exactly is merely doing a variation of the basic formula, be it "Boy meets girl, boy loses girl because boy finds out the girl is a nun," or "Boy meets boy" or "Girl meets girl."

Basic springboards are only as trite and mundane as your characters, your plot, and your resolution. To avoid clichés, ask yourself the following questions about your lovers. Then make sure that most of the answers you come up with are fresh, innovative, and maybe a little offbeat.

Who are the lovers? What kind of people are they? How do they think, feel, react? Do either or both have any hangups or inhibitions, and if so, how will it affect their relationship?
What circumstances bring the lovers together?
What attracts one to the other?
Have either one or both ever been in love before, and if so, how would that affect this relationship?
Do they know how each feels about the other, and if not, how do you plan to have them discover their own feelings as well as the other's feelings?
Are either or both lovers free and able to make a commitment to the other? Already married? Other problems?

What triggers the romance?

Are there problems or secrets from the past that could affect the relationship and its eventual outcome?

Who or what creates dissension between the lovers?

Do your lovers have sex with one another in your story? With others? What about the sex scenes you write that will make them fresh, exciting, tender, passionate, erotic?

Are your sex scenes explicit enough in dialogue and in description to make the reader feel he or she is there watching?

Does the love scene or sex scene take place in a usual or unusual location?

Answer each question carefully. Any one of them can make your story transcend the obvious and the clichéd.

Along with basic love story premises, this chapter includes lists to spark some story alternatives you might not have considered. I suggest you read the chapter before coming to any decisions. Once you've read this chapter, I suggest the following:

1. Establish your theme and what your love story is about, or, if your love story is part of another story, how it fits in. A glance at the list of attractions, involvements, and relationships might aid you in that decision.

2. Develop the premise into a beginning, middle, and end, or decide on a premise and then develop your principal characters so they can tell you how they would handle their romantic involvement and what conclusion they would reach. The list of the most romantic roles and romantic qualities might add to the biographies you have done. Also check the lists on where and how lovers meet and the lists of usual and unusual romantic locations.

3. Once you've developed your plot or characters, check the list of problems and obstacles the lovers might have to overcome and the list on how people overcome romantic problems and barriers.

4. As you develop your story, you might want to examine the list of things associated with romance. It might spark something you overlooked.

LOVE STORY PREMISES

The following is a list of premises from which you can develop a story. Premises are just that and nothing more. How they are developed, peopled, plotted, and resolved is the difference between a hackneyed story and one that is new and fresh.

A member of one sex loves a member of the opposite sex who is not aware that the other exists.

Two people from different worlds, cultures, classes, ethnic groups, economic strata, religions, or nationalities find themselves attracted to one another.

Two weak people find strength and love in one another.

Two people, each engaged to another person, fall in love.

Two childhood sweethearts rediscover each other and those old feelings.

Two people, each jilted by former lovers, are drawn to one another.

An employee falls in love with his or her employer.

An employer falls in love with his or her employee.

A jealous person asks a trusted friend, associate, or hired person to watch the jealous person's fiancé. The spy falls in love with the person he or she watches.

A couple who never considered themselves more than good friends discovers their feelings run much deeper.

A divorced or separated couple discovers how much they really care for one another.

Two people, each secretly terminally ill, fall in love.

An individual falls in love with a photograph of another and seeks that person.

Lovers are kept apart by a family feud, rival gangs, etc.

Lovers are forced apart by a misunderstanding.

Lovers are separated because of another person's deceit.

A young person falls in love with an older person.

An older person falls in love with a younger person.

A brief encounter occurs between two people who know their love can never be.

Lovers are separated by war or a disaster.

Lovers are separated by misfortune.

Lovers find themselves competitors.

Trials and tribulations of homosexual or bisexual lovers.

Lovers try to avoid commitment.

BREATHING LIFE INTO THE BASICS

There is hardly a basic plot that hasn't been done.

Almost every story written is a variation on a theme, but there are many ways to take a basic premise and breathe new life into it.

For example, take the premise, "Two lovers are kept apart by a family feud." That's straight out of *Romeo and Juliet*. However, when two lovers came from opposing gangs in the musical and film *West Side Story*, the plot took on a whole new light by contemporizing Shakespeare's story and changing the family feud to a feud between street gangs.

A similar switch was done in the classic *Abie's Irish Rose*, where the families were of different religious beliefs. A few years ago, a writer adapted a true newspaper story about two young mentally retarded lovers who wanted to marry but were kept apart by their families. The same premise would work if the two lovers were of different races or were kept apart because of economic or political differences.

Once the motive, characters, and circumstances have been altered, the plot, by sheer necessity, must take a different road, becoming a new and fresh story.

In *Romeo and Juliet*, the two lovers were young teenagers. The story would be significantly different if the two lovers were more mature and were being kept apart by their children.

With new problems to overcome and a different resolution, Shakespeare's *Romeo and Juliet* could take on not only a new look but a whole new perspective.

Let's take another premise, "An employee falls in love with an employer."

A pretty trite idea, but with women in top executive positions today, what if the employer is a woman and the employee is a male chauvinist who loves her but resents her being his superior, and in attempting to reverse the roles, almost loses the woman he loves? How the male chauvinist deals with the situation offers a myriad of possibilities in developing the story and the resolution.

Take another premise, "Lovers are forced apart by a misunderstanding." In the film *An Affair to Remember*, two lovers agree to separate to find out if they really care for one another. Should their feelings for one another remain the same, they plan to meet at an appointed time and place a year later. The day arrives, but the woman has an accident on the way to the appointment and is rushed to the hospital moments before the man arrives. The man arrives. Unaware of what happened, he believes the woman chose not to come. He assumes she has terminated their romance, and so he leaves. Sometime later, he sees her in a wheelchair and discovers what happened on her way to meet him that night. They are reunited.

Let's suppose you want to use a similar premise, but instead of deciding to separate and meet later, they are forced to separate temporarily. Then, before they can get together, a situation arises that causes one to think the other has had a change of heart.

For example, suppose a false news item links one of the lovers with someone else, and the other assumes their love is over. Or suppose the man suffers some misfortune and believes he would be a burden to his love. What if an unforeseen duty or obligation prevents one lover from contacting the other, or what if the woman learned she was bearing his child and didn't show up because she didn't want him to feel trapped into marriage? There are a multitude of things that could happen to lead to the misunderstanding. What options do you have after the misunderstanding takes place?

One of the lovers could marry someone else.

The feeling of rejection leads one to a desperate act.

The former lovers become enemies.

One of the lovers seeks revenge for being rejected.

Pride causes each of the lovers to claim they didn't show up at the appointed time and place.

Years later the man meets the son he never knew was his.

Alternative directions are limitless.

What if the lovers were of different races? How would that alter the basic premise? Could it open your story to new directions?

What if the two lovers were elderly, and their children convinced them they were being foolish? The characters, their age, and their children's interference would give the story a whole new complexion.

In the film *Laura*, a detective investigates what appears to be a murder case and falls in love with a portrait of the woman who was supposedly murdered. Later in the story we find she is still alive and that someone resembling her was murdered in her stead.

Suppose we use the device of a man falling in love with a photograph or painting of a woman and lose the rest of the *Laura* premise. What if a man sees the picture and sets out to find her? The search could take him anywhere in the world.

Or:

It could become an obsession that blinds that individual from a lover who waits in the wings.

He could find the woman only to learn she's already married or promised to another.

The seeker finds the woman and discovers the face he fell in love with is now disfigured, or he meets a woman whose face is disfigured and doesn't know she's the woman in the photograph.

Another possibility is that as the individual seeks the person in the photograph, an antagonist, having some ulterior motive, doesn't want the woman found. It surely would intensify the search and increase the suspense and drama.

Your love story could turn into a mystery, an espionage story, or anything you choose, and although it began with a photograph of a woman, your story would be substantially different from *Laura*.

PROBLEMS AFFECTING ROMANTIC INVOLVEMENTS

The road to romance is usually bumpy, often complicated by problems brought on by the lovers themselves. Other problems may be foisted upon the lovers by events beyond their control.

The following lists some of the problems that might arise in the course of a romance.

Abuse
Addiction
Children from prior marriage
Class differences
Cultural differences
Distrust and suspicion
Divorce
Dominance
Educational differences
Ethnic differences
Financial problems
Frigidity
Frustration
Immorality
Impotence
Indifference
Indiscretion
Individual needs
Infidelity
Influence of friends
Influence of parents
Interference by family
Interference by friends
Jealousy
Lack of commitment

Life styles
Love triangle
May-December romance
Misunderstandings
One outgrows the other
Overwork
Personal ambition
Personality clashes
Political differences
Prior marriage
Professional disagreement
Psychological problems
Racial differences
Rape
Rejection
Religious differences
Remarriage
Rigidity
Secrets
Separation
Sexual drive
Social differences
Stress
Work habits

TYPES OF ATTRACTIONS, INVOLVEMENTS, AND RELATIONSHIPS

Love means many different things. To most it means an intense affection for one another based on mutual respect and common interests. To others it's an intense attraction based on sexual desire or a need to possess. Below is a list of some of the needs and emotions that bring lovers together.

Childhood crush
Common interests
Common needs
Desire to possess
Hero worship

Infatuation
Intellectual attraction
Intrigue
Long-lost lovers reunite
Love of children

Love-hate relationship
Marriage of convenience
Maternal complex
May-December romance
Moral strength
Mutual respect
Need for affection
Obligation
Obsession
Outgrowth of platonic friend

Paternal complex
Physical strength
Prearranged relationship
Professional interests
Sacrificial love
Sexual desire
Similarity to a former lover
Sincere affection
Stability
The attraction of opposites

TYPES OF LOVE

Bisexual
Heterosexual
Homosexual
Love of a child
Love of a parent

Love of a sibling
Maternal
Paternal
Platonic
Unrequited

WHERE AND HOW LOVERS MEET

At sports events
At school
At shop counters
At bars
At weddings
At parties
At conventions
At resorts
On blind dates
By sharing an experience
Through newspaper or
     magazine ads
Through computer matching
Through dating services
In waiting rooms

In parks
In restaurants
Through marriage brokers
On airplanes
On trains
On beaches
On cruises
On buses
As pen pals
Sharing a ride, car pool, taxi
In singles groups
Through friends or relatives
Through work or profression
Through accidents

THINGS PEOPLE DO TO OVERCOME ROMANTIC PROBLEMS AND BARRIERS

Admit one's true feelings
Alter his or her personality
Appease the other
Attain status
Attempt to appear younger

Attempt to be something
     they're not
Be there in time of need
Become more romantic
Change religious belief
Compromise

Confess indiscretion	Play upon other's guilt
Create an obligation	Play on sympathy
Create a romantic atmosphere	Reconcile differences
Develop a common interest	Rid self of bad habit
Develop understanding	Sacrifice for another
Devise means of meeting	Seek advice from friends
Eliminate the competition	Seek financial success
Improve physical appearance	Send gifts
Increase their knowledge	Take a stand
Learn to share	Use devious means
Make a commitment	Use sexuality
Make another jealous	Use tenderness

MOST ROMANTIC AND UNROMANTIC ROLES AND QUALITIES

Romantic characters have been drawn from every aspect of life. The following lists represent fictional roles and qualities that appear to be both the most appealing and the most unappealing in novels, films, and television shows.

Most Romantic Male Roles

Adventurer	Outdoorsman
Artist	Pilot
Athlete	Pirate
Cowboy	Playboy
Defender of the right	Soldier of fortune
Detective	Sophisticated thief
Historical hero	Spy
Hunter	Swashbuckler
Idealist	Underdog
Loner	War hero
Mr. Lucky gambler	Writer

Most Romantic Male Qualities and Characteristics

Adventurous	Heart of gold
Compassionate	Mysterious
Courageous	Sensitive
Devil-may-care attitude	Sophisticated
Free spirited	Strong silent type
Funny	Tough
Handsome	Worldly

Most Unromantic Male Qualities and Characteristics

Abusive	Cowardly
Boastful	Cruel
Cheater	Fortune hunter

Jealous
Lustful
Narcissistic
Self-serving

Sneaky
Uncaring
Weak
Womanizer

Most Romantic Female Roles

Adventuress
Animal lover
Ballerina or Dancer
Country girl
Glamour girl
Historical heroine
Idealist
Independent type

Mistress
Playgirl
Poor little rich girl
Royalty
Royalty in exile
Society girl
Spy
Working girl seeking success

Most Romantic Female Qualities and Characteristics

Beauty
Charm
Feisty
Free-spirited
Good figure
Independent
Intelligent

Loyal
Passionate
Sense of humor
Sensitive
Sensuous
Unpredictable
Warm

Most Unromantic Female Qualities and Characteristics

Cheater
Demanding
Devious
Dictatorial
Envious
Flirtatious
Gold digger
Jealous
Materialistic

Nag
Narcissistic
Questioning
Rumor monger
Self-serving
Two-faced
Vengeful
Weak
Whiner

STORY ELEMENTS ASSOCIATED WITH ROMANCE

"Our song"
Adultery
Anniversaries
Beauty
Being jilted
Candlelight
Candy
Carrying a torch
Champagne
Courtship

Cupid
Dear John letters
Desire
Diary
Dinner for two
Dreams
Elopement
Embracing
Engagement
Engagement rings

Fidelity
First impressions
Flowers
Former boyfriends
Former girlfriends
Hand-holding
Heart
Hideaways
Honeymoons
Hope chests
Infatuations
Island paradise
Jealousy
Kissing
Living together
Love at first sight
Love letters
Love songs
Loyalty
Making up
Marriage
Matchmaking
Memories

Moonlight cruises
Moonlight strolls
Moonlit night
Photographs
Physical attraction
Poetry
Puppy love
Responsiveness
Sandy beaches
Sensuality
Sentimental items
Sexual encounters
Soft lights
Soft music
Sweethearts
Tenderness
The other man
The other woman
Touching
Triangles
Valentine's Day
Wedding bands
Wedding gowns

USUAL ROMANTIC LOCATIONS

Amusement park
Art gallery
Bedroom
Champs Elysées
Concert in the park
Country inn
Cruise ship
Dance floor
Deserted island
Farm
Favorite restaurant
Ferry boat
Festival
Fireplace
Fishing cabin
French chateau
French Riviera
Gazebo
Hideaway
High-rise penthouse
Hollywood Bowl

Horse-drawn carriages
Hotel room
Italian villa
Lake or lakeside
Lakeside cottage
Lovers' lane
Moonlight sailing
Moonlit beach
Mountain cabin
Mountain top
Parks
Picnic grounds
Private yacht
Rolling hills
Rooftop
Rose garden
Sidewalk cafe
Ski lodge
South Seas island
Wharf

UNUSUAL ROMANTIC LOCATIONS

A crowded subway station
A manufacturing plant
Amusement park ride
Atop high-rise construction
  site
Battle zone under fire
Cemetery
Closet
Crowded airline terminal
Crowded bus
Crowded bus terminal
Crowded elevator
Crowded railroad station
Crowded store
Empty classroom
Empty elevator
Empty hospital room
Empty sports stadium
Empty stage
Escalator

Glass elevator
Haunted house
Ice rink
Mortuary
Museum
Opposite sex's club
Public library
Raft adrift
Raging storm
Rear seat of a police car
Restroom
Store window
Street blocking traffic
Supermarket
Suspended scaffold
Taxi in traffic
The back of a truck
The opposite sex's gym
Under water
Vacant theater

11

Marriage and the Family

Marriage and other relationships in a family bring the writer opportunities brimming with every human emotion—love, anger, fear, joy, sorrow, frustration, jealousy and, at times, hate.

It is an arena that often promises and delivers loyalty, devotion, and responsibility but can also bring pain and anguish, abuse, incest, infidelity, and murder.

Family life has its light and dark sides.

It can often be warm, tender, at times comedic, at other times tragic.

It is an area that almost every human being is familiar with, so writer beware. The family sitcom on television is escape entertainment. Though at times sitcoms have realistic situations and problems, seldom is family life as simple as TV makes it appear.

If your drama is to be real, your characters must be real.

Whenever possible, draw upon your own relationships and experiences as well as others you know of. Divorce, family, and domestic courtrooms are also excellent places to gain an insight into real people involved in marital and family disputes.

Research gathered from family counselors and social workers can also be valuable and help inspire a story.

Marital and domestic problems vary depending on the circumstances of those involved. A married couple could be newly-married, married less than five years, or married between five to fifteen years, fifteen to twenty-five years, or over twenty-five years.

They could be a working couple, one spouse working, one spouse or both retired, or neither working—unemployed or independently wealthy. In any of these cases, the couple might or might not have children.

They could be married for the first time, married before and divorced or widowed, or be bigamously married. They could have children from a previous marriage, no other family members, or one or both could have come from a large family. They could be from different economic, social, or ethnic backgrounds.

Their marriage could have followed a brief encounter, been a marriage of convenience, begun in school, been prearranged, or followed a traditional courtship.

The couple might face any of the following marital problems:

Adjustment to one another
Difficulty in communication
Religious differences
Financial problems
Age differences
Social differences
Growing apart
Frigidity
Sexual problems
Infidelity, adultery
Separation
Boredom
Business or professional pressures
Psychological or medical problems
Homosexuality
Creative differences
Jealousy or suspicion
Parental dependency or parental interference
Inability to have children
Children
Family secrets
Unemployment or professional setback
Different goals or desires
Interference by relatives, friends
Moving due to spouse's job situation

The following lists concern marriage and the family. Please refer to the "marital status" and "family members" lists in the character development section for characters associated with marriage and family.

PROBLEMS ASSOCIATED WITH SEPARATION AND DIVORCE

Legal battles, legal fees
Custody of children, effect upon children
Community property settlement, alimony
Other man or other woman
Effect upon job or profession, finances
Siding of friends, family, children
Child support
Adapting to single life, living alone, dating
Hostility, anger, frustration
Fear of or inability to make another commitment

PROBLEMS ASSOCIATED WITH BECOMING WIDOWED

Sense of loss
Readjustment to being single
Guilt
Loneliness
Beginning life over, dating
Will, probate, inheritance
Conflict with family over inheritance
Financial problems
Single parent
Moving to new surroundings
Inability to cope

MARITAL PROBLEMS

Adoption
Boredom
Cheapness
Child abuse, verbal or physical
Childbirth
Children's habits, friends, school, grades, appearance, attitude
Death
Domination by one spouse
Ex-spouse
Family finances, income, education expenses, taxes, bills, etc
Illness, mental or physical
Infidelity, adultery
Interference of parents
Lack of privacy
Living above means

Loss of a child
Moving
Parental abuse, verbal or physical
Parent/offspring disputes
Raising children
Rape
Responsibility for parents
Spousal abuse, verbal or physical
Stepchildren
Trouble with relatives
Unemployment

FAMILY PROBLEMS

Acceptance or rejection of an outsider
Addiction to alcohol, drugs
Communication
Death
Disagreements over aims, goals, ambitions, finances
Disapproval of act of a family member
Family black sheep
Family business
Family member moving in or out
Family moving to new home
Family pride, honor
Family secrets
Favoring one family member over another
Financial problems
Following in family footsteps
Friends of the family
Illness
Inheritance
Interference
Jealousy
Overbearing or domineering family member
Separation of family
Sharing responsibilities
Skeleton in family closet

PROBLEMS AFFECTING FAMILY MEMBERS

Parents

Becoming dependent on their grown children
Concern about the welfare of their own parents
Concern over children's education, financial responsibility
Concern over the friends with whom their children associate
Difficulty in accepting their children as responsible adults

Difficulty in cutting the umbilical cord
Having a lost, kidnapped, or runaway child
Having their grown children interfere in their lives
Having their lives run by their grown children
Interference in their family life by their own parents
Lack of ability to properly communicate with their children
Making changes that can affect their children, their parents
Setting a good example for their children
Trying to run their children's lives
Trying to give their children advantages in life

Offspring

Being from a previous marriage or having a sibling from one
Being a bad seed (evil offspring) or having a bad seed
Being or having a jealous sibling
Being irresponsible or having an irresponsible sibling
Being responsible or having a responsible sibling
Being adopted or having an adopted sibling
Being abused by parent or sibling
Being mistreated or having sibling mistreated by parent
Being a child of foreign-born parents
Being a brother or sister involved in sibling rivalry
Having a brother or sister lost, kidnapped or a runaway
Being a disowned offspring or having disowned sibling
Having been spoiled or having sibling spoiled by parent
Having or being the overprotective brother or sister
Having overprotective parents
Having or being the bratty brother or sister
Having or being the domineering brother or sister
Having parents who do not understand
Being the offspring of a widowed parent
Being the offspring or siblings who fight over inheritance
Being the offspring of disreputable parent(s)
Being the offspring of famous parent(s)
Being the product of divorced parents

Grandparents

Abuse or mistreatment by children or grandchildren
Custody of grandchildren upon death of children's parents
Fear of dependency upon children or grandchildren
Forced dependency upon children, grandchildren
Interference in lives by children or grandchildren
Need or desire for independence
Rejected or ignored by children

ASSOCIATED WITH MARRIAGE

Bachelor party
Best man
Courtship
Devotion
Engagement ring
Fidelity
Home
Honeymoon
Love

Maid of honor
Marriage license
Responsibility
Wedding cake
Wedding gown
Wedding invitations
Wedding ring
Wedding shower
Wedding vows

ASSOCIATED WITH FAMILY

Anniversaries
Baby
Baby shower
Bar or bat mitzvah
Birthdays
Church
Confirmation
Crib
Dancing lessons
Family album
Family arguments
Family black sheep
Family burial plot
Family business
Family car
Family debt
Family feud
Family friends
Family get-togethers
Family heirloom
Family history

Family inheritance
Family look-alike
Family photographs
Family picnics
Family reunions
Family tree
Family vacations
Grandparents
Holidays, graduations
Home repairs
Housework
Letters from home
Long-lost relative
Music lessons
Nursery
Pregnancy
Pride
Privacy
Raising children
Relative
Toys

ASSOCIATED WITH CHILDHOOD

Allowance
Baby carriage
Baby clothes
Baby pictures
Being scolded
Best friend
Birthday parties
Child's first steps
Clubhouse
College

Crib
Dolls
Elementary school
Family talks
Favorite toy or doll
First bicycle
First dance
First date
First flowers
First job

First love	Long pants
First sexual encounter	Own telephone
First spanking	Prom dress
First time drove family car	Ran away from home
First torch	School prom
Games played	School teachers
High school	School teams
Hobbies	Sled
Junior high	Toys
Kindergarten	Trouble

TEENAGE PROBLEMS

Teenage problems can be serious as well as comedic. (See Chapter Twelve, Comedy, for comedic teen problems.)

Few teenagers view their problems as humorous. To the average teenager, his or her problems are as big and important as any problem an adult may face. The following are lists of dramatic problems teenagers could face.

School

Athletics	Peer pressures
Bullies, gangs	Popularity with opposite sex
Communication with peers	Pregnancy
or teachers	Proms, dances, school events
Dating	Scholarships
Drugs and alcohol	Sex
Grades, tests	Teen romances
Language barriers	Teen suicide

Parental

Abuse	Illness
Alcoholism or drug use	Lack of communication
Allowance	Loss of use of family car
Being foreign-born	Part-time job
Death of a parent	Restrictions, domination
Divorce	Runaway siblings
Finances	Single-parent home
High expectations	

Appearance

Clothes	Parental disapproval of
Complexion	appearance
Weight	Physical limitations
Beauty or handsomeness	Friendships
Depression	

YOUNG SINGLES' PROBLEMS

As with teenagers, young singles have their share of dramatic problems as well as lighter ones. The following lists problem areas of young singles that make for dramatic themes.

Abortion
Adjustment to living away from home
Being expected to follow in father's footsteps
Being unable to leave home
Breaking up a romance
Changes in lifestyle
Competition to succeed
Continuing post education for special degree
Cost of living
Facing the realities and practicalities of life
Failing at school or work
Getting caught up in the drug culture
Getting engaged
Going back to school
Having to take over the family business opposed to own desires
Having to serve time in the military (see Chapter Seventeen,
    The Military)
Living together
Loss of a parent or parents
Maintaining independence
Pregnancy
The professional athlete out of college (see Chapter Thirteen,
    Sports)
Relationships and commitments
Romance (see Chapter Ten, The Love Story)
Sex, safe sex
The sibling rivalry continues
Single parenthood
Trying to live up to family expectations
Trying to meet the right member of the opposite sex
Unable to get position educated and trained for

SENIOR CITIZEN PROBLEMS

As medical science has increased the length of life, so has it added problems for the aged.

For comedic problems associated with the elderly, please refer to Chapter Twelve, Comedy. As with teenagers and young singles, there is a lighter side, of course, but the list on the following page sets forth the more serious problems affecting the elderly.

Abuse or disregard by grown children
Adjustments to changing times
Being considered "over the hill"
Depression and despair
Desire and attempt to remain independent
Difficulty in surviving on pension, social security
Fear of becoming dependent on children, family
Fear of death
Forced retirement
Going back to school
Illness and disability
Interference by grown children, grandchildren
Loneliness
Loss of family/spouse/job/friends
Old age homes
Patronization by grown children
Remarriage
Romance
Separation from the more familiar
Starting a new business
Traveling around the world for the first time
Trying to get a job

12

Comedy

Comedy comes in many forms, whether as prose fiction or as a script for television or theatrical films: sitcoms, where the comedy stems from both the running characters and the episode's situation; light, sophisticated comedy films; slapstick comedy; verbal comedy and satire; burlesque and out-and-out farce.

Comedy is best when it stems from a situation or from a character which is so well created that it dictates how the comedy develops.

Laurel and Hardy were perfect examples of that. So was Charlie Chaplin's Little Tramp and Jackie Gleason's Ralph Kramden and Poor Soul characters.

Here is a list of characteristics that can help make for a good comedic character:

A wimp
A character suffering a phobia
A character with false dignity
A backfire practical joker
A gullible character
A quick-witted character
A character with an allergy
A bungler
A deadpan, no reaction individual
A long-suffering individual
A constantly frustrated individual

An extremely naive individual
An overly suspicious individual
A schemer
A bull-in-a-china-shop
A liar
A know-it-all
A showoff
A person scared of his own shadow
A wisecracker
A well-meaning but ineffective person

These are just a few possible characteristics you might consider for a comedic character you are building.

Now let's look at the things that make for slapstick or physical comedy. Remember, all physical comedy need not be like slipping on a banana peel.

Physical comedy includes many subtleties such as a dirty look, a double take, etc. It would be impossible to list every piece of business that makes for physical comedy, but here are some things associated with physical comedy that might suggest a situation, sequence, or reaction:

Becoming involved with something that is sticky or gooey
Being doused with water, flour, etc.
Losing part or all of clothes in public
Trying to make progress on a slippery surface
Having to handle a difficult or cumbersome object
Hitting the wrong object
Juggling a valuable or dangerous object
Trying to operate an unfamiliar or runaway vehicle
    or piece of equipment
Attempting to accomplish some task and making it worse
    or having it backfire
Trying desperately not to appear to be a "fish out of water"
Trying to appear sober or trying to do something complicated
    while intoxicated
Trying to maintain one's dignity at an inopportune time
Trying to perform some feat without attracting attention and only
    drawing more attention to oneself
Knocking off someone's wig or toupee
Accidentally falling into a pool, mud, or newly poured cement

As previously stated, physical comedy need not be slapstick. Physical comedy can be accomplished by a take, a look, a subtle reaction or movement, whereas slapstick is much broader. If you're into slapstick, I suggest you study the films and videos of:

Abbott and Costello	Buster Keaton
Milton Berle	The Keystone Kops
Sid Caesar	Harry Langdon
Cantinflas	Laurel and Hardy
Charlie Chaplin	Jerry Lewis
Chevy Chase	Harold Lloyd
Chester Conklin	The Marx Brothers
Leon Errol	The Ritz Brothers
Fernandel	Peter Sellers
Jackie Gleason	Red Skelton
Danny Kaye	The Three Stooges

BASIC COMEDY SITUATIONS

Comedy results from the marriage of a good comedic character and a good comedic situation.

An important thing to remember, of course, is that what happens to a comic character is usually only funny to the viewer, not to the character. To the character, the problems must be serious. The more serious they are to the character, the funnier they are to the reader or audience.

These are some of the situations your comedic character might find himself or herself in:

Assumed to be someone other than self and going along with it
Assuming incorrectly one is in the right place or with the right
    people
Assuming the role of another person
Assuming a position one is not qualified for
Attempting to meet someone who is difficult to meet
Attempting to avoid someone
Baby-sitting a monstrous child
Being wrongly convinced one knows what is happening
Being discovered in a place one shouldn't be
Believing mistakenly that one is going to die soon
Believing oneself to be jinxed
Bragging about something one won't do, then having to do it
Building a reputation on a false basis
Coming up with or being suckered into a get-rich-quick scheme
Discovering one made two dates at the same time
Doing something to excess and suffering the consequences
Doing something while trying not to be observed doing it
Doing something to please an employer
Forgetting someone's birthday

Finding self in possession of something dangerous or
the property of another
Innocently giving the right information to the wrong person
Looking after someone else's property
Losing sense of taste, smell
Making a bet and then trying to win it
Misplacing something important and forgetting where
Mistaken identity
Mistaking a message, note or instruction
Not knowing the person one is criticizing is the
person being talked to
Not realizing a life is at stake
Pretending to know someone
Proceeding on a false assumption
Receiving wrong information that can be life threatening
Sharing space with someone he or she dislikes
Showing jealousy based on false suspicions
Telling a small lie that gets out of hand
Thinking one is well-protected when that's not the case
Trying to adjust to a lifestyle not accustomed to
Trying to be in two places at the same time
Trying to break a habit
Trying to bring the wrong two people together
Trying to cover up for another's mistake and getting caught
Trying to fulfill an almost impossible task
Trying to get a raise
Trying to get an invitation
Trying to get rid of something that keeps showing up
Trying to get self fired
Trying to hide someone who shouldn't be there
Trying to keep a secret
Trying to keep out of trouble and by doing so getting
into more of the same
Trying to lose weight
Trying to regain possession of something given or thrown away
Trying to return something to an owner who doesn't want it

EMBARRASSING SITUATIONS

Accidentally blurting out a secret
Being discovered as an impostor
Being trapped into trying to perform an impossible feat
Being discovered in improper dress
Being caught in a lie
Being caught with someone one swore one wouldn't be
caught dead with

Being discovered in a compromising position by a spouse or lover
Being discovered in the wrong place at the wrong time
Being discovered hiding in closet, under bed, etc.
Boasting about an accomplishment not really achieved
Meeting someone you claimed to know intimately but who is
    actually a total stranger
Coming face-to-face with wife and mistress (or husband and lover)
    and neither knows about the other
Coming to an unfounded conclusion
Discovering one is a sleepwalker or -talker
Discovering the clothing one had been wearing is now missing
Eating with or entertaining someone and being unable to pay
Finding self inferior in strength to someone who
    appears much weaker
Finding self played for a sucker
Getting hand caught in the cookie jar
Having to explain the presence of some object
Inviting two enemies to same function or party
Literally being caught with pants down
Making an accusation that proves unfounded
Mentioning name in sleep of someone other than
    one's sleeping with
Performing an act or service and then finding it's the wrong
    place or for the wrong people
Playing hooky and then being discovered
Secret diary is exposed that reveals many intimate details
Someone assumes gift was meant for them when it was actually
    purchased for someone else
Someone showing up who wasn't supposed to be there
Suddenly realizing one made the same promise to two
    different people
Talking about someone one thinks is absent only to find
    that person is present
Telling off someone only to find that person is
    immediate superior
True identity is exposed
Trying to prevent spouse and mistress from meeting
Trying to impress another only to be deflated
Unable to produce something that had been entrusted
    for safekeeping

THE FISH-OUT-OF-WATER

The turnabout, role reversal, or fish-out-of-water formula often offers excellent comedic situations. It places a primary character in a problem situation that is usually fraught with comedic adjustments that must be made.

This concept many times results in the character plunging into a new lifestyle and learning something about the other side of life. *The Beverly Hillbillies*, *Green Acres*, *Some Like It Hot*, *Tootsie*, and *Victor/Victorio* are excellent examples of this concept.

Here are a few ideas for turnabouts you might use:

American in foreign country unfamiliar with language
   or customs
City person taking up rural lifestyle
Elderly person attending college
Employer assuming role of employee
Enlisted man believed to be an officer
Executive suddenly finding self a laborer
Extremely young person attending college
Female forced to live the life of a male
Foreigner in America, unfamiliar with language and customs
Former crook trying to go straight, having a difficult time of it
Laborer suddenly cast into role of an executive
Landlubber at sea
Law enforcement officer working undercover
Maid or butler who changes roles with mistress or master
Male forced to live the life of a woman
Marrieds pretending to be single
Mistaken identity and then assuming that identity
Peasant who is believed to be royalty
Poor person suddenly cast into great wealth or society
Priest, nun, monk, etc. living a secular life
Royal person becoming or pretending to be a peasant
Rural person in the big city
Secretary posing as employer
Single couple pretending to be married
Someone pretending to be a priest, nun, etc.
Unwed person suddenly burdened with a child
Wealthy person now in poverty
Young person assuming position of authority

COMEDIC PROBLEMS OF THE ELDERLY

Being put out to pasture	Driving
Clinging to the past	Grandchildren
Doing things their way	Interference by children

May-December romances
Memory
Modern technology
Movement
New morals
Not acting their age

Plastic surgery
Reliving the good old days
Romance
Sex
Today's cost of living
Young upstarts

COMEDIC PROBLEMS OF YOUTH AND TEENAGERS

Allowance/money
Borrowing the family car
Bullies
Cleanliness
Clothing
Concern about the future
Crushes
Current music
Current trends
Drag racing
Drinking
Driving lessons
Drugs
Family chores
Family problems
Fraternities
Getting own car
Grandparents
Homework
Invasion of privacy
Junk food
Lack of communication
Older brothers/sisters
Own room
Parents

Part-time jobs
Parties, dances
Peer pressure
Personal belongings
Puppy love
Report cards
Scholarships
School
School prom
Sex
Siblings
Single parent
Sleepaway camp
Slumber parties
Social activities
Sports
Teachers
Teen magazines
Telephone
The older man or woman
The opposite sex
Use of the bathroom
Use of the TV
Vacation time

COMEDIC PROBLEMS OF FAMILIES

Age differences
Bickering
Boredom
Divorce
Family rules
Family secrets
Financial problems
In-laws
Lack of communication

New additions
Offspring from different
    marriages
Parental concern
Personal tastes
Romances of single parent
    affecting children
Second marriages
Separation

Sibling differences
Single-family households
Skeletons in the family closet

Social differences
The family car
Visitation rights

COMEDIC PROBLEMS OF YOUNG SINGLES

Ambition
Competition related to
 romance
Competition related to work
 or profession
Considering marriage
Coping with failure
Coping with success
Dating
Financial problems
Hang-ups
Homosexuality
Living alone
Meeting the opposite sex
Moving out or away from
 home
Old friends, new friends

The older man
The older woman
Political differences
Relationship with parents
Religious differences
Reunions
Romantic involvements
Roommates
Sex
Single parenthood
Social difference
Starting a new life
The working man
The working woman
The workplace
Trends
Vacations

ODD-COUPLE RELATIONSHIPS

Age differences
Ambitious/lazy
American/foreigner
Big city/small town
Brothers-in-law/sisters-in-law
Business or professional
 competitors
Civilian/military
Cultural differences
Earthling/alien
Employer/employee
Ex-husbands/Ex-wives
Fathers-in-law
Former enemies

Former lovers
Religious/atheistic
Heterosexual and homosexual
Intellectual differences
Introvert/extrovert
Male/female platonic friends
Mothers-in-law
Neat/sloppy
Optimist/pessimist
Political differences
Racial differences
Realist/dreamer
Wealthy/poor

13

Sports

THE SPORTING LIFE

If you're looking for an arena, theme, hobby, or interest for one or more of your characters, sports should not be overlooked.

Sports offers drama, suspense, and action. Hundreds of millions of people around the globe are involved in sports, as fans or participants.

To help round out a character, consider an interest in a sport, either as a participant or an observer. Because some sports provide a great deal of drama, action, and suspense, you might consider a sport as the central theme or background for a story or film.

The film *Bull Durham* examined the life, trials, and tribulations of characters involved in minor league baseball. It offered humor, sex, and an insight into the lives of people involved in that arena. *Chariots of Fire* was an excellent story that dealt with the drive and ambition of those involved in the Olympics during the 1920s. Films such as *Champion*, *The Harder They Fall*, and *Rocky* examined the fight game.

Sports has a built-in audience and readership and should not be overlooked as the basis of a story or as an added interest for one of your characters.

In this section you will find lists of competitive sports (team and singles) and sports in general. You will also find brief descriptions of many of these sports, including positions, equipment, and rules.

You will also find bibliographies and a list of organizations you might wish to contact for further information.

AMATEUR AND SPECTATOR SPORTS

Characters involved in sports might be spectators, amateur participants, or professionals. Sports most often associated with characters who participate as amateurs include:

Archery	Jogging
Badminton	Lawn bowling
Ballooning	Parachuting
Bicycling	Ping-Pong
Billiards	Polo
Boating	Pool
Bowling	Sailing
Darts	Scuba diving
Dirt biking	Shuffleboard
Flying	Skiing
Free-falling (skydiving)	Softball
Gliding	Surfing
Golf	Swimming
Handball	Target shooting
Horseback riding	Tennis
Horseshoes	Volleyball
Hunting	Walking
Ice-skating	Water polo

Major spectator sports include:

Baseball	Ice hockey
Basketball	Jai alai
Bowling	Rodeo
Boxing	Roller derby
Bullfighting	Skiing
Dog racing	Soccer
Football	Stock car racing
Formula one racing	Tennis
Golf	Track events
Horse racing	Wrestling

PRIVATE CLUBS AND SPORTS FACILITIES

Athletic fields	Bike clubs
Auto clubs	Bike paths
Auto tracks	Bowling clubs
Beach clubs	Country clubs
Beaches	Flying clubs

Golf clubs
Handball courts
Hunting clubs
Ice rinks
Polo clubs
Private gyms
Race tracks

Rifle ranges
Roller rinks
Running tracks
Shooting clubs
Ski resorts
Tennis clubs
Yacht clubs

SPORTS STORY THEMES

The following is a list of themes and subjects that might serve as the basis for a character or story involving sports.

Education versus sports
Gambling
Winning at all costs
Injuries in sports
From the minors to the majors
Olympics—going for the gold
Overcoming a mental or physical handicap
Grandstanding
Relationships (coach, players, romance, managers, trainers)
The will to win
The comeback
Stress
Endurance
Record setters/Record breakers
Cheating
The challenge
Feuds
Daredevils
The big money in sports
Yesterday's hero
International competition
From worst to first
The fan
The love of the game
Sports as a cold, hard business
The fix
One goal—to make it to the pros
The sailor against the sea
The hunter and his prey
Steroid use
The master and the apprentice

TEAM SPORTS—COMPETITIVE

Badminton (doubles)
Basketball
Bobsledding
Bowling
Cricket
Curling
Football
Hockey (ice, field,
    roller skates)
Jai alai
Lacrosse
Lawn bowling
Paddle tennis (doubles)
Polo
Relay racing
Roller derby
Rowing
Rugby
Soccer
Table tennis (doubles)
Team handball
Team ice-skating
Tennis (doubles)
Tobogganing
Volleyball
Water polo
Wild water boating
Yachting

SINGLE SPORTS—COMPETITIVE

Air racing
Auto racing (stock, formula,
    sports car, drag,
    midget car)
Badminton
Ballooning
Bicycle racing (track, road)
Billiards
Bowling
Boxing
Bullfighting
Canoe racing
Clay pigeon shooting
Crossbow archery
Darts
Dirt bike racing
Discus
Diving
Dogsled racing
Fencing
Field archery
Figure skating
Flying
Free-falling
Gliding
Golf
Gymnastics (vault, parallel
    and uneven bars, balance
    beam, rings, pommel
    horse, floor exercises,
    trampolining)
Hammer
Handball
High jump
Horseshoe pitching
Hurdles
Ice-skating
Javelin
Judo
Karate
Kayak racing
Long jump
Motocross
Motorcycle racing
Paddleball
Parachuting
Pistol shooting
Pole vaulting
Pool
Potato-sack racing
Rifle shooting
Rodeo
Roller skating

Running (dash, mile,
     marathon,
     cross-country)
Sailing
Shot put
Shuffleboard
Skateboarding
Skiing (alpine, downhill,
     slalom, jumping, speed,
     cross-country)
Soapbox racing

Speed skating
Surfing
Swimming
Table tennis
Tennis (singles)
Walking
Waterpolo
Waterskiing
Weight lifting
Wheelbarrow racing

SPORTS NOT NECESSARILY COMPETITIVE

Badminton
Bicycling
Billiards
Bowling
Darts
Diving
Fishing (deep sea, spear,
     fresh water)
Flying
Free-falling
Gliding
Golf
Hunting
Paddle tennis
Parachuting
Pool

Running
Sailing
Scuba diving
Shuffleboard
Skateboarding
Skating (ice, roller, blade)
Skeet and trap shooting
Skiing
Surfing
Swimming
Target shooting (rifle, pistol,
     archery, skeet)
Tennis
Walking
Waterskiing
Yachting

ANIMAL SPORTS

Cockfighting (illegal in U.S.)
Dog racing
Dog sled racing
Dogfighting (illegal in U.S.)
Harness racing (trotting, pacing)
Horse jumping
Horse racing (flat, turf, thoroughbred, quarter horse)
Steeplechasing

FOOTBALL

National Conference Teams

Eastern Division
Dallas Cowboys
New York Giants
Philadelphia Eagles
Phoenix Cardinals
Washington Redskins

Central Division
Chicago Bears
Detroit Lions
Green Bay Packers
Minnesota Vikings
Tampa Bay Buccaneers

Western Division
Atlanta Falcons
New Orleans Saints
Los Angeles Rams
San Francisco 49ers

American Conference Teams

Eastern Division
Buffalo Bills
Indianapolis Colts
Miami Dolphins
New England Patriots
New York Jets

Central Division
Cincinnati Bengals
Cleveland Browns
Houston Oilers
Pittsburgh Steelers

Western Division
Denver Broncos
Kansas City Chiefs
Los Angeles Raiders
San Diego Chargers
Seattle Seahawks

NATIONAL FOOTBALL
(teams and team offices)

NFL League Office
280 Park Ave.
New York, NY 10017
www.nfl.com

Arizona Cardinals
P.O. Box 888
Phoenix, AZ 85001

Atlanta Falcons
One Falcon Pl.
Suwanee, GA 30024

Baltimore Ravens
11001 Owings Mills Blvd.
Owing Mills, MD 21117

Buffalo Bills
One Bills Dr.
Orchard Park, NY 14127

Carolina Panthers
800 S. Mint St.
Charlotte, NC 28202-1502

Chicago Bears
Halas Hall @ Conway Park
1000 Football Dr.
Lake Forest, IL 60045

Cincinnati Bengals
One Bengals Dr.
Cincinnati, OH 45204

Cleveland Browns
76 Lou Groza Blvd
Berea, OH 44017

Dallas Cowboys
One Cowboys Pkwy
Irving, TX 75603

Denver Broncos
13655 Broncos Pkway
Englewood, CO 80112

Detroit Lions
1200 Featherstone Rd.
Pontiac, MI 48342

Greenbay Packers
P.O. Box 10628
Greenbay, WI 54307

Indianapolis Colts
P.O. Box 535000
Indianapolis, IN 46253

Jacksonville Jaguars
One Alltell Stadium Pl.
Jacksonville, FL 32202

Kansas City Chiefs
One Arrowhead Dr.
Kansas City, MO 64129

Miami Dolphins
7500 SW 30th St.
Davie, FL 33314

Minnesota Vikings
9520 Vikings Dr.
Eden Prarie, MN 55344

New England Patriots
60 Washington St.
Foxboro, MA 02035

New Orleans Saints
5800 Airline Dr.
Metairie, LA 70003

New York Giants
Giants Stadium
E. Rutherford, NJ 07073

New York Jets
1000 Fulton Ave.
Hempstead, NY 11550

Oakland Raiders
1220 Harbor Bay Pkwy
Alameda, CA 94502

Philadelphia Eagles
3501 S. Broad St.
Philadelphia, PA 19148

Pittsburgh Steelers
300 Stadium Circle
Pittsburgh, PA 15212

St. Louis Rams
One Rams Way
St. Louis, MO 63045

San Diego Chargers
P.O. Box 609609
San Diego, CA 92160

San Francisco 49ers
4949 Centennial Blvd.
Santa Clara, CA 95054

Seattle Seahawks
11220 NE 53rd St.
Kirkland, WA 98033

Tampa Bay Buccaneers
One Buccaneers Pl.
Tampa, FL 33607

Tennessee Titans
460 Great Circle Rd.
Nashville, TN 37228

Washington Redskins
P.O. Box 17247, Dulles Intl.
Airport
Washington, DC 20041

COLLEGE FOOTBALL BOWLS
Aloha Bowl—Honolulu, HI
Blockbuster Bowl—Miami, FL
California Bowl—Fresno, CA
Citrus Bowl—Orlando, FL
Copper Bowl—Tucson, AZ
Cotton Bowl—Dallas, TX
Fiesta Bowl—Tampa, FL
Freedom Bowl—Anaheim, CA
Gator Bowl—Jacksonville, FL
Hall Of Fame Bowl—Tampa, FL
Holiday Bowl—San Diego, CA
Independence Bowl—Shreveport, LA
John Hancock Bowl—El Paso, TX
Liberty Bowl—Memphis, TN
Orange Bowl—Miami, FL
Peach Bowl—Atlanta, GA
Rose Bowl—Pasadena, CA
Sugar Bowl—New Orleans, LA

FOOTBALL STADIUMS
Anaheim Stadium, Anaheim, CA, Los Angeles Rams
Arrowhead Stadium, Kansas City, MO, Kansas City Chiefs
Astrodome, Houston, TX, Houston Oilers
Atlanta-Fulton County Stadium, Atlanta, GA, Falcons
Busch Memorial Stadium, St. Louis, MO, Cardinals
Candlestick Park, San Francisco, CA, 49'ers
Cleveland Stadium, Cleveland, OH, Browns
Giant Stadium, East Rutherford, NJ, Giants
Jack Murphy Stadium, San Diego, CA, Chargers
Kingdome, Seattle, WA, Seahawks
Lambeau Stadium, Greenbay, WI, Packers
Los Angeles Coliseum, Los Angeles, CA, Raiders
Memorial Stadium, Baltimore, MD, Baltimore Ravens
Metropolitan Stadium, Edina, MN, Vikings
Mile High Stadium, Denver, CO, Broncos
Orange Bowl, Miami, FL, Miami Dolphins
Pontiac Stadium, Detroit, MI, Lions
Rich Stadium, Buffalo, NY, Colts
Riverfront Stadium, Cincinnati, OH, Bengals
Robert F. Kennedy Stadium, Washington, DC, Redskins
Schaefer Stadium, Foxboro, MA, New England Patriots
Shea Stadium, New York, NY, New York Jets
Soldier Field, Chicago, IL, Bears
Superdome, New Orleans, LA, Saints

Tampa Stadium, Tampa, FL, Buccaneers
Texas Stadium, Dallas, TX, Cowboys
Three Rivers Stadium, Pittsburgh, PA, Steelers
Veterans Stadium, Philadelphia, PA, Eagles

Field and Equipment

A football field is $53^1/_3$ yards wide and 120 yards long. The goal lines are 100 yards apart with ten yards of end zone at either end of the field.

Yard lines run from sideline to sideline every five yards and are numbered at ten yard intervals from ten to fifty with marks running along both sidelines down the field.

The football is 11.7 inches long and weighs 15 ounces.

Players' Equipment

Helmet
Face mask (attached to helmet)
Jersey and numbers (first digit of number indicates position)
Chest protector
Shoulder pads
Rib and kidney padding
Regulation pants
Below-the-belt padding
Metal jockey cup
Thigh padding
Shin padding
Lightweight shoes (regulation)

Objective of the Game

Two teams of eleven players each attempt to score points by putting the ball across the opposing team's goal line (six points for touchdown, one point for a conversion following a touchdown), or by kicking goals across the opposing team's goalposts (three points).

The team scoring the most points wins. In professional football, the period of play is sixty minutes, consisting of four fifteen-minute quarters, with a timeout between the second and third quarters. Each team is allowed three one and one half minute time-outs per half plus injury time-outs that are not counted. In the event of a tie at the end of the fourth quarter, the first team to score in overtime wins.

Officials

The referee is the chief official. The umpire is responsible for equipment and the scrimmage line.

Linesmen are responsible for encroachment by either team, and offsides by operating on each side of the field, changing at halftime.

Chain crews measure the distance needed for a first down.

The line judge on the side opposite the linesman is responsible for the toss, the score, time-outs, and illegal shifts or movements behind the line of scrimmage.

The field judge is responsible for loose balls, forward passes, and kicks from scrimmage.

The back judge operates on the same side of the field as the line judge and checks the number of defensive players at the snap of the ball and the eligibility of pass receivers on his side of the playing field.

Teams

There are eleven players on each team. There cannot be more than eleven players from each team on the field during play. Each team has defensive and offensive squads and special teams for kickoff, field goal and punt plays. Unlimited substitutions are allowed.

Scrimmage Positions

The line

Ends are at each end of the scrimmage line (tight end, split end, defensive end). Tackles are next position in from the ends (defensive, offensive). Guards are next position in from the tackles (defensive, offensive). The center is in the center of the line of scrimmage (defensive, offensive).

The backfield positions

The quarterback is behind the center (defensive, offensive). Linebackers are behind the quarterback.

When the offensive team is on the field, the linebackers are running backs. When the defensive team is on the field, the linebackers are defensive backs, corner backs, or safeties.

Each team also has a punter, used when the team having possession of the ball must punt; a field goal kicker, who specializes in kicking field goals; a team manager, a head coach, offensive and defensive coaches, assistant coaches, trainers, a doctor, and other personnel.

For more detailed information regarding plays, passes, time-outs, kickoffs, and more specific rules of the game, contact the National Football League, 410 Park Avenue, New York, NY 10022.

Suggested Reading

Ford Hovis. *The Sports Encyclopedia.* New York: Praeger
    Publishing, 1976.
The Design Group. *Rules of the Game.* New York: Bantam
    Books, 1976.

MAJOR LEAGUE BASEBALL
www.majorleaguebaseball.com

Commissioner's Office
245 Park Ave., 31st fl.
New York, NY 10167

AMERICAN LEAGUE

(teams and team offices)

American League Office
350 Park Avenue
New York, NY 10022

Anaheim Angeles
2000 Gene Autry Way
Anaheim, CA 92806

Baltimore Orioles
333 W. Camden St.
Baltimore, MD 21201

Boston Red Sox
4 Yawkey Way
Boston, MA 02215

Chicago White Sox
333 W 35 St.
Chicago, IL 60616

Cleveland Indians
2401 Ontarion St.
Cleveland, OH 44115

Detroit Tigers
2121 Trumball Ave.
Detroit, MI 48216

Kansas City Royals
1 Royal Way
Kansas City, MI 64141

Minnesota Twins
34 Kirby Puckett Pl.
Minneapolis, MN 55415

New York Yankees
Yankee Stadium
Bronx, NY 10451

Oakland Athletics
7677 Oakport, # 200
Oakland, CA 94621

Seattle Mariners
83 South King St.
Seattle WA 98104

Tampa Bay Devil Rays
1000 Ballpark Way
St. Petersburg, FL 33705

Texas Rangers
1000 Ballpark Way
Arlington, TX 76011

Toronto Blue Jays
1 Blue Jays Way #3200
Toronto, Ont. M5V 1J1

NATIONAL LEAGUE
(teams and team offices)

National League Office
350 Park Ave.
New York, NY 10022

Arizona Diamondbacks
401 E. Jefferson St.
Phoenix, AZ 85004

Atlanta Braves
755 Hank Aaron Dr.
Atlanta, GA 30315

Chicago Cubs
1060 W. Addison St.
Chicago, IL 60613

Cincinnati Reds
100 Cinergy Field
Cincinnati, OH 45202

Colorado Rockies
2001 Blake St.
Denver, CO 80205

Florida Mariners
2267 NW 199th St.
Miami, FL 33056

Houston Astros
P.O. Box 288
Houston, TX 77001

Los Angeles Dodgers
1000 Elysian Park Ave.
Los Angeles, CA 90012

Milwaukee Brewers
P.O. Box 3099
Milwaukee, WI 53201

Montreal Expos
4549 Ave. Pierre de Couberin
Montreal, Que H1V 3N7

New York Mets
123-01 Roosevelt Ave.
Flushing, NY 11368

Philadelphia Phillies
3501 S. Broad St.
Philadelphia, PA 19148

Pittsburgh Pirates
P.O. Box 7000
Pittsburgh, PA 15212

St. Louis Cardinals
250 Stadium Plaza
St. Louis, MO 63102

San Diego Padres
8880 Rio San Diego Dr.
San Diego, CA 92112

San Francisco Giants
3 Com Park @ Candlestick Pt.
San Francisco, CA 94124

Diamond and Equipment

A baseball is approximately nine inches in circumference, weighing about five ounces. Baseball bats are traditionally made of wood (usually ash or hickory), however, because of the shortage of wood and for ecological reasons, it is rumored that wooden bats will soon be replaced by aluminum. Gloves include the catcher's mitt, first baseman's mitt, and fielding gloves worn by the pitcher, baseman, and outfielders.

Baseball fields consist of an infield (the diamond) and the outfield.The infield diamond consists of home plate where the catcher is positioned and the pitcher's mound sixty feet six inches from home plate. The distance between the bases is ninety feet in the major leagues.

The shortstop plays between second base and third base just outside of the infield.

The outfield consists of grass or Astroturf outside the infield diamond and is played by a right fielder, a center fielder, and a left fielder.

The distance from home plate to the fence differs among ballparks.

Games are nine innings long, although a game can go into as many extra innings as necessary until one side breaks a tie.

Officials

There are four umpires. The head umpire wears mask and a chest protector as he stands behind the catcher at home plate. He judges strikes and balls and is the overall judge on all decisions. The other umpires stand near first base, second base, and third base.

A statistical recorder maintains the records and details of each play.

Dress

All team members wear regulation uniforms with their team colors and insignia.

The catcher wears a face mask, chest protector, shin guards, and a protective cup.

Each fielder uses a leather glove or mitt on his ball-catching hand.

Baseball shoes have spikes.

Players in the field wear a soft baseball cap.

Players at bat must wear a plastic batting helmet.

For more detailed information about the game's rules, write the Baseball Commissioner's Office, 350 Park Avenue, New York, NY 10022; the National League Office and the American League offices are at the same address.

Suggested Reading

The Design Group. *Rules of the Game.* New York: Bantam
   Books, 1976.
Ford Hovis. *The Sports Encyclopedia.* New York: Praeger
   Publishing, 1976.

BASKETBALL

The National Basketball Association

Eastern Conference, Atlantic Division
Boston Celtics (MA)
Charlotte Hornets (NC)
New Jersey Nets (NJ)
New York Knickerbockers (NY)
Philadelphia 76ers (PA)
Washington Bullets (DC)

Eastern Conference, Central Division
Atlanta Hawks (GA)
Chicago Bulls (IL)
Cleveland Cavaliers (OH)
Detroit Pistons (MI)
Indiana Pacers (IN)
Milwaukee Bucks (WI)

Western Conference, Midwest Division
Dallas Mavericks (TX)
Denver Nuggets (CO)
Houston Rockets (TX)

Miami Heat (FL)
San Antonio Spurs (TX)
Utah Jazz (UT)

Western Conference, Pacific Division

Golden State Warriors (CA)
Los Angeles Clippers (CA)
Los Angeles Lakers (CA)
Phoenix Suns (AZ)
Portland Trailblazers (OR)
Sacramento Kings (CA)
Seattle Supersonics (WA)

**NATIONAL BASKETBALL
ASSOCIATION**
www.nba.com

League Office
National Basketball Association
Olympic Tower, 645 5th Ave.
New York, New York 10022

Atlanta Hawks
One CNN Center, #405
Atlanta, GA 30303

Boston Celtics
151 Merrimac St.
Boston, MA 02114

Charlotte Hornets
100 Hive Dr.
Charlotte, NC 28217

Chicago Bulls
1901 W. Madison
Chicago, IL 60612

Cleveland Caviliers
1 Center Court
Cleveland, OH 44115

Dallas Mavericks
777 Sports St.
Dallas, TX 75207

Denver Nuggets
Pepsi Ctr, 1000 Chopper Pl.
Denver, CO 80204

Detroit Pistons
Two Championship Dr.
Auburn Hills, MI 48326

Golden State Warriors
1011 Broadway
Oakland, CA 94607

Houston Rockets
Two Greenway Plaza, #400
Houston, TX 77046

Indiana Pacers
125 S. Pennsylvania St.
Indianapolis, IN 46204

Los Angeles Clippers
1111 Figueroa St.
Los Angeles, CA 90037

Los Angeles Lakers
555 Nash St.
Los Angeles, CA 90245

Miami Heat
One SE 3rd Ave., #2300
Miami, FL 33131

Milwaukee Bucks
1001 N. 4th St.
Milwaukee, WI 53202

Minnesota Timberwolves
600 1st Ave. North
Minneapolis, MN 55401

New Jersey Nets
390 Murray Hill Parkway
E. Rutherford, NJ 07073

New York Knickerbockers
Two Pennsylvania Plaza
New York, NY 10121

Orlando Magic
Two Magic Pl.
8701 Maitland Summit Blvd.
Orlando, FL 32801

Philadelphia 76ers
First Union Ctr., 3601 S. Broad
Philadelphia, PA 19148

Seattle Supersonics
190 Queen Anne Ave., #200
Seattle, WA 98109

Phoenix Suns
201 E. Jefferson
Phoenix, AZ 85004

Portland Trailblazers
One Center Ct., #200
Portland, OR 97227

Sacramento Kings
One Sports Pkwy
Sacramento, CA 95834

San Antonio Spurs
100 Montana St.
San Antonio, TX 78203

Toronto Raptors
40 Bay St., #400
Toronto, Ontario M5J2X2

Utah Jazz
301 W. South Temple
Salt Lake City, UT 84101

Vancouver Grizzlies
800 Griffith Way
Vancouver, B.C. V6B 6G1

Washington Wizards
718 7th St. NW
Washington DC 20004

Court and Equipment

Both college and professional basketball courts are ninety-four feet long and fifty feet wide. Games are played on wood floors. The basketball is made of leather and is nine inches in diameter. Two suspended netted baskets, ten feet above the floor, are at each end of the court. Baskets are eighteen inches in diameter and hang from a metal ring or hoop that is attached to a fifty-four-inch backboard made of wood or transparent material. A center line divides the court. A free throw or foul lane is twelve feet wide and is located at each end of the court with the free throw line fifteen feet from the basket.

Technical equipment required for the game includes a scoreboard indicating the score, time-outs remaining, personal and team fouls; stopwatches or clocks including game clock, time-out clock, twenty-four second shot clock that times the interval a team is allowed to hold the ball before a scoring attempt and the ten-second clock that times when, as play begins or resumes, a ball must be moved past mid-court.

Each team consists of five players: one center, two guards, and two forwards. Although most substitutions only require that a player report his name and number to the referee, there are additional rules governing substitutions under certain conditions.

Each team also has a team manager, a head coach, an assistant coach, a trainer, ball or water boys, and a team doctor.

Dress

Each team has distinctive colors and emblems or insignia on two sets of uniforms, one for home games, one for away games. Uniforms consist of shorts, sleeveless jerseys, and sneakers. Shirts are numbered one to fifteen and usually bear the team name and the players last name.

Officials

Officials dress in officials' uniforms. Officials include a referee, an umpire, a scorekeeper, a timekeeper, and a 24-second clock operator. The referee and umpire work at opposite ends of the court, changing places following each foul involving a free throw or a jump ball. Referees and umpires use whistles and hand signals to indicate fouls, rule infractions, jump balls, etc.

Objective of the Game

The objective is to score more points than the opposing team within the prescribed time of play. Game begins with a jump ball. The team in possession of the ball attempts to get the ball down court to the opposing team's basket and score by putting the ball through the basket. The defensive team must try to steal the ball, intercept a pass, or otherwise prevent the offensive team from scoring.

Game Time

Professional basketball consists of four 12-minute quarters. There is a time-out between the second and third quarters.

Ball Holding Time

The team in possession of the ball must attempt a shot at the basket within twenty-four seconds of possession of the ball, or the ball is turned over to the opposing team.

Time-outs

Each team is allowed two one-minute time-outs per half. Twenty-second injury time-outs are not charged against a team. Time-outs called by an official automatically stop the clock and are not charged against either team.

Scoring

A basket scores two points, or three points if made from outside the perimeter. One point is given for each free throw or foul shot. In the event of a tie at the end of regulation play, the game goes into five-minute overtime periods until one team is leading at the end of a period.

Penalties

Penalties give the opposing team free throws or possession of the ball. Technical fouls can be called by the referee against a player or coach for certain infractions or disrespect to an official.

There are many types of fouls, penalties, and rules in professional, college and high school basketball. I recommend more research if you are describing the game in detail. Contact the League Office of the National Basketball Association at 410 Park Ave., New York, N.Y.

Suggested Reading

The Design Group. *Rules of the Game.* New York: Bantam, 1976.

Ford Hovis. *The Sports Encyclopedia.* New York: Praeger Publishing, 1976.

ICE HOCKEY

National Hockey League

WALES CONFERENCE, ADAMS DIVISION
Boston Bruins (MA)
Buffalo Sabres (NY)
Hartford Whalers (CT)
Montreal Canadiens (Quebec)
Quebec Nordiques (Quebec)

WALES CONFERENCE, PATRICK DIVISION
New Jersey Devils (NJ)
New York Islanders (NY)
New York Rangers (NY)
Philadelphia Flyers (PA)
Pittsburgh Penguins (PA)
Washington Capitals (DC)

CAMPBELL CONFERENCE, NORRIS DIVISION
Chicago Black Hawks (IL)
Detroit Red Wings (MI)
Minnesota North Stars (MN)
St. Louis Blues (MO)
Toronto Maple Leafs (Ontario)

CAMPBELL CONFERENCE, SMYTHE DIVISION
Calgary Flames (Alberta)
Edmonton Oilers (Alberta)
Los Angeles Kings (CA)
Vancouver Canucks (British Columbia)
Winnipeg Jets (Manitoba)

Next to jai alai, hockey is the fastest professional sport, and along with football, one of the most physical of team sports. Ice hockey action moves up and down the rink even more rapidly than basketball. It is also a game that requires two major skills: speed skating and the ability to handle the stick. A third might be added: the free-for-all fighting that often breaks out.

Hockey Rink and Equipment

An official ice hockey rink is two hundred feet in length, including the ten feet behind each of the goal nets, and eighty-five feet wide, encircled by boards approximately four feet high. In international competition, the rink is one hundred feet wide.

There are nine face-off spots on the ice, each spot one foot in diameter. One spot is in the center of the rink, one is on each side of the goals at both ends of the rink, and four face-off spots are between the blue lines, two near each blue line on opposite sides of the rink.

There are three important markings on the ice. In professional hockey, the center of the rink is divided in half by a dashed red line and into thirds by two unbroken blue lines. These lines are used by the referee to determine specific infractions. Goal nets are centered on each of the two goal lines spanning the width of the rink, one at each end of the rink. Goalposts rest on stakes set in the ice and are six feet wide and four feet high. Team benches are located across the rink from one another at approximately center rink, just outside the fence.

The team benches can be occupied by no more than nineteen, including team members, managers, coaches, doctor and trainers. The coach is confined to the area of his team bench. A penalty box has space for eight players.

Players

A team may have fifteen uniformed players, a goalkeeper, and a spare goalkeeper. Players must wear numbers in addition to team insignia, and a list of those players must be provided the referee and scorekeeper prior to the start of the game.

Each team has six members, a goalie or goalkeeper, a right defense, a left defense, a right wing, a left wing, and a center.

Dress and Equipment

Teams dress in distinctive uniforms consisting of a long sleeved shirt, shorts over pants, stockings, and ice skates of approved design. Each player wears protective equipment including shoulder pads, elbow pads and shin pads, all worn under the uniform. Players also wear gloves; headgear is optional in professional ice hockey. The goalkeeper wears additional protective equipment, as the puck travels at speeds up to one hundred miles an hour. A goalkeeper wears a face mask, a chest protector, leg guards, and a large floppy mitt similar to a baseball first baseman's mitt to field pucks.

Each player carries a hockey stick, the shaft of which is four feet, five inches long with the projecting blade of the stick one foot, two and one half inches in length and three inches in width. The goalkeeper's stick shaft is four feet, five inches in length, one foot, two and one half inches long from the center portion of the shaft to the end of the projecting blade, which is one half inch wider than other players' regulation sticks.

Game Time

Games are three periods of twenty minutes each. In the event of a tie, there is an overtime period. In the Stanley Cup playoffs, tie games are decided in as many overtime periods as necessary. Timing clocks stop when goals are scored, when infractions are committed, when the puck is hit out of the rink, or when an injury is sustained. There are intermissions between periods.

Objective of the Game

The game begins with a face-off at the center of the rink. The referee tosses the puck, a vulcanized circular piece of hard rubber three inches in diameter, to the ice. The team with possession of the puck attempts to score by passing the puck down the ice and hitting it into the opposing team's goal. The team with the higher score wins the game, one point for each goal.

Penalties and Penalty Shots

For penalty shots, the puck is placed on the center face-off spot. All opposing players are withdrawn behind the center line as a lone player goes down the ice toward the opposing team's goal and goalie, who must remain in his crease until the puck crosses the blue line. At that time, the goalkeeper may attempt to prevent the puck from entering the goal cage.

There are many rules and penalties in professional ice hockey. I recommend further study before writing about the game.

For rules, regulations and answers to specific questions, contact the NHL League Office, Sun Life Building, Montreal, Quebec, Canada.

Suggested Reading

The Design Group. *Rules of the Game.* New York: Bantam, 1976.

Ford Hovis. *The Sports Encyclopedia.* New York: Praeger Publishing., 1976.

BOXING

Boxing, also known as prizefighting, is one of the most watched spectator sports. It is also extremely controversial with respect to some of the brutal punishment fighters suffer, in some cases resulting in brain damage and even death.

Unsavory characters have been and still are involved in boxing, including managers, promoters, trainers, and mobsters. It is a sport also noted for hangers-on who profit by the fighter's quest for bigger and bigger purse money and championships.

Boxing itself is an art. Fighters and sluggers are more apt to just go at one another and ignore the more sophisticated nuances of boxing.

In professional boxing the fighter is only allowed to strike blows with his gloves. Hitting with any other part of the fighter's body is a foul, as is hitting below the belt, tripping, striking an opponent after the bell ending the round has sounded, hitting an opponent who is outside the ropes enclosing the ring or who is down, or continuing to strike an opponent after the referee has ordered the fighters to separate.

Time

A professional boxing match consists of three to fifteen rounds, each round three minutes in length with one-minute rest periods between rounds. Each round ends at the sound of the bell. Amateur boxing rounds last two to three minutes with one-minute rest periods between rounds and usually have a three-round limit.

Rules

When a fighter is knocked down, the opponent must go to a neutral corner while the referee counts to ten. If the fighter who has been knocked down gets to his feet and the referee agrees to let the fight continue, the boxer in the neutral corner and his opponent resume the fight. Should the fighter be unable to get to his feet before the count of ten or should the referee decide that the fighter who has been knocked down is physically incapable of continuing, the fight is ended and the opponent declared the winner.

When a fighter is unable to respond after the count of ten, it is declared a knockout. When the fallen fighter or his trainer, the referee, or the ring physician decides the fight should end because of injury to that fighter, the bout is called a technical knockout.

Ring and Equipment

Boxing takes place within a three-roped ring with a canvas floor over rubber or felt. Most professional rings are twenty feet square and have approximately one foot, six inches of space between the ropes. A stool for the boxer to sit on between rounds is placed in each boxer's corner when the bell sounds ending the round and withdrawn when the bell sounds beginning the next round.

Officials

Bouts are officiated by a referee, two judges, a timekeeper, and official seconds (up to four for each professional boxer).

Dress and Equipment

Boxers wear boxing trunks (colors must differ from opponent's). Professionals are allowed up to eighteen feet, two inches of soft bandage of eleven feet by one inch zinc oxide tape, no more than nine feet below middle-class weight. Knuckles are not allowed to be taped. Boxing gloves weigh eight ounces in professional and amateur boxing; six ounce gloves are used by professional welterweights and under; ten ounce gloves are used by heavyweights in some countries. Boxers also use gumshields or mouth protectors, cup protectors, and boxing boots.

Scoring the Fight

Scoring is done by the referee and two ringside judges. Fights decided by points or rounds are called "decisions." In the "round" system of scoring, the fighter believed to have won that round is awarded one point. At the conclusion of the bout, the points are totaled, and the fighter with more rounds or points is declared the winner. If the rounds totaled reveal no conclusive winner, the fight is called a split decision or draw. There are also point systems, but they are seldom used in major professional bouts.

Maximum Weights for Professional Boxing

Flyweight: 112 lbs
Bantamweight: 118 lbs
Featherweight: 126 lbs
Lightweight: 135 lbs
Welterweight: 147 lbs
Middleweight: 160 lbs
Light heavyweight: 175 lbs
Heavyweight: Over 175 lbs

Maximum Weights for Amateur Boxing

Light Flyweight: 106 lbs
Flyweight: 112 lbs
Bantamweight: 119 lbs
Featherweight: 125 lbs
Lightweight: 132 lbs
Light welterweight: 139 lbs
Welterweight: 147 lbs
Light middleweight: 156 lbs
Middleweight: 165 lbs
Light heavyweight: 178 lbs
Heavyweight: Over 178 lbs

For further information on boxing and its rules and regulations, contact one of the following boxing organizations.

The World Boxing Council, Genova 33, Oficina 503 Colonia Juarez Cuauhtemoc, 06600, Mexico City DF, Mexico.

The World Boxing Association, 412 Colorado Avenue, Aurora, Illinois 60506.

The United States Boxing Association, 134 Evergreen Pl., 9th Floor, East Orange, New Jersey 07018.

The International Boxing Association, 134 Evergreen Pl., 9th Floor, East Orange, New Jersey 07018.

SOCCER

The Game

Soccer is a field game using a ball, played by two teams, each team consisting of eleven players (including goal tenders).

Objective of the Game

To kick the ball into the opponent's goal, with the team scoring the most goals declared the winner.

The Field

The playing field is 50 by 100 yards wide and 100 by 30 yards long. Netted goal posts are at each end of the field with each goal area enclosed in the larger penalty area. The touch lines and goal lines are part of the playing field. Flags on posts 5 feet high are placed at each corner of the field. Flags on either side of center field are optional.

Playing Time

Two halves consisting of 45 minutes each with teams changing sides after the first half. Half time is approximately 5 minutes.

Playing the Ball

Except for throw-ins, the goal tender is the only member of the team allowed to play with his arms or legs and then only in the penalty area. Players may use their feet, head, thighs, or chest. A coin is tossed for selecting the team that will kick off. A goal is scored when the ball yposts, assuming the goal has been achieved within the rules of the game.

A ball is considered to be out of play when it crosses the boundaries or when play has been stopped by the Referee. The ball is then "thrown in" along the touchline where the ball went out of play. The ball is awarded to the last team to have touched the ball before it went out of play. No goal can be made by a "throw-in."

Kicks

There are a number of different kicks.

A *goal kick* is awarded to the defending team if and when the ball crosses their goal line after last having been touched by the opposing team. The kick may be attempted by any member of the defending team, including its goal tender. No goal can be scored directly by a goal kick.

A *corner kick* is awarded to the attacking team if or when the ball crosses the goal line having last been touched by the defending team. It is taken from the corner circle by the corner flag. In this case, a goal *can* be scored directly from a corner kick; however, the kicker may not play the ball until it has been touched by another player.

A *free kick* is taken from where the offense has taken place.

A *direct free kick* is where the player awarded the kick can make a direct score. An *indirect free kick* is one in which a goal cannot be scored until the ball has been touched by another player.

Penalties and Infringements

An *indirect free kick* is awarded for charging, dangerous play, for obstructing an opponent while not playing the ball, for charging the goal tender, for dissenting with the Referee's decision, or for entering or leaving the game without proper notification of the Referee.

A *penalty kick* is one in which any offense incurs a direct free kick and is punished by a penalty kick to the opposing side when the offense is committed by a defending player in his or her own penalty area. The kick is taken from the penalty spot. It is awarded for dissenting with the Referee's decision, for entering or leaving a game without permission of the Referee, and for ungentlemanly conduct.

Fouls and Misconduct

Holding, tripping, charging the ball, or kicking, striking, or pushing an opponent.

There are many special rules for types of kicks, infringements, etc. The National Soccer Association (NSA) should be contacted for an official rule book.

Officials

A Referee controls the game with the assistance of two Linesmen. The Referee acts as time keeper, maintains a record of the game, stops the game on account of injuries, enforces the rules of the game, and may terminate the game because of inclement weather or other problems.

The Linesmen, one on each touchline, indicate if the ball is out of play, determine which side should have possession of the ball, and put the ball back into play by a corner kick, a throw, or a goal kick. They can raise flags to indicate an infringement but can be overruled by the Referee.

Substitutions

Players may be substituted, usually not more than one or two, and must be named prior to the beginning of the game. Once replaced by a substitute, the original player may not return to the game.

A Few Words to the Wise

If you're writing about a sporting event in the past, properly identify the teams and leagues, and the rules of the game at that time. For the latest information on major sports, try *Sports Illustrated* magazine, especially the annual preview issues on football, baseball, and basketball.

Suggested Reading

The Design Group. *Rules of the Game.* New York: Bantam Books, 1976.

Ford Hovis. *The Sports Encyclopedia.* New York: Praeger Publishing, 1976.

HORSE RACING

Basically there are two types of horse racing, flat racing and steeplechase, although there are very few steeplechase races held in the United States.

Flat races are run on either dirt or grass (turf) on oval tracks, some with a more complex pattern to allow for a variety of starting points, with races run for 6 furlongs, $6^1/_2$ furlongs, 7 furlongs, 1 mile, $1^1/_8$ miles, and $1^1/_2$ miles (a furlong is $^1/_8$ mile or 220 yards).

The main officials are known as Stewards, while other officials have such titles as the Racing Secretary who is in charge of the course and the meet, the Weighing Officer in charge of the weighing in and the weighing out, the Handicapper who arranges the weights for handicap races, and the Judges who declare the results at the finish of the race.

Racing categories include races for horses that have never raced before, maiden races for horses who have never won a race, claiming races where a horse may be claimed for a specified price, allowance races, stakes races, special handicap races, and championship races such as the Breeders Cup and other major competitions.

In flat racing, horses and jockeys come out of a chute at the start of the race. Each horse and jockey has been pre-assigned a numbered chute, called "the post." The chute's number denotes the "post position" of that horse and jockey.

When the flag is dropped, the chute automatically opens, releasing the horses and their jockeys. The length of the race determines whether the horses race down a stretch or if they go two turns of the track. The first horse to reach the Finish Line is declared the Winner, the second horse is considered to have "Placed," and the third horse to come across the finish line is said to have "Shown." Payoffs are made on Win, Place, and Show bets.

Jockeys must be licensed and they may be substituted before or after the weigh-out providing there is no undue delay in changing jockeys.

Horse categories

A horse's age is based on the 1st day of the calendar year (i.e., beginning January 1) in which the horse was foaled. Females are considered to be Fillies until the age of 5 years and called Mares thereafter.

Male horses are Colts to the age of 5 and are called Horses after that. A male horse that has been castrated is called a Gelding.

Horse's saddle

Saddle, girth, and surcingle, stirrup irons, leathers or webs, and a number cloth.

Jockey dress

A crash helmet or cap (compulsory), a shirt and riding pants in the owner's colors, boots, spurs, and a whip.

Glossary

Apprentice: Also known as a "Bug Boy," a beginning jockey, the "bug" signifying a special weight allowance.

Backstretch: The far side of the track

Beat odds: Term applied to a horse that finished in a higher position than in the betting.

Beyers: A rating given to horses based on their last performance.

Blinkers: Flaps worn by the horse to prevent peripheral vision so that he cannot see the other horses but only the track in front of him.

Bore-out: Bearing to the right. "In" would be to the left.

BPR: The horse is better than previously raced.

Breezing: When a horse runs with little or no effort.

Broke in a tangle: Horse does not break out of the gate in clear running position.

Broke in the air: When a horse jumps at the start of the race.

BTL: A work or race that was better than thought.

Calks/Stickers: Special horseshoes believed to be better when running on turf or muddy track.

Chalk: An odds-on favorite going off at very low odds.

Claiming: A race in which all horses entered can be purchased for the claiming price of the race.

Claimproof: For some reason the horse cannot be claimed.

Class: The class held by the horse, such as being a Maiden, i.e. not having won its first race, or not having raced in claiming races, allowance races, stakes races, handicap races, etc.

Closer: A horse that comes up sharply near the end of the race.

Colors: The colors worn by the jockey that denote the stable he or she is riding for.

Conditions horse: Horses entered in an Allowance race that barely fit the qualifications.

Corded up: When a horse is unable to stand due to a leg muscle spasm.

Daisycutter: A horse that runs on the turf.

Distance: The length of the race, from 4 to 7 furlongs, 1 mile, $1\frac{1}{8}$ miles, $1\frac{1}{4}$ miles, to $1\frac{1}{2}$ miles.

Dwelt: When a horse is reluctant to leave the gate.

Eased: Horse did not finish the race and no final time was recorded.

FF: Designates a horse that finished with the fastest fractions.

First time starter: A horse that is racing for the first time against more experienced horses.

FS: Means the fastest spurt in the last $1\frac{1}{8}$ of a mile.

Furlong: An eighth of a mile.

Green: Inexperienced horse.

Handicap: Consideration of all the information about the horses in a given race in an attempt to figure out the likely winner.

Handily: Means an easy win with the jockey using the whip.

Hat trick: Winning three races in a row.

Horses for courses: Horses that show a preference for certain race tracks.

Hung: The horse lost his drive.

In-the-money: A horse that finished 1st, 2nd, or 3rd.

Inquiry: Officials examine a race for violations. There can be a Steward's inquiry or an inquiry called by a jockey.

Inside post position: Horse running close to the rail.

Jail: A restricted period after a horse has been claimed. If a horse races within 30 days of being claimed, it must run at a 25% higher price.

Lasix: Medication used to treat horses that are bleeders.

Layoff or regency: A horse's frequency of racing, for example, how long it has been between races.

Lick: Early speed.

Live horse: A horse that is expected to give a top performance.

Lone 'F': Leading field by a large margin.

Longshot: A horse that is being bet at long odds; it is not expected to win but has an outside chance.

Lugged in: When horse veers to his left. 'Out' would be to veer to the right.

Maiden win: Horse's first win.

Main track: The dirt track.

Morning glory: Horse does well in morning workout but not in race.

Morning line: The estimated odds appearing on the board and in the program.

Odds-on: Refers to favorite; wager is usually less than even money.

Off-track: Can mean a track known to be less than fast, because of rain. Also can refer to betting at a track or gaming establishment other than where the race is being run.

Open: A race that has no restrictions.

Overlay: When odds created by betting are higher than the morning line. An "underlay" means the exact opposite.

Pace: The time in which the leading horse is running.

Poles: The poles designate the parts of the mile. Quarter poles are red and white, eighth poles are green and white, sixteenth poles are black and white.

Post time: The time the race begins.

Purse: The total amount of prize money for the race.

Rank: Horse is not running properly.

Regated: When a horse breaks through the gate before the start of the race and must be reloaded.

Regency: The racing activity or experience of the horse.

Released from claiming jail: Horse is now allowed to race after having been claimed in a claiming race and was subsequently restricted under the rules of the Racing Commission until it is permitted to race again under new colors.

Router: A horse that performs exceedingly well at one mile or more.

Saver: A bet to back up another bet.

Shadow roll: Sheepskin or roll of cloth across horse's nose to prevent shadows.

Short: Means horse was racing well in the stretch but then lost energy.

Split a field: When a horse has beaten half the horses in a race.

Sprinter: Horse that runs best under a mile.

Stick: A horse with late speed or stamina.

Sulked: Horse refuses to run.

Surface: The condition of the track or surface the horse is racing on; for example, dirt or turf.

Tag: Another name for a claim.

Tookup: When the jockey has to slow his mount when blocked.

Turf race: Horses racing on grass as opposed to the main track.

Two turns: Any race requiring the horse to make two turns on the track.

Used: A term applied to pushing the horse too early in the race.

Washy: Horse is perspiring heavily because of nervousness.

Wet: Horse that is washy.

Wide: When horse is near the inner rail, causing it to have to travel farther around the track.

Wire-to-wire: Horse wins from start to finish.

Workouts: The time the horse raced at various lengths during training.

Wraps: The cloth bindings worn by a horse around lower legs for protection and indicating some weakness in the horse's leg(s).

Horse Racing Tracks

Aiken, Aiken, SC
Ak-Sar-Ben, **Ak-Sar-Ben Field**, Omaha, NE
Albuquerque, **Highland Station**, Albuquerque, NM
Aqueduct, Jamica, NY
Arlington Park, Arlington Heights, IL
Atokad Park, South Sioux City, NE
Almoral Park, Crete, IL
Bendera Downs, Bendera, TX
Bay Meadows, San Mateo, CA
Belmont Park, Jamaica, NY
Beuiah Park, Grove City, OH
Birmingham Race Course, Birmingham, AL
Blue Ribbon Downs, Sallisaw, OK
Calder Race Course, **Carol City**, Opalacka, FL
Canterbury Downs, Shakopee, MN
Carolina Cup, **Colonial Cup**, **Springdale Course**, Camden, SC
Charleston Cup, Charleston, SC
Charles Town Races, Charles Town, WV
Churchill Downs, Louisville, KY
Columbus, Columbus, NE
Columbus Steeplechase, Columbus, GA
Dayton Days, Dayton, WA
Delaware Park, Wilmington, DE
Del Mar, Del Mar, CA
Delta Downs Race Track, Vinton, LA
Detroit Ladbroke, Livonia, MI
Dueling Grounds Race Course, Franklin, KY
Ellis Park, Henderson, KY
Evangelline Downs, Lafayette, LA
Fair Grounds, New Orleans, LA
Fair Hill Races, Elkton, MD
Fairmount Park, Collinsville, IL
Fairplex Park, Pomona, CA
Fair Hills Race Meet, Fair Hills, NJ
Ferndale, Ferndale, CA
Finger Lakes, Canadaigua, NY
Flathead Fairgrounds, Kalispell, MT
Fonner Park, Grand Island, NE
Foxfield, Charlottesville, VA

Fresno, Fresno, CA
Garden State Park, Cherry Hill, NJ
Gillespie County Fair, Fredricksburg, TX
Golden Gate Field, Albany, CA
Grand National Steeplechase, Butler, MD
Grants Pass, Grants Pass, OR
Great Falls, Great Falls, MT
Gulfstream, Hallandale, FL
Harbor Park, Grays Harbor County Fair, Elma, WA
Hawthorne Race Course, Cicero, IL
Hialeah, Hialeah, FL
Hollywood Park, Inglewood, CA
Horseman's Track, Lexington, KY
Jefferson Downs, Kenner, LA
Juarez Racetrack, El Paso, TX
Klamath County Fairgrounds, Klamath Falls, OR
La Mesa Park, Raton, NM
Laurel Race Course, Laurel, MD
Les Bola Park, Boise, ID
Lincoln Nebraska State Fair, Lincoln, NE
Lone Oak Park,Oregon State Fairgrounds, Salem, OR
Longacres, Renton, WA
Los Alamitos, Costa Mesa, CA
Lousiana Downs, Bossier City, LA
Marshfield Fair, Marshfield, ME
The Meadowlands, East Rutherford, NJ
Metrapark Race Track, Billings, MT
Monmouth Park, Oceanport, NJ
Montpellier Hunt Races, Montpellier Station, VA
Mountaineer Park, Chester, WV
Mount Pleasant Meadows, Mount Pleasant, MI
Northhampton, Northhampton, MA
Oaklawn Park, Hot Springs, AR
Oak Tree (At Santa Anita), Arcadia, CA
Orange County Racing Fair, Costa Mesa, CA
Penn National Race Course, Grantville, PA
Philadelphia Park, Bensalem, PA
Pimlico Race Course, Baltimore, MD
Platfair, Spokane, WA
Pleasanton, Pleasanton, CA
Portland Meadows, Portland, OR
Prairie Meadows, Altonna, IA
Prescott Downs, Prescott, AZ
Remington Park, Oklahoma City, OK
Rillito Downs, Tucson, AZ
River Downs, Cincinnati, OH

Rockingham Park, Salem, NH
Ruidoso Downs, Ruidoso Downs, NM
Sacramento (Cal State Fair) , Sacramento, CA
Salem Fairgrounds, Salem, OR
San Juan Downs, Farmington, NM
Santa Anita Park, Arcadia, CA
Santa Fe Downs, Santa Fe, NM
Santa Rosa, Santa Rosa, CA
Saratoga, Saratoga, NY
Solono County Fair, Vallejo, CA
Sonoma County Fair, Santa Rosa, CA
Sportsman's Park, Cicero, IL
Stockton, Stockton, CA
Strawberry Hill Races, Richmond, VA
Suffolk Downs, East Boston, MA
Sun Downs, Kennewick, WA
Sunland Park, Sunland Park, NM
Tampa Bay Downs, Oldsmar, FL
Thistledown, Cleveland, OH
Timonium, Timonium, MD
Trinity Meadows, Weatherford, TX
Turf Paradise, Phoenix, AZ
Turfway Park, Florence, KY
Waltsburg, Waltsburg, WA
Walla Walla, Walla Walla, WA
The Woodlands, Kansas City, KS
Wyoming Downs, Evanston, WY
Yakima Meadows, Yakima, WA

AUTOMOBILE RACING

AUTOMOBILE-RELATED ABBREVIATIONS

AAA	American Automobile Association
ACO	Automobile Club de l'Ouest
ACGBI	Automobile Association of Great Britain and Ireland
ADAC	Allgemeine Deutsche Automobil Club
AIACR	Association Internationale des Automobiles Clubs Reconnus
ACF	Automobile Club de France
ACCUS	Automobile Competition Committee for the U.S.
aiv	automatic inlet valve(s)
ALAM	Association of Licensed Automobile Manufacturers
AMOC	Aston Martin Owners' Club
ARCA	Automobile Racing Club of America
AVUS	Automobil-Verkehrs-und Übungs-Strasse

BARC	British Automobile Racing Club
BBC	British Broadcasting Corporation
bhp	brake horsepower
BMC	British Motor Corporation
BRDC	British Racing Drivers' Club
BRSCC	British Racing and Sports Car Club
BRTDA	British Rally and Trials Drivers' Association
CRA	California Racing Association
CASC	Canadian Automobile Sports Club
cc	cubic centimeters
ci	cubic inches
CV	cheval vapeur (French: horsepower)
CSI	Commission Sportive Internationale
DIN	Deutsche Industrie Normen
dohc	double overhead camshaft
eoi	exhaust over inlet (valves)
ET	elapsed time
FEMA	Fédération Européene du Modélisme Automobile
FF	Formula Ford
FFSA	Fédération Française du Sport Automobile
FI	Fuel injected
FIA	Fédération Internationale de l'Automobile
FISA	Federazione Italiana delle Scuderie Automobile
FJ	Formula Junior
ft	feet
ft	fastest time of the day
4wd	four wheel drive
fwd	front wheel drive
GP	Grand Prix
GPDA	Grand Prix Drivers' Association
GT	Gran Turismo
hp	horsepower
ht	high tension (magneto ignition)
ifs	independent front suspension
IMCA	International Motor Contest Association
in	inch(es)
ioe	inlet over exhaust (valves)
irs	independent rear suspension
JCC	Junior Car Club
kg	kilogram(s)
km	kilometer(s)
KNAC	Koninklijke Nederlandse Automobiel Club
kph	kilometers per hour
lt	low tension (magneto ignition)
lwb	long wheelbase
MCC	Motor Cycling Club

min	minute(s)
mm	millimeter(s)
moiv	mechanically operated inlet valve(s)
mpg	miles per gallon
mph	miles per hour
MRP	Midland Racing Partnership
NACC	National Automobile Chamber of Commerce
NART	North American Racing Team
NASCAR	National Association for Stock Car Auto Racing
NORRA	National Off Road Racing Association
ohc	overhead camshafts
ohv	overhead valve(s)
oiv	overhead inlet valve(s)
PS	Pferde Stärke (German: horsepower)
psi	pounds per square inch
RAC	Royal Automobile Club (England)
RN	Route Nationale
rpm	revolutions per minute
RSAC	Royal Scottish Automobile Club
SAE	Society of Automotive Engineers
sec	second(s)
SFI	Sequential fuel injection
SL	Super legera (super light)
Spl	Special
sv	side valve(s)
SCCA	Sports Car Club of America
TT	Tourist Trophy
USAC	United States Automobile Club
VSCC	Vintage Sports Car Club
wb	wheelbase
yd	yard(s)

Abbreviations that indicate the Country of Manufacture of Automobiles:

A	Austria
AUS	Australia
CDN	Canada
CH	Switzerland
CS	Czechoslovakia
D	Germany, West
DDR	Germany, East (formerly)
E	Spain
F	France
GB	Great Britain
I	Italy
J	Japan

NL	Holland
NZ	New Zealand
PL	Poland
S	Sweden
SU	Union of Soviet Socialist Republics (formerly)
US	United States of America
ZA	South Africa

AUTO RACING TRACKS *(listed by state)*

ALABAMA
Birmingham—Birmingham International Raceway
Talledega—Alabama International Speedway

ARIZONA
Phoenix—FasTrack International Speedway, Manzanita
Park Speedway

CALIFORNIA
Bakersfield—Mesa Marin
Chula Vista—South Bay Speedway
Costa Mesa—Orange County International Speedway
Corona—Corona Raceway
Gardena—Ascot Park
Hanford—Kings Fairgrounds Speedway
Irwindale—605 Speedway
Long Beach—Long Beach Grand Prix Circuit
Monterey—Laguna Seca Raceway
Palmdale—Los Angeles County Raceway
Placerville—Placerville Racetrack
Riverside—Riverside International Raceway
Rosemond—Willow Springs Raceway
Saugus—Saugus Speedway
Sonoma—Sears Point Raceway
Visalia—Plaza Park Raceway

COLORADO
Englewood—Englewood Speedway
Erie—Colorado National Speedway

DELAWARE
Dover—Dover Downs International Speedway

FLORIDA
Daytona Beach—Daytona International Speedway

GEORGIA
Atlanta—Atlanta International Raceway
Gainesville—Road Atlanta

IDAHO
Meridian—Meredian Speedway

ILLINOIS
Du Quoin—Du Quoin State Fairgrounds
Granite City—Tri-City Speedway
Hinsdale—Santa Fe Speedway
Rockford—Rockford Speedway
Springfield—Illinois State Fairgrounds, Springfield Speedway

INDIANA
Clermont—Indianapolis Raceway Park
Fort Wayne—Memorial Coliseum
Indianapolis—Indianapolis Motor Speedway, Indiana
    State Fairgrounds
Kokomo—Kokomo Speedway
Salem—Salem Speedway
Schereville—Illiana Motor Speedway
Terre Haute—Action Track Speedway
Winchester—Winchester Speedway

IOWA
Cedar Rapids—Hawkeye Downs
Des Moines—Iowa State Fairgrounds
Knoxville—Knoxville Speedway

KANSAS
Kansas City—Lakeside Speedway
Wichita—81 Speedway

KENTUCKY
Lost Creek—Lost Creek Speedway
Louisville—Fairgrounds Motor Speedway

MICHIGAN
Brooklyn—Michigan International Speedway
Hartford—Hartford Motor Speedway
Marne—Berlin Raceway

MISSOURI
Odessa—I-70 Speedway
Sedalia—Missouri State Fairgrounds

NEBRASKA
Lincoln—Midwest Speedway
Omaha—Sunset Speedway

NEW JERSEY
Trenton—Trenton Speedway

NEW YORK
Elbridge—Rolling Wheels Raceway

Fulton—Fulton Raceway
Syracuse—New York State Fairgrounds
Watkins Glen—Watkins Glen Grand Prix Circuit
Weedsport—Weedsport Speedway

NORTH CAROLINA
Charlotte—Charlotte Motor Speedway
North Wilkesboro—North Wilkesboro Speedway
Rockingham—North Carolina Motor Speedway

OHIO
Cincinnati—Tri-County Speedway
Columbus—Columbus Motor Speedway
Dayton—Dayton Speedway
Findlay—Millstream Motor Speedway
Hartford—Sharon Speedway
Lexington—Mid-Ohio Sports Car Course
Lima—Limaland Motor Speedway
New Bremen—New Bremen Speedway
Rossburg—Eldora Speedway
Toledo—Toledo Speedway

OKLAHOMA
Enid—Enid Speedway

PENNSYLVANIA
Harrisburg—Penn National Race Course
Pocono—Pocono International Raceway
Reading—Reading Fairgrounds
Selinsgrove—Selinsgrove Speedway
Williamsgrove—Williamsgrove Speedway

SOUTH CAROLINA
Darlington—Darlington International Raceway

SOUTH DAKOTA
Brookings—Brookings Speedway
Huron—State Fairgrounds Speedway

TENNESSEE
Bristol—Bristol International Speedway
Nashville—Fairgrounds Motor Speedway

TEXAS
College Station—Texas World Speedway

UTAH
Provo—Suntana Raceway
Salt Lake City—Salt Flats

VIRGINIA
Martinsville—Martinsville Speedway

WISCONSIN
Elkhart Lake—Road America
Hales Corners—Hales Corners Speedway
Kaukauna—Wisconsin International Speedway
Madison—Capital Super Speedway
Milwaukee—Wisconsin State Fair Speedway
Shawano—Shawano County Fairgrounds
Sun Prairie—Angell Park Speedway
West Salem—LaCrosse Interstate Speedway

For further information regarding auto racing and track information, either contact the track directly or contact the appropriate legislative organization listed:

American Hot Rod Association, 4701 College Blvd., Leewood, KS 66211

Championship Auto Racing Teams (CART), 3321 W. Big Beaver Rd., Suite 205, Troy, MI 48084

International Hot Rod Association, P.O. Box 3558, Bristol, TN 37620

International Motor Sports Association, 32365 Mally Dr., Madison Heights, MI 48071

NASCAR, P.O. Box K, Daytona Beach, FL 32015

National Hot Rod Association, 10639 Riverside Dr., North Hollywood, CA 91602

SCORE International (off-road racing), 31356 Via Colinas, Suite 111, Westlake Village, CA 91362

14

Medicine

THE WRITER IN THE MEDICAL ARENA

As a writer, I learned a long time ago that research is essential if your writing is to be credible. Having written many episodes of the television series *Medical Center*, I began to feel like a medical student because of the research I had to do for my stories to pass the scrutiny of the series' technical advisor and the viewers of the series.

For example, in writing an episode about sudden infant death syndrome (SIDS), I not only became involved with the organizations dealing with the parents of children who succumbed to SIDS but found myself one day at the county morgue watching more than six hours of autopsies on SIDS infants. Through that research I discovered which infants were most at risk for SIDS, the effect of the unexpected deaths on the infants' families, and that, in some cases autopsied that day, a forty-nine cent bulb syringe might have prevented the demise of the infant.

Good, solid research provides the reader or viewer an insight to a subject they might never have known, and it gives your story added drama.

This chapter cannot provide you with the necessary research for the medical aspects of your story. That would take a complete and up-to-date medical library and interviews with doctors and other specialists familiar with the illness you are writing about. This chapter can help acquaint you with the various aspects of medicine and hospitals. To ensure credibility, consult a specialist.

If one of your characters ingests poison, there is a list of simple treatments. Another lists manias, fears, obsessions, and phobias you might wish to use as an Achilles' heel for one of your principal characters.

Still another lists communicable diseases. This could involve a hospitalized patient or a character running amuck somewhere, a walking time bomb that could cause an epidemic.

Last is a comprehensive list of the departments and clinics, medical, technical, and administrative personnel in a major medical center.

How would you use this information? Suppose you are writing a story or a screenplay that takes place in a hospital. You should be aware of the departments and personnel in that locale. Although the list contains a number of highly specialized departments, it could encourage you to learn what departments and equipment might be found in the hospital you're writing about.

Suppose you were writing a story about a woman's pregnancy. You might be concerned with such areas as obstetrics, prenatal care, maternal-fetal diagnosis, labor and delivery, pediatric I.C.U., the newborn nursery, the family waiting room, etc.

What if the unexpected arises, some complication during pregnancy or the birth of the infant? Here's a chance to increase the drama. You could refer to the list of afflictions, illnesses, and diseases, and once the complication has been chosen look up the medical or surgical specialty that would deal with the complication.

Remember, the lists merely offer suggestions for your consideration, a voice saying, "Hey, how about this for a complication?" The actual research must be done by you.

FROM TYPEWRITER TO STETHOSCOPE

You don't have to be a doctor or medical student to write a medical story, but it sure would help. The next best thing is to either know a doctor who can help you with your research or to begin doing your own.

The Writer's Partner is not a medical dictionary or medical manual. The purpose of this section is to help familiarize you with medical specialties, medical and surgical supplies, ailments, illnesses and diseases, manias, phobias, obsessions and fears, the staff and equipment in an emergency room, the usual cases brought into emergency, emergency room slang, and the departments in a major medical center.

HOW TO USE THIS MEDICAL SECTION

There are many ways to utilize the information on the following pages. One, of course, is the selection of the illness from which your character might suffer.

A list is included of doctors, dentists, and specialists who might treat the illness or disease you've selected. As it would be impossible to list all the tests and treatments for the illness you choose, do further research once you've chosen the particular condition your story will involve.

The list of manias, fears, obsessions, and phobias might apply to one of your characters, possibly as an Achilles' heel a character has to deal with at a crucial moment.

The communicable diseases listed might create a problem within a hospital or might suggest a character who is unaware of having the disease.

The medical center divisions are presented to give you an idea of the immensity of such an establishment. To the writer whose story takes place in a medical center, the list of departments, personnel, and clinics should paint a picture of the locale of your story. Even if a small part of your story takes place there, this information would still be of value.

DOCTORS, DENTISTS, AND OTHER SPECIALISTS

Allergist
Anesthesiologist
Anesthetist
Audiologist
Bacteriologist
Bronchoscopist
Cardiologist
Cardiovascular surgeon
Chiropractor
Cytologist
Dentist
Diagnostician
Electroencephalogist
Embryologist
Endocrinologist
Endodontist
Endoscopist
Ephebriatrist
Epidemiologist
Esophagologist
Gastroenterologist

Geriatrician
Gynecologist
Hematologist
Hydrotherapist
Hypnologist
Immunologist
Internist
Laryngologist
Lobotomist
Microbiologist
Neonatalogist
Nephrologist
Neurologist
Neuropathologist
Obstetrician
Oncologist
Ophthalmologist
Oral surgeon
Orthodontist
Orthogamist
Orthopath

Orthopedist
Orthopsychiatrist
Otolaryngologist
Otologist
Ovariotomist
Parasitologist
Pathologist
Pediatrician
Periodontist
Pharmacologist
Physiotherapist
Plastic surgeon
Proctologist
Psychiatrist

Psychoanalyst
Psychosomaticist
Pulmonologist
Radiologist
Rheumatologist
Rhinologist
Roentgenologist
Serologist
Stomologist
Syphilologist
Toxicologist
Urologist
Virologist

FIRST AID EQUIPMENT AND PROCEDURES

Adhesive tape
Antiseptics
Artificial respiration
Baking soda for bee sting
Bandages
Coagulants
Cool applications and drinks for sunstroke
Decongestants
Disinfectants
Elevating the legs for fainting
Emetics (raw eggs, milk)
Gauze
Heat
Ice pack
Incision and sucking for snake bite
Isolation and rest
Loosened clothing
Lowering the head for shock
Massage
Mouth-to-mouth resuscitation
Nitroglycerin for angina
Oxygen
Pressure on cut artery or tourniquet nearer heart
Reclining position
Smelling salts
Splint
Tea or coffee
Tourniquet
Wet dressing

MEDICAL / SURGICAL SUPPLIES

Adhesive bandages
Adhesive tape
Air-driven bone saws
Anesthesia equipment
Aspirator
Bandage scissors
Bandages
Blackhead extractors
Blood pressure machine
Blood transfusion equipment
Bone chisels
Bone gouging forceps
Bone holding forceps
Brain cystoscopes
Bullet probe
Cardiogram equipment
Catheters
Clamps
Colostomy bags
Colostomy receptacle
Commode
Cotton
Cotton balls
Crile forceps
Cryoprobes
Curette
Cuticle nippers
Deaver retractor
Denhardt mouth gag
Doppler electrocardiogram
Doptone
Ear forceps
ECG probes
Echocardiogram
Elastic bandages
Electric shock equipment
Endotracheal catheter
Gigli saw
Graefe cystotome
Graefe strabismus hook
Hard cast material
Hemostatic scissors
Hypodermic needles
Hypodermic syringe

Incontinence bags
Intestinal forceps
Intravenous tubes
Iris scissors
Lancet
Laryngoscope
Laser-beam knives
Lens spoon
Lewis lens loop
Lister bandage scissors
Littaurer stitch scissors
Magnetic resonance imaging
  (MRI)
Mayo dissecting scissors
Microscope
Mouth and ear light
Nails
Nasal forceps
Needle folder
Neurological hammer
Obstetric forceps
Operating scissors
Ophthalmoscope
Orthopedic chisels
Orthopedic gauges
Oscillometers
Otoscope
Oxygen masks
Oxygen tanks
Oxygen tent
Percussion hammer
Pins
Plexor
Precision forceps
Prescription blanks
Pus basin
Rankin-Kelly forceps
Reflex hammer
Retractor
Scale
Scalpel
Scarificator
Slings
Soft cast material

Sperm analyzer
Sphygmomanometer
Splints
Staples
Sterile gloves
Sterile masks
Sterilization box
Stethoscope
Subcutaneous saw
Surgical saw
Surgical scissors
Surgical shears
Surgical snippers
Sutures
Swabs

Symballophone (double
    stethoscope)
Thomas splint
Timing watch
Tongue depressors
Tongue-seizing forceps
Tonometer
Trephine saw
Tuning fork
Tweezers
Ultrasonic pulse detectors
Ultrasound
Ureameter
Utility forceps
X-ray machine

TREATMENTS FOR CHEMICAL POISONING

Alum water
Ammonia
Baking soda in water
Charcoal
Epsom salts
Induced vomiting
Ipecac
Lemon juice
Lime in water

Mustard water
Oils
Oxygen
Raw egg white
Salt water
Soap suds
Starch solution
Vinegar

MANIAS, OBSESSIONS, AND PHOBIAS

Acrophobia: fear of height.
Agoraphobia: fear of open spaces.
Ailurophobia: fear of cats.
Ansatrophobia: fear of kissing.
Anthrophobia: fear of society.
Autophobia: fear of loneliness.
Bacteriophobia: fear of germs.
Claustrophobia: fear of closed places.
Coitophobia: fear of intercourse.
Compulsion: obsessive urge to act.
Dipsomania: craving for alcohol.
Egomania: preoccupation with own self.
Euphoria: excessive, unrealistic feeling of happiness.
Gymnophobia: fear of nakedness.
Hagiophobia: fear of sacred things.
Haptephobia: fear of being touched.
Heliophobia: fear of exposure to the sun.

Hypochondria: excessive fear of ill health.
Kleptomania: compulsive urge to steal.
Megalomania: obsessive desire for wealth, power.
Monophobia: fear of being alone.
Mythomania: compulsion to lie or exaggerate.
Narcissism: self love.
Necromania: excessive preoccupation with dead bodies.
Necrophobia: fear of the dead.
Neophobia: fear of new things, ideas.
Nymphomania: female's excessive sexual desires.
Oedipus complex: excessive attachment to parent.
Paranoia: delusions of being persecuted.
Pedophilia: unwholesome interest in children.
Phobophobia: fear of being afraid.
Pyromania: excessive compulsive desire to set fires.
Pyrophobia: fear of fire.
Satyriasis: male's excessive sexual desires.
Schizophrenia: delusions in escaping from reality.
Taphephobia: fear of being buried alive.
Thanatophobia: fear of death.
Traikaideaphobia: fear of the number thirteen.
Xenophobia: fear of strangers.
Zoophobia: fear of animals.

CAUSES OF DEATH

Accidents	Immolation
Assassination	Live burial
Burning	Loss of blood
Cement overcoat	Lye vat
Choking	Old age
Disease	Poisoning
Drowning	Scalping
Euthanasia	Shooting
Execution	Stabbing
Garroting	Strangulation
Gassing	Suffocation
Hanging	Suicide
Heart attack	War

DISEASES OF CHILDHOOD

Chickenpox	Roseola
Diphtheria	Scarlet fever
German measles	Smallpox
Measles	Tetanus
Mumps	Tuberculosis
Poliomyelitis	Whooping cough

COMMUNICABLE DISEASES

AIDS
Anthrax
Athlete's foot
Botulism
Bubonic plague
Chancre
Chicken pox
Cholera
Common cold
Conjunctivitis
Consumption
Dengue fever
Diphtheria
Dysentery (amoebic)
Dysentery (bacillary)
Encephalitis
Filariasis
Gonorrhea
Green monkey fever
Hepatitis (type A, type B, and
   non-A, non-B)
Herpes
Impetigo
Infectious mononucleosis

Lassa fever
Leprosy
Lyme disease
Malaria
Meningitis
Mumps
Poliomyelitis
Rabies
Rheumatic fever
Rocky Mountain fever
Scarlet fever
Smallpox
Staph infection
Strep infection
Syphilis
Systemic fungal infections
Tick fever
Toxoplasmosis
Trichinosis
Tuberculosis
Typhoid fever
Typhus
Yellow fever

AFFLICTIONS, ILLNESSES, AND DISEASES

Abscess
Acidosis
Acne
Alcoholism
Allergies
Alzheimer's disease
Amnesia
Angina pectoris
Apoplexy
Appendicitis
Arteriosclerosis
Arthritis
Asthma
Atrophy
Backaches
Bends
Beriberi
Blindness

Blood poisoning
Boils
Bone fractures
Botulism
Brain damage
Bright's disease
Bronchitis
Bruises
Burger's disease
Burns
Bursitis
Callous
Cancer
Cataracts
Catarrh
Cerebral palsy
Chills
Colic

Colitis
Constipation
Convulsions
Corns
Coronary disease
Cough
Croup
Deafness
Delirium tremens
Dementia praecox
Dermatitis
Diabetes
Diarrhea
Dislocation
Dropsy
Dyslexia
Earache
Eczema
Edema
Embolism
Emphysema
Epilepsy
Food poisoning
Frostbite
Gallstones
Gangrene
Gastritis
Gastroenteritis
Gingivitis
Goiter
Gout
Hangover
Hay fever
Hemophilia
Hemorrhoids
Hernia
High blood pressure
Hives
Hodgkin's disease
Hypertension
Hyperthyroidism
Hypothyroidism
Hysteria
Ileitis
Indigestion
Insomnia

Jaundice
Kidney disease
Kidney stones
Laryngitis
Lockjaw
Lou Gehrig's disease
Lumbago
Malnutrition
Mastoiditis
Meningitis
Mental retardation
Multiple myeloma
Multiple sclerosis
Muscular dystrophy
Necrosis
Nephritis
Nervous breakdown
Neuralgia
Neuritis
Nosebleed
Obesity
Osteomyelitis
Parkinson's disease
Pellagra
Phlebitis
Piles
Pleurisy
Pneumonia
Poisoning
Pulled muscle
Pulled tendon
Pyorrhea
Radiation poisoning
Rheumatism
Rheumatoid arthritis
Rhinitis
Ringworm
Scurvy
Seasickness
Seborrhea
Shingles
Sinusitis
Sleeping sickness
Slipped disk
Spasm
Sprain

St. Vitus' dance
Stress
Sunstroke
Swelling
Tapeworm
Thrombosis
Tonsillitis

Toothache
Trichinosis
Tumor
Ulcer (peptic, duodenal)
Uremia
Uremic Poisoning
Varicose veins

MAJOR HOSPITAL / MEDICAL CENTER DEPARTMENTS

Administration
Ambulatory Care Center
Anesthesia Pain Center
Anesthesiology
Antepartum Testing
Arrhythmia Center
Audio-Visual Services
Audiology
Bed Reservations
Belongings Desk
Biliary Disease Center
Biofeedback
Biomedical
Biomedical Engineering
Birth Certificates
Birth Control Clinic
Birth Defects Center, Medical Genetics
Blood Bank
Blood Donor Facility
Blood Gas Lab
Blood Replacement
Burn Center
Business Office
CPR (Cardiopulmonary Resuscitation)
Cafeteria
Cancer Center, Comprehensive
Care Unit/Chemical Dependency
Career Counseling
Carpenter Shop
Cashier
Cast Room (Orthopedics)
Central Files
Central Processing
Central Registry
Chaplaincy Department
Child Psychiatry

Child and Family Study Group
Chronic Pain Management Program
Clinical Engineering
Coffee Shop
Community Relations
Conference Rooms
Continuing Medical Education
Credit Union
Cystic Fibrosis
Cytogenics Lab
Cytology Lab
Deaf Callers
Decedent pathology:
  Autopsy
  Morgue
Decontamination
Department of Medicine
Diabetes:
  Insulin Pump Program
  Out-Patient Education
  Program Education Center
  Research
Diagnosis Related Group
Diagnostic Radiology
Diagnostic X ray
Dialysis Unit
Discharges
Doctors' Message Center
EEG (Electroencephalography)
Electron Microscope
Emergency Cardiac Life Support
Emergency Dial Code (Code Blue, Code Red)
Emergency Medical Services
Emergency Room Registration
EMG (Electromyography)
EMI (Brain Scanner)
Employment Health Services
Endocrine Lab
Endocrinology
Endocrinology Research
Endoscopy (GI)
Endoscopy (Surgery)
Enterostomal Therapy
Environmental Services
Food and Nutrition Services:
  Cafeteria

Catering
Clinical Dietetics
Commissary
Daily Menu Recording
Kosher Kitchen
Meals on Wheels
Nutrition Counseling Center
Personnel
Quality Control
Storeroom
Training Office
Frozen Autologous Blood Program
Gastrointestinal (GI) Lab
Gastroenterology Department:
   Lab
   Metabolic Support Team
   Nutrition Center
   Research
Geriatrics Program:
   Senior Care Program
   Senior Resource Center
Graphic Arts Department
Gynecology Department:
   Oncology
   Surgery
Hazardous Waste
Heart Diagnostic Center
Hematology/Oncology (adults)
Hematology/Oncology (pediatrics)
Hemodynamic Monitoring
Histopathology
Histotechnology
Hospice Program
Human Resources Department
IV (Intravenous Therapy)
In-Patient Admissions
Infectious Diseases
Information Center
Information Services:
   Administration
   Project Control
Information Systems Department:
   Administration
   Applications
   Computer Room
   Data Center

Scientific Data Center
Financial Processing
Microcomputer Support
Network Hotline
Operations
Production Control
Technical Support
Inhalation Therapy
Intensive Care Units
   CICU-Cardiac intensive care unit
   CICU Triage
   CSICU-Chest surgery intensive care unit
   DACU-Dialysis Acute Care Unit
   MICU-Medical intensive care unit
   NICU-Neonatal intensive care unit
   PICU-Pulmonary intensive care unit
   RICU-Respiratory intensive care unit
   SCU-Surgical care unit
   SICU-Surgical intensive care unit
Internal Audit Department
Internal Communications:
   Current Lines
   Lifelines
   Speakup
Interpreter Services
Labor and Delivery
Laboratories:
   Ambulatory Care
   Biochemistry Research
   Biophysics
   Blood Bank
   Blood Donor Facilities
   Blood Replacement
   Cardiovascular
   Catheterization
   Chemistry
   Clinical
   Cytology
   Diabetes
   Electron Microscope Endoscopy
   Endocrinology
   GI
   Gastroenterology
   Hematology
   Histocompatibility
   Histology

Histopathology
Immunology
Lab Computer Facility
Medical Oncology
Metabolic
Microbiology
Neonatal Blood Gas
Noninvasive
Ophthalmology
Outpatient
Pacemaker
Peripheral Vascular
Phlebotomy
Pulmonary
Rheumatology
Serology
Toxicology
Triage
Vascular
Vivarium
Laboratory
Laser Surgery
Library
Lifeline Emergency Response System
Linen Services
Lithotripsy
Lobby
Lobby desk
Lost and Found
Mail Room
Materials Support Department:
  Central Processing
  Receiving
  Records
  Reprographic/Forms Print Shop
  Retention
  Storeroom
  Transportation Services
Maternity:
  Delivery Room
  Fathers' Waiting Room
  Patient Care
  Pre-admitting
  Tours
  Women's Center
Medical Education:

Continuing Medical Education
Graduate Medical Education
Medical Library
Medical Photography
Medical Records:
  Admissions and Discharge Records
  Birth
  Government Agencies
  Hospital
  Legal
  Patient Insurance
  Physician
  Project Studies
  Reports Chart
  Requisitions
  Transcription and Distribution
  Tumor Registry
Medical Social Services
Mental Health Inpatient Admissions
Mental Health Outpatient Admissions
Message Center (Physicians)
MRI (Magnetic Resonance Imaging)
Nephrology Department:
  Teaching
  Transplantation
Neurophysiology Department:
  Audiology
  Brainstem Evoked Response
  Visual Evoked Response
Nuclear Medicine:
  Nuclear Cardiology
Nursery
Nursing Services:
  Ambulatory Care
  Cardiology MedicaVSurgery
  CICU
  Community Health
  Continuing Education
  Diabetes Outpatient
  Director of Nursing Services
  Emergency Care
  Enterostomal Therapy
  Floor
  Hospice
  IV Team
  Labor and Delivery

Medical/Teaching
MICU
Neonatal PICU Pediatrics
New Graduate Program
Nursery
OR Services
Order Nurse
Ortho Technicians
Parent/Child Health
Patient Education
Recruitment and Retention
Rehab and Ambulatory Care
Rehabilitation
Research and Development
SCU
SICU
Special Projects
Nursing Stations
Occupational Therapy
Out-Patient Admissions
Outpatient Infusion Center
Pathology and Lab Medicine Department:
    Anatomic Pathology Division
    Autologous Frozen Blood Program
    Decedent Path Study
    Histology Special Stains Lab
    School of Medical Technology
    Surgical Pathology
Payment Processing
Pharmacy
Phonocardiography:
    In- and Out-Patient
Physical Therapy
Physicians' Dressing Rooms
Physicians' Lounges
Post-op Holding
Pre-admissions-Obstetrics
Pre-op Holding
Radiation
Radiation Therapy
Recovery Rooms
Refunds
Rehabilitation Department:
    Biofeedback
    Occupational Therapy
    Physical Therapy

Psychological Services
Speech Therapy
Renal Stone Center
Repair Services
Research Departments
Safety and Security Services
Scientific Data Center
Smoking Cessation Program
Substance Abuse
Surgical Admissions Testing Office
TMHC (The Mental Health Center)
Tay-Sachs Program
Teen-Line Cares
Tissue Lab
Transplantation Services
Ultrasound
Urology
Volunteer Services
Weight Control Program
X ray

Clinics

Allergy
Ambulatory Care Center
Breast Clinic
Cardiac
Colo-rectal
Crisis Clinic
Dental
Dermatology
Diabetic
Eating Disorders
Endocrine
ENT
Enterostomal Therapy
Eye/Optometry
Family Planning Clinic
GI
General Medicine
Gynecology Clinic
Head and Neck
Hematology
Infectious Disease
Neurology
Neurosurgery
Oncology
Orthopedic
Pediatric
Peripheral Vascular
Podiatry
Psychiatric Clinic
Prenatal-Postpartum
   (Obstetric)
Renal Hypertension
Rheumatology
Sleep Disorders
Surgery
Swallowing Clinic
Thoracic Disease
Triage (walk-in)
Urology

Cardiology

Administration
CICU Professional Services

Cardiac Rehabilitation
Cardiovascular Lab
Cardiovascular Research
Cardiovascular Surgery
Catheterization Lab
ECG (Electrocardiography)
Heart Family Program
Hemodynamic Monitoring
Holter Monitoring
Noninvasive Lab (Echocardiology)
Nuclear Cardiology, Stress Testing
Pacemaker and Cardiac Stress Lab
Physical Consulting

Chief Residents

Medicine
Obstetrics/Gynecology
Pediatrics
Surgery
Chief of Staff

THE ER (EMERGENCY ROOM)

The primary function of an emergency room is to treat surgical and medical emergencies.

Patients are seen on the priority of need. Those facing a life and death crisis and those in shock are treated first. Consultations, should they be necessary, are made with staff specialists.

Followup care is provided by the patient's physician or a member of the staff.

Lab and X-ray technicians also have important roles in emergency rooms.

X rays are read by the physician on duty, who calls for immediate ("stat") assistance if necessary. X rays may also be read by the chief of radiology or other specialists if the results are uncertain.

Nurses in ER usually work eight-hour shifts, but often work overtime. A chief ER nurse may be assisted by dozens of registered nurses, practical nurses, and nurse's aides, depending on the size of the emergency department. In rare cases, nurses are summoned from other floors.

Interns spend approximately four months in the ER during their internships. Interns handle simple treatments and are supervised in more complicated procedures. Major surgical procedures are performed in ORs (operating rooms).

In large hospitals and medical centers, ER physicians work there full-time. ER Staff (including those summoned to the ER when necessary) include:

Ambulance driver
Assistant pathologist
Cardiac specialist
Chest surgeon
Chief ER nurse
Chief house physician in
 charge of ER
Chief of internal medicine
Chief ob-gyn resident
Chief of ophthalmology
Chief of Trauma and ER
 services
DDS (dental surgeon)
ER physician
ENT (ear, nose and throat
 physician)
Head and neck surgeon
Interns
Lab technicians
Neurosurgeon
Nurse's aide
Paramedics liaison office
Plastic surgeon
Psychiatrist RN (registered
 nurse)
Trauma/pediatric liaison
 nurse
Triage/disaster unit
X-ray technicians

Cases Often Seen in Emergency Rooms

Abdominal conditions:
  acute bowel obstruction
  appendicitis
  cholecystitis
  dissecting aneurysm
  diverticulitis
  ileitis
  perforated bowel
  perforated duodenal ulcer
  peritonitis
  ruptured or leaking aneurysm
  strangulated hernia
  volvulus
Bronchial asthma
Burns
CVA (cerebral vascular accident, or "stroke")
Carbuncles
Cardiac arrest
Cardiac arrhythmia
Cellulitis
Coma
Corneal abrasions
Coronary infarction

Dislocations
Fractures
Frostbite
Gallbladder and kidney stones
Gunshot wounds
Heatstroke
Hemorrhage:
   GI (gastrointestinal)
   GU (genitourinary)
   pulmonary
Hysteria
Ingested articles
Infections
Lacerations
Lymphangitis
Massive physical traumas
Nosebleeds
Overdose
Poisoning
Puncture wounds and splinters
Removal of embedded particles
Seizure disorder
Shock
Sprains
Stab wounds
Stroke
Surface bleeding
Swallowing
Thrombophlebitis
Urinary retention

MEDICOLEGAL TERMS

Abdomen: the belly; the trunk below the diaphragm.

Accouchment: childbirth.

Ache: a dull, continuous pain.

Acoustics: pertaining to hearing, sound.

Acute: severe but not chronic.

Addict: one who is addicted.

Adhesion: the process of union between surfaces.

Agony: intense pain of body or mind. The act of dying.

Ailment: a slight or chronic illness.

Alcohol: a colorless, volatile inflammable liquid which is the intoxicating principle in fermented and distilled liquors.

Alcoholism: intoxication produced by alcohol. It is acute when induced by excessive consumption at one time. It is chronic when the use of spirits results in significant physical and psychological impairment, especially as seen in the deterioration of social relationships.

Algesia: severe pain.

Alienist: psychiatrist specializing in legal aspects of psychiatry.

Alignment: bringing into line.

Alopecia: baldness.

Amentia: severe mental retardation, marked by stupor, apathy, and lack of knowledge of surroundings.

Amnesia: loss of memory.

Ampule: a small, sealed flask which usually contains one dose of a hypodermic medicament.

Amputation: the cutting off of a whole or part of a limb.

Analgesia: loss of pain sensation.

Analysis: the process of breaking up a chemical compound and recognizing its constituents.

Anaphia: the absence of sense of touch.

Anaphrodisia: absence of sexual feeling.

Anatomy: the structure of the body and its parts.

Anemic: lack of blood corpuscles, or hemoglobin.

Anesthesia: a partial or complete loss of sensation, with or without consciousness, due to disease, injury, or administration of a drug.

Anesthetic: an agent used to remove the sensation of pain. It may be local, such as novocaine, procaine, or cocaine; or general, such as ether, chloroform, nitrous oxide, or ethylene.

Antemortem: before death.

Antepartum: before childbirth.

Antenatal: before birth.

Anterior: before, in relation to time or space.

Antidote: an agent to neutralize a poison or counteract its effects.

Antiseptic: substance used to clean tissue, destructive to the germs which cause disease.

Antitoxin: a substance produced biologically to counteract the effect of toxins.

Anus: the inferior opening of the alimentary canal; the fundament.

Aorta: the main artery leading from the heart.

Aperture: an orifice or opening.

Apex: the conical end of the heart or lung.

Apoplexy: a sudden internal hemorrhage; if cerebral, often followed by paralysis.

Appendix: a wormlike structure, projecting from the junction of two portions of the intestinal tract.

Artery: a blood vessel which carries blood away from the heart except the pulmonary artery. Arteries carry red or aerated blood.

Arthritis: a term applied to the disease of a joint.

Articulation: a joint. Also the mechanism of speech.

Assimilate: the absorption and incorporation into the body of digested food products.

Autopsy: the examination of a dead body to determine the cause of death.

Bifid: separated into two parts, or possessing two legs.

Bilateral: relating to, or having two sides.

Binet test: a test to determine the mental age of a child by asking a series of questions considered proper for normal children of that age and grading the child accordingly. Revised versions were the Binet-Simon scale and the Stanford-Binet Test.

Bleeder: a sufferer from hemophilia or other disorder of the blood.

Blood pressure: the pressure with which the blood is pumped by the heart through the blood vessels.

Burn: a lesion caused by heat, electricity, chemicals, or friction. Classified as first degree, where only the superficial layer of skin is involved, such as ordinary sunburn; second degree, where the deeper layer of skin is involved; third degree, where all layers and possibly the underlying muscles and tendons are involved. Its healing may result in scar or pigmented area.

Buttock: the prominence of the lower back or either hip region.

Cadaver: a corpse; dead body.

Caesarean section: taking a child from the womb through an opening cut in the abdomen of the mother.

Caffeine: a stimulant drug derived from coffee or tea.

Calorie: a unit of heat.

Cancer: a malignant new growth. Carcinomas arise in epithelial tissues, sarcomas in mesodermal tissues.

Cannabism: habituation to or poisoning with hemp or hashish.

Carbolic: a poisonous acid; phenol.

Carbon monoxide poisoning: the result of the inhalation of the odorless poisonous element contained in exhaust gases of automobiles or incompletely oxidized fuel in a dampered furnace or fireplace. The victim is profoundly unconscious, the skin is red, and breathing deep and noisy. The pulse is full and rapid.

Cardiac: relating to the heart.

Castrate: to remove the testicles or ovaries.

Catalepsy: a hysterical state in which an individual assumes a state of waxy rigidity of the limbs, which can be placed in any attitude and will be maintained thus for a long period of time. In this state, the patient is insensitive to pain.

Causa mortis: in anticipation of death.

Cell: a minute structure; the unit of all plant and animal life.

Centimeter: one one-hundredth of a meter; two-fifths of an inch.

Chancre: a sore which appears as a first manifestation of infection with syphilis.

Charlatan: a quack.

Chloroform: a sweet-smelling general anesthetic agent; not frequently used at present due to possibility of liver damage.

Cholera: an epidemic infectious disease characterized by profuse watery stools, vomiting, muscle pains and collapse.

Chronic: denoting a disease of slow continuance and long duration.

Circumcision: the operation of removing the foreskin from the penis as a sanitary or religious measure.

Clot: the plug which forms to stop bleeding, due to reactions in the blood when exposed to air. A clot in the blood vessels of the brain may cause a stroke, paralysis or death.

Coagulation: clotting; also, a process of destroying tissues, such as warts, tumors, and tonsils, by applying heat to them.

Coca leaves: leaves of the coca plant, primarily grown in Central America and Asia, which produce cocaine.

Cocaine: a drug formerly used as a local anesthetic. It is a habit-forming drug and from a legal standpoint it is considered a narcotic. It has a bitter taste and cooling effect on the tissues. Usually sniffed or taken hypodermically. Called "snow," "c," "happy dust," "sleigh ride, " "coke."

Codeine: a morphine or opium derivative used to allay pain. A habitforming drug, but not commonly used by addicts.

Coition: sexual intercourse.

Coitus: sexual intercourse.

Color blind (chromatodysopia): total or partial inability to perceive colors independent of the capacity for distinguishing light, shade, and form. Generally thought to be due to inefficiencies of the retinal cone receptors.

Coma: a state of profound unconsciousness in which the patient cannot be aroused. This may be due to a poison, alcohol, diabetes, brain injury, or kidney disease.

Complex: a group of symptoms which when joined together are characteristic of a certain disease. In psychiatry, it denotes a group of unpleasant experiences which are forced into the unconscious mind.

Complication: an intercurrent condition which arises in the course of a disease, either as a result of the disease itself or from extraneous sources.

Concussion: a condition of the brain which is brought about by injuries involving falls, in which the head is struck directly, or shaken violently when the body lands on a part, such as the buttocks.

Congestion: an abnormal collection of blood or fluid in a part or organ due to an obstruction of its blood vessels, inflammation caused by injury, or failure of an organ, e.g., heart failure.

Contagion: a mode of transmission of an infectious disease, either by direct contact with a patient or through a third party.

Contusion: a bruise or the reddening of the skin, without breakage of it, due to a direct forceful blow.

Convulsion: a violent contraction of groups of muscles which are not under the patient's control, sometimes caused by brain injuries.

Copulation: the act of uniting in sexual intercourse.

Corpus: body.

Cremation: reducing a corpse to ashes by means of fire.

Cutis: skin.

Cyst: a bladder; an abnormal sac containing fluid, gaseous or cheesy matter.

Degenerate: to fall to a lower level of mental or physical functioning.

Delirium: a mental disturbance, often with confusion, disorientation and hallucinations.

Delusion: a false belief which persists despite contrary evidence.

Dementia: a decline in intellectual functioning.

Dermis: the skin.

Diagnosis: the determination of the nature of disease.

Digitalis: a drug used as a heart stimulant.

Dipsomania: a recurring compulsion to drink excessive amounts of alcohol.

Dope: any drug that causes stupefaction.

Dotage: the intellectual decline in old age.

Drug: a substance employed in medicine for the treatment of disease. A narcotic.

Ecstasy: a mental state in which there is exhilaration, a rapturous expression, and loss of pain sense.

Embryo: the human fetus in its first three months of life.

Epilepsy: a chronic disease characterized by seizures or convulsions of varying severity, sometimes with unconsciousness, frothing at the mouth, and in its later stages associated with mental disturbances. (Cause unknown, or from tumor, injury, or vascular disease).

Ether: a volatile drug used for general anesthesia.

Exhibitionist: a person who has an impulse to show the sex organs to a member of the opposite sex.

Exitus: death.

F.R.C.S.: Fellow of the Royal College of Surgeons (United Kingdom).

Facies: facial expression, especially when characteristic of a disease.

Faint: an attack of temporary unconsciousness.

Feeble mindedness: common term for mental deficiency. A mental condition rather than a disease.

Fever: a rise in body temperature over 98.6 F or 37.5 C.

Fistula: a pathological tract leading from an abscess cavity or a gut to the skin surface.

Focus: a term applied to a point from which infection spreads to the other parts of the body.

Forensic medicine: use of medical knowledge as evidence in a trial or investigation.

Formaldehyde: a pungent irritating gas used in embalming.

Formula: a recipe for the compounding of a prescription.

Freudian: pertaining to Freud's theory that unpleasant experiences and sexual desires are not reacted to, but depressed into the unconscious mind, and manifest themselves symbolically in later life during dreams.

Genesis: the origin or process of coming into being.

Gestation: pregnancy.

Giddy: dizzy.

Gland: a secreting organ.

Gonorrhea: a venereal disease of the sexual tract, caused by the gonococcus, characterized by profuse discharge, burning, pain and frequency of urination.

Graft: anything inserted into another thing so as to become an integral part of the other, such as a skin graft or bone graft.

Gynecology: the specialty of diseases of women.

Halitosis: bad breath.

Hallucination: A subjective perception of something which does not exist.

Hashish: an intoxicating, habit-forming drug, similar to marijuana in effect, extracted from hemp, the use of which is illegal in the U.S.

Hermaphrodite: a person with both female and male genital organs.

Hemorrhage: profuse bleeding. Discharge of blood from wounded or ruptured blood vessel.

Hemostat: a drug or an instrument to stop bleeding.

Heredity: the transmission of certain characteristics from parent to offspring.

Heroin: an opium derivative. A narcotic, habit-forming drug. It is a coarse, white powder and has a bitter taste, taken hypodermically or by sniffing it, or through the mouth. Called "h," or "horse," among other names.

Hypersexual: overactive or overdeveloped sexually.

Hypnosis: a condition resembling sleep or trance, produced through intense concentration on one idea.

Hypodermic: an injection under the skin layer.

Hysteria: a psychic condition marked by various symptoms ranging from nervous instability to fits of causeless crying and laughing.

Idiot: a person who has been without understanding from his nativity. Obsolete.

Imbecile: one who is born with a mental capacity which does not go to a higher level than that of an average seven-year-old child as determined by the Benet-Simon tests. Both the term and the test are now obsolete.

Infanticide: the criminal destruction of a newborn child after it has established an independent existence.

Insanity: unsoundness of mind due to disease; mental alienation or derangement; a morbid psychic condition resulting from disorder of the brain. Primarily legal rather than a medical term.

Insomnia: inability to sleep.

Intoxication: the state of being poisoned; the condition produced by the administration or introduction into the human system of a poison. In popular use, "acute alcoholic poisoning."

Jugular: the main vein at the side of the neck.

Kahn test: a method of examining blood to determine the presence of syphilis. Developed in 1923.

Kline test: a rapid method of examining blood to determine the presence of syphilis. Developed in 1926.

Lateral: on the side of, generally meaning the outer side.

Laudanum: opium derivative, the drug is a dark brown liquid used to allay pain or induce sleep.

Lead poisoning (painter's colic): an acute or chronic disease of workers in lead products or others who ingest lead, characterized by vomiting, cramps, diarrhea, and local paralysis.

Leprosy: a contagious disease known since biblical times, characterized by severe skin and nerve lesions. Also, Hansen's disease.

Lethargy: a condition resembling profound slumber from which the patient may be aroused but promptly relapses again.

Leucocyte: a white blood cell.

Lockjaw (tetanus): generally, a complication of wounds which have been contaminated with street dirt, which contains the spores of the tetanus bacillus. Deep puncture wounds such as those caused by nails, gunpowder, firecrackers, and bullets are particularly susceptible. The disease is characterized by severe spasm of all the muscles of the body, causing the body to be bent back like a bow, and the jaw held clenched tight.

Lysol: a commercial antiseptic.

Malignant: tending to result in death or deterioration.

Malpractice: the mistreatment of disease or injury through ignorance, carelessness, or criminal intent.

Mania: a mental disorder characterized by hyperactivity, rapid passage of ideas, and exaltation.

Manipulation: the process used in restoring motion to joints.

Marijuana: hallucinogen extracted from a species of hemp. It is either smoked or chewed.

Median: middle.

Medical jurisprudence: the application of medical and surgical knowledge to the principles and administration of the law. It comprises all medical subjects which have legal aspects.

Melancholia: a mental disease marked by apathy, mental sluggishness, depression, and indifference to one's surroundings. Obsolete.

Menopause: the period in a woman's life when the menstrual period ceases. The end of the reproductive period.

Mesial: middle.

Mesmerism: hypnotism.

Metabolism: the chemical processes which go on in the body, i.e., the building up and breaking down of tissue.

Microbe: a single-celled organism, either animal or vegetable.

Midriff: the mid-abdomen, waist.

Midwife: a woman who attends at the delivery of a baby.

Miscarriage: the giving of birth to a fetus which has been carried from four to six months. This may be caused by falls, injuries or disease.

Morphine: a habit-forming narcotic drug derived from the juice of a species of poppy (an opium derivative).

Myopia: nearsightedness.

Narcotic peddler: a person who sells narcotic drugs, such as opium, without a lawful permit. In general usage, the name applies to sellers of cocaine also.

Narcotic addict: also called "dope fiend," "hophead," snowbird," etc. One addicted to the use of narcotic drugs or cocaine.

Narcotic: a drug for the production of profound sleep and loss of sensation (stupor); fatal in large doses. Underworld terms are: "junk," "smack," "stuff."

Natal: relating to birth.

Neurasthenia: nervous breakdown; an exhaustion of the nervous system.

Normal: the usual and according to rules or standards.

Obstetrics: the specialty which treats conditions arising during and after pregnancy.

Olfactory: relating to the sense of smell.

Opium: the dried juice obtained from parts of certain poppies. A habit-forming drug. A brownish, gummy substance similar in appearance to thick molasses, smoked in an opium pipe. The least harmful of narcotic drugs.

Organic: the opposite of functional. A condition is organic when there is a pathological change in the tissue or organ.

Orthopedics: literally, "straight child." The specialty which treats skeletal diseases, deformities and injuries.

Os: orifice or bone.

Ossification: formation of bone.

Osteopathy: treatment by manipulation of the bones, muscles, and nerve centers.

Ovary: one of a pair of small, almond-sized organs in a woman, found in the pelvis on either side of the uterus; the egg-producing organs.

Ovum: the egg that is produced by the ovary every twenty-eight or so days during a woman's fertile life.

Pain: a feeling of physical or mental distress causing suffering.

Paralysis: a loss of the voluntary use of a muscle due to injury to its nerve supply, by disease or accident.

Parasite: an animal or vegetable organism which lives on another and derives its nourishment therefrom.

Paroxysm: a spasm or convulsion.

Pathogenesis: the mode of origin of any disease.

Pathology: the branch of medicine which deals with changes wrought by disease.

Pediatrics: the branch of medicine which deals with the diseases of children.

Pedology: the study of children.

Penis: the male organ of procreation.

Perspiration: a fluid secreted by the sweat glands of the skin, which contains many of the waste products of metabolism.

Peyote: made from mescal cactus plant. Effect similar to marijuana except longer lasting and more deadening.

Pharmacist: one who prepares and dispenses prescription drugs.

Pharmacology: the study of the action of drugs.

Pharmacopoeia: a standard listing of the strength and purity of drugs and directions for their preparation.

Phenol: carbolic acid, a powerful antiseptic and poison.

Phobia: an unreasonable dread or fear of something.

Physique: the build of the body.

Poison: any substance which, when introduced into the animal organism produces morbid, noxious, or deadly effects, or is injurious to health or life.

Post obit: after death.

Postmortem: an examination of the body after death.

Postcibal: P.C. on a prescription, meaning after meals.

Posterior: behind in time or place.

Pregnancy: the period between the time of fertilization of the ovum and the time of delivery of the child (usually 280 days or 9 calendar months).

Psychiatrist: a doctor of medicine specializing in psychiatry.

Psychiatry: the study of diseases of the mind and their treatment.

Psychology: the science of behavior.

Psychoneurosis: a minor mental disease not as serious as insanity.

Psychopath: a person with a limited sense of social and moral obligation; often, one who seeks immediate gratification through criminal means.

Psychosis: a disorder of the mind; insanity.

Puberty: the age at which the reproductive organs begin to function; thirteen to sixteen years in boys, twelve to fourteen years in girls. By law, presumptive puberty is often set at twelve years for girls and fourteen years for boys.

Pulse: the intermittent dilation of an artery which is synchronous with the heartbeat.

Quack: one who pretends to have a knowledge of medicine.

Quarantine: the period of time during which a person who has an infection or contagious disease is isolated. Also, a place where ships from foreign shores are detained while passengers and crew are examined for contagious diseases.

Quinine: a bitter drug derived from cinchona bark used in the treatment of malaria.

Rabies: hydrophobia.

Radium: a very rare metallic radioactive element which is extracted from pitchblende.

Rape: the unlawful carnal knowledge of a woman by a man, forcibly and against her will.

Recipient: a patient who receives transfused blood from a donor.

Respiration: an automatic act of drawing fresh air, containing oxygen, into the system and expelling foul air, containing carbon dioxide, from it.

Rigor mortis: a condition of stiffening of the dead body beginning three to four hours after death and disappearing gradually over forty-eight to sixty hours; due to chemical changes in the muscles.

Sadist: one who derives sexual pleasure from inflicting pain by beating, maltreatment, humiliation, and even homicide.

Sedative: a drug which calms or quiets nervous excitement.

Sense: the faculty of perceiving a stimulus; consciousness.

Sex: the sum of the peculiarities of structure and function that distinguish a male from a female organism; the character of being male or female.

Sexual inversion: obsolete term for homosexuality.

Sexual perversion: gratification of sexual desires through unusual or abnormal practices.

Sexual intercourse: carnal copulation of male and female, implying actual penetration of the organs of the latter.

Shock: a state of mental and physical collapse attendant upon severe physical injury, or great emotional disturbance.

Sleep: a physiological state of relative unconsciousness.

Somnambulism: the performance of complete acts while in a state of sleep.

Spasm: a cramplike muscular contraction of a person or organ.

Statutory rape: sexual intercourse with a female under statutory age. The offense may be either with or without the female's consent.

Sterile: unable to reproduce or bear progeny; barren.

Strychnine: a bitter poisonous drug, used in minute quantities to stimulate the appetite.

Syphilis: a venereal disease (vulgarly called "the pox") of peculiar virulence, infectious by direct contact, capable of hereditary transmission, and the source of various other diseases, and, directly or indirectly, of insanity.

Tactile: relating to the sense of touch.

Temperature: the normal temperature of the human is 37.5 degrees Celsius or 98.6 degrees Fahrenheit. Elevation of this temperature is fever.

Therapeutics: the branch of medicine which deals with the administration of drugs and other methods of treatment of disease.

Transfusion: the injection of blood from one individual, the donor, to another individual, the recipient.

Traumatic: relating to an injury or wound caused by infliction of force, such as a blow or fall.

Trunk: the body, exclusive of the head and extremities; also, the main stem of a blood vessel, or nerve.

Truss: the mechanical device used for the retention of a hernia.

Tumor: any swelling. Also, a growth within or on any tissue which has no useful function.

USP: United States Pharmacopoeia.

Ultraviolet light: light generated by a mercury quartz lamp of short wave length. It is the element of sunlight which produces burning of the skin.

Urine: the excretion of the kidneys. Under normal conditions between one and four pints are passed in a day.

Uterus: the womb.

Vaccinate: to inoculate with vaccine to protect against small pox; protective inoculation with any vaccine. To inject a killed culture of a specific bacterium as a means of curing a disease caused by that microorganism.

Vagina: the genital canal of the female, the vulva being at its outer opening.

Varicose veins: dilated veins, common in the lower extremities. Brought about through a failure of the valves in the veins to sustain the weight of the column of blood in them.

Vein: a thin-walled vessel which carries impure dark blue blood back to the heart. The only exception is the pulmonary vein which carries bright red arterial blood from the lung to the heart.

Venereal: relating to or arising from sexual intercourse.

Vivisection: any experiment performed on a living animal which requires cutting into it, or injecting drugs into it, or feeding it drugs, in order to note their effects.

Vomit: the forcible ejection of the contents of the stomach.

Wasserman test: a test performed upon a specimen of blood or spinal fluid from a person suspected of suffering from syphilis. Developed in 1906.

Wound: a break in the continuity of the skin by injury.

X ray: the popular term applied to a negative photographic film or plate which is used for diagnosing or treating diseases or injuries of different parts of the body.

MEDICAL STORY IDEAS

A young person who is mildly mentally retarded is torn between his family's over-protection and a young woman who believes he is capable of marriage and a normal life.

The only chance for a patient to survive upcoming surgery is the patient's will to live, but doctors are at a loss to find out why the patient lacks the incentive.

A female patient remains comatose after surgery. Tests fail to show any physiological reason, and her doctor suspects she is catatonic because of a psychological problem.

An operation is in progress when an earthquake hits, and there is no way the surgery can be terminated. Meanwhile, the staff tries to evacuate the patients when the building shows signs of collapsing.

A doctor faces a moral dilemma about whether to save the life of a convict slated for the gas chamber.

A mentally disturbed man terrorizes a hospital, blaming the staff for the death of his wife, child, parent.

Cosmetic surgery so drastically alters a patient's personality that it almost breaks up his or her home life, and the blame is placed on the surgeon.

A faith healer is hospitalized but refuses the surgery necessary to save his or her life.

A shortage of kidneys for transplant forces the transplant committee of the hospital to chose between a young patient and a member of the hospital's medical staff or a wealthy middle-aged contributor to the new cardiac wing.

The life of a yet-to-be-born infant depends on the pregnant mother telling her husband the expected baby is not his.

A surgeon tries to hide his own debilitating illness from his peers and continues to practice surgery, endangering his patients.

One member of a blind married couple learns that he or she has an excellent opportunity to see again through a new surgical procedure. How will the marriage be affected once one can see after both have been blind since birth?

A child is in desperate need of a transplant. The father is the only compatible donor but is an escaped convict on the run.

A pregnant woman opposed to abortion is found to be a carrier of muscular dystrophy. Her unborn child faces a fifty-fifty chance of being born dystrophic. Her husband insists she give birth, but her doctor is for abortion.

A patient suffers hysterical blindness. The cure is locked inside his or her head and if unlocked could destroy his or her family

A surgeon receives a note just prior to performing surgery that his wife has been kidnapped and will be killed unless the surgeon lets the patient die on the operating table.

A child desperately needs surgery. One parent is for the surgery, the other against it, and the surgery is delayed until the court decides.

An emergency room attempts to cope following a major catastrophe.

A hospital where nurses and other staff are out on strike attempts to stay open.

The mortality rate at a hospital is far beyond normal and the Mortality Committee wants to know why.

While the patient's life hangs in the balance, a conflict arises between two doctors with different ideas as to how the patient should be treated.

15

Crime

CRIME PAYS

One of the most lucrative subject areas for the writer, for print, television, or the big screen is crime, a writing arena I have been heavily involved in for many years, as can be noted by my *Writer's Complete Crime Reference Book,* published by Writer's Digest Books (1990). No crime writer should be without it.

Crime stories fall into several categories: the mystery, as in Agatha Christie's stories; the cop story, as in the straight police novels; private-eye stories, e.g., Parker's *Spencer* series; the caper story, as in *The Thomas Crown Affair.*

Crime stories are either open stories or closed stories, the open story being the format in which both the protagonist's and antagonist's sides of the story are revealed to the reader or the viewer. In some instances, TV's *Columbo* for example, the investigator has a good idea who the villain is. It's merely a matter of how he catches him. In the closed story, the reader or the viewer learns what is happening along with the protagonist.

All mysteries (whodunits) are closed stories or they wouldn't be mysteries. Cop stories and private-eye stories can be open or closed, whereas the caper is most often an open story.

Protagonists in crime stories fall into three categories. First, the protagonist might work for a law enforcement agency, e.g., city police, sheriff's department, district attorney's office, a federal agency, or military law enforcement. Second, a protagonist might be a private investigator. And third, a protagonist might be a lawyer, an investigating reporter, someone accidentally involved in a crime, or a protagonist who, for some vested interest, chooses to become involved in a criminal investigation.

Antagonists in crime stories fall into a number of categories:

Amateur criminals
Psychotic criminals
Blue-collar criminals
Serial killers
Organized crime figures
Street gangs
Professional criminals
White-collar criminals

CRIMES AND CRIMINAL ACTIVITIES

Armed robbery
Arson
Art theft
Assault
Bribery
Burglary
Child molestation
Computer theft
Conspiracy
Counterfeiting
Drug trafficking
Embezzlement
Extortion
Forgery

Fraud
Gambling
Hijacking
Homicide/murder
Kidnapping
Larceny
Loan-sharking
Piracy
Prostitution
Racketeering
Rape
Robbery
Smuggling
White slavery

MOTIVES FOR CRIME

Anger
Compulsion
Coverup
Destruction of evidence
Framing another
Getting rid of a witness
Greed
Insanity

Jealousy
Lust
Prevent discovery of crime
Profit
Protecting another
Revenge
Temporary insanity
Thrill

ACTS ASSOCIATED WITH CRIME

Alter appearance of crime
Alter identity
Appear to have no motive

Attempt to flee
Destroy evidence
Discredit another

Double cross accomplice
Establish an alibi
Fence stolen merchandise
Frame another
Get rid of body
Get rid of weapon
Get rid of witnesses

Go into hiding
Remove prints from scene
Squeal on accomplice
Start fire to cover crime
Take a hostage
Tamper with evidence
Threaten witnesses

PROTAGONIST'S MOTIVES FOR BECOMING INVOLVED IN THE CRIME STORY

Aid another
Attorney for defense
Bring crime to police's
    attention
Claim a reward
Curiosity
Get a story
Hired as bounty hunter
Hired to find suspect
Mistaken identity

Prevent own demise
Protect another from harm
Prove a crime was committed
Prove another's innocence
Prove own innocence
Regain possession of stolen
    object
Revenge for another's demise
Self-defense
Settle an old score

METHODS OF MURDER

Beating
Burning
Burying alive
Crushing
Decapitating
Drowning
Gassing
Hanging
Hit and run

Overdosing
Poisoning
Shooting
Smothering
Spearing
Stabbing
Strangling
Torturing
Witholding medication

MURDERERS

Addictive: one who becomes violent and kills under the influence
    of his addiction.
Avenging: one who receives aggressive relief from a relationship.
Compulsive: one unable to control or prevent violent
    aggressive behavior.
Passive/aggressive: one who absorbs painful hostility
    and then explodes.
Sadistic: one who receives sexual gratification from the
    act of murder.
Sociopathic: one who wages war against society.
Temporary psychotic: one suffering great passion or
    mental illness.

HOMICIDE AND MURDER

Homicide is the act of taking the life of another. A criminal homicide is a homicide that is neither excusable nor justifiable. A criminal homicide is considered to take place at the scene of the act, although the victim may die elsewhere. In a criminal homicide, death must occur within a year and a day and must be as a result of the injury sustained by the act. There must be premeditation, intent to kill or to commit bodily harm; the perpetrator must be engaged in a dangerous act with wanton disregard for human life, such as robbery, rape, aggravated assault, etc.

Murder: killing with malice aforethought or premeditation. The law presumes all homicides brought to trial to be murder unless the accused can prove there was an excuse or the act was justifiable.

Manslaughter: an unlawful and felonious killing without premeditation or malice aforethought.

Voluntary manslaughter: the unlawful killing of another committed in the heat of passion caused by adequate provocation. It is not murder even though there was intent to kill or commit great bodily harm.

Involuntary manslaughter: an unlawful homicide without intent to kill, e.g., as in negligence or while perpetrating an offense other than burglary, rape, robbery, or aggravated assault.

Excusable homicide: the outcome of an accident or misadventure while doing a lawful act in a lawful manner and without negligence, for example, a hunter shooting a concealed person. A homicide committed in self-defense while protecting own life or another is justifiable if grounds actually exist. If grounds do not actually exist but are believed to be in good cause, the act is excusable. For example, if a person is threatened or intimidated with a lethal weapon and believes the weapon will be used to take his life, the killing is excusable by reasonable mistake of fact.

Justifiable homicide: "authorized" killing to prevent the commission of a felony such as rape, robbery, etc., or the escape of an armed perpetrator while performing a legal duty under the scope of authority and without negligence, such as a law officer having authorization to shoot to kill under prescribed conditions or the carrying out of a legal death sentence. A soldier shooting and killing the enemy in wartime is justifiable homicide.

FORENSIC SCIENCE

Forensic science is the application of science to the law. The forensic sciences apply scientific skills of examination and evaluation to the resolution of legal issues. Law is the common core of the forensic sciences. To be effective, the forensic scientist must not only be an expert in the skills of the discipline, but must also be able to communicate findings in courts of law and administrative tribunals. There are ten main disciplines of forensic science, all of which require at least a bachelor's degree.

Criminalistics: the analysis, identification, and interpretation of physical evidence. The primary aim of the criminalist is to provide an objective application of the natural and physical sciences to physical evidence in the reconstruction of events to prove a crime, and to connect or eliminate a suspect and/or victim with that crime.

Forensic anthropology: the application of standard techniques of physical anthropology in identifying skeletal or other remains.

Forensic engineering: the application of scientific principles to the investigation, analysis, and reconstruction of physical events.

Forensic odontology: the branch of dentistry which deals with the proper handling and examination of dental evidence, and the proper evaluation and presentation of dental findings.

Forensic pathology/biology: the investigation and interpretation of injury and death resulting from violence as in homicides, suicides, or accidents, or death occurring suddenly, unexpectedly, or in an unexplained manner.

Forensic psychiatry and behavioral science: the application of psychiatry and psychology to legal issues.

Forensic toxicology: in a medicolegal context, the study and understanding of the harmful effects of external substances introduced into living systems.

General: a variety of emerging disciplines and investigative subspecialties are included in this discipline.

Jurisprudence: the study and practice of the law.

Questioned documents: the scientific examination of handwriting, typewriting, printing, ink, paper, and other aspects of documents to answer legal questions concerning the document, its author, and its authenticity.

CRIME SCENE INVESTIGATION

The following steps are taken in most crime scene investigations. In the event of a homicide or murder, the homicide division is in charge of the investigation.

Artist sketches crime scene.
Bag and tag evidence.
Check last twenty-four hours of victim's life.

Describe missing articles.
Determine means of entry.
Determine angle at which weapon was used.
Dust for prints.
Establish time of death.
Identify suspect(s).
Identify victim.
Issue APB (All Points Bulletin) on suspect(s).
Medical examiner/coroner examines the body.
Question witnesses separately.
Remove body for post mortem.
Search for motive.
Search for physical evidence.
Search for trace evidence.
Search for weapon(s).
Secure the crime scene.
Seize questioned documents.
Take still photos of crime scene.
Take report of first officer on scene.
Take video of crime scene.

All homicides are considered murders unless the investigator concludes otherwise. A complex process involving the police, prosecutors, perhaps a grand jury, and trial and appeal courts determines if the homicide is murder, manslaughter, voluntary manslaughter, involuntary manslaughter, excusable, or justifiable.

The first twenty-four hours following a homicide are the most important. Each day that passes without an arrest lessens the chance to solve the crime and apprehend the guilty party.

On the following pages are a number of premises for crime stories. Bear in mind, they are only premises. The approach you take, who your protagonists and antagonists are, completes the notion. Where you place the story, the characters you people it with, the actions you plot out for your characters, how they handle the obstacles placed in their paths, and your own unique twists can provide a fresh and exciting climax to your story, a story different from any other with the same premise.

PLOT PREMISES

A doctor in love with the wife of one of his patients is drawn into the wife's scheme to kill her husband.

An individual trades identities with a dying person to inherit a fortune.

A witness to a murder is committed to a psychiatric hospital and is systematically driven mad.

A police officer goes undercover to investigate charges of brutality in a prison and is terrorized by a prison guard or is recognized by an inmate the officer was responsible for sending to prison.

A psychopath kidnaps the child of the police officer who sent him away.

A factory is plagued by loan sharks.

Bank robbers kidnap a bank official overnight, planning to have the banker open the vault the following morning.

Fugitives or escapees take over a farm, a small town, or a resort.

A stroke victim witnesses a crime, but has difficulty communicating what he or she saw.

An innocent person is drawn into a compromising position in order to be blackmailed, and then sets out to find and kill the blackmailer.

A criminal is on the run from a gang he double-crossed.

A young man, seeking to impress a young woman, turns to a life of crime.

An innocent family is murdered, with the exception of one son who was away at the time, and the police cannot find a motive for the murders.

A judge's family is threatened or kidnapped to force the judge to render an innocent verdict in a case he or she is hearing.

Police seeking to identify a Jane Doe learn that she has multiple personality disorder.

A private investigator unwittingly is hired by organized crime to find someone who ran off with their money.

A cop finds his partner is on the take.

Detectives puzzle over a half-finished manuscript to discover the killer of the author.

A special tactical squad trained for anti-terrorist assignments plots a daring rescue of a planeful of hostages.

A police officer is framed when the man he shoots in self-defense is found without a weapon.

The death of a corporation president in an airplane crash draws the attention of a detective who doesn't believe the crash was an accident.

A killer who wants to be caught plays cat-and-mouse games with a police officer by sending him clues before each crime he commits.

A woman kills her twin sister, then assumes her identity.

A group of veterans carries out a daring robbery using military techniques.

A man kills his wife's lover and then discovers he killed the
wrong man.

An escaped convict fakes his death to elude the police.

A number of veterans, all once part of the same outfit, are being
killed off one by one—but by whom and why?

A mercy killing—or was it?

A kidnapper picks up a ransom but drops dead before returning to
where he or she was holding the victim, and police have no clue
where the victim is.

An overly ambitious person who will stop at nothing—including
murder—finds someone even more ambitious is trying to
murder him.

A murder occurs in every town in which a professional football
team plays while on the road, and a sports reporter suspects
there is a connection.

A handicapped person is alone in a house with a psychopath.

A person without any known enemies is pursued by a
would-be killer.

A crime writer or a policeman plots the perfect murder and then sets
out to accomplish it.

A slasher seeks out successful businesswomen, but is the slasher a
man or a woman?

Police have to find the killer of a young gang member before a gang
war breaks out.

A detective uses a Hollywood special-effects man to trap a killer.

A reporter facing a libel suit tries to prove the story he wrote was
true, and in doing so finds himself accused of the murder of the
man who was suing him.

A former narc seeks the dealer who turned the narc's dead sister into
an addict and prostitute.

Patients are dying in St. Martin's hospital, but not of the illnesses
that hospitalized them.

Someone is blackmailed into committing murder.

A hunter is hunted.

A killer has multiple personality disorder, and only one personality
knows of the killing.

Someone overhears a murder plot but has no idea who the killer is
or the identity of the victim.

A hit man arrives by plane, dead from a heart attack. The police
know he was a hired killer with a contract, but on whom? And
who will be his replacement?

A rape victim tries to get police to stop her husband from
killing the rapist.

A supposedly "clean" and highly successful person turns to murder to cover a sordid past.

Police seek a criminal who carries a communicable disease that could cause an epidemic.

A police officer tries to find the young punk who stole his gun and is using it to commit robbery and murder.

A private investigator stalks a killer while the killer's brother (or father) stalks the private eye.

Two teenagers steal a car for a joyride and find a body in the trunk.

When a teenager refuses to join a neighborhood street gang, he and his parents become terrified targets of the gang.

A police officer finds out his teenaged daughter is an addict, and the daughter refuses to reveal who turned her on to drugs.

A street gang terrorizes a high school principal for coming down on one of their own.

A surgeon becomes richer each time one of his heart patients dies, but the police can't prove any connection.

A fraternity hazing—or was it murder?

A group of militant policemen take the law into their own hands.

A detective flying off on vacation finds his vacation short lived when one of the passengers aboard the jet is murdered.

When the police close in on a hit-and-run driver, the driver is murdered by another occupant of the car to make sure his or her identity isn't revealed.

A recent widow who is left a fortune finds her late husband isn't really late, just suffering from amnesia in a small hospital, and she plots to kill him before he regains his memory and her inheritance.

A compulsive rapist/killer poses as a cop.

Two young men who had been inseparable friends as kids now find themselves enemies; one's a cop and the other a crook.

LET'S PLAY "WHAT IF?"

Changing or adding a few details can give any of the ideas above a novel twist.

For example, let's take the first premise. What if the doctor and the doctor's lover were of the same sex? Or what if the patient's spouse accuses the doctor of malpractice because of the way the patient died, giving the spouse both an inheritance and a malpractice award to share with the real lover?

In another premise, escaped convicts take over a town or a person's home, but what if the escapees were youngsters from a reform school or a group of female escaped cons? Or suppose the home they take over belongs to a Mafia crime lord?

Suppose that instead of a psychopath kidnapping a cop's child, it's a robot that had been ordered destroyed.

Bette Davis did a film many years ago in which her character killed her twin sister and assumed her identity. What if a twist were added? What if the sister who takes on the other's identity finds the sister she killed was guilty of murder and now she faces jail and possible electrocution for a murder she didn't commit? Or what if the sister she now pretends to be was marked for murder by someone else?

What if, instead of committing a robbery, a group of veterans uses their talents and military techniques to conquer crime in a certain city?

As I have indicated many times, a change in approach, in characters (types, sex, age) in location and in time can vastly alter what might have appeared to be a trite premise. Play with these premises or other familiar plots and see what happens when you ask yourself, "What if?"

SUGGESTED READING

Alison, H.C. *Personal Identification*. Boston, MA: Holbrook Press, 1973.

Blum, Richard. *Deceivers & Deceived*. Springfield, OH: Chas. Thomas Publishing, 1972.

Brown, Robert. *The Electronic Invasion*. New York: J.F. Rider Publishing, 1967.

Cooper, Paulette. *Medical Detectives*. David McKay Co., Inc.,

Dictionary of American Underworld Lingo. New York: Citadel Press, N.D.

Farr, Robert. *The Electronic Criminals*. New York: McGraw Hill, 1975.

Fisher, Barry, Arne Svensson, and Otto Wendell. *Techniques of Crime Scene Investigation*. New York: Elsevier Science Publishing, 1987.

Hall, J. *Inside the Crime Lab*. Englewood Cliffs, NJ: Prentice Hall, 1974.

Haunts, Marshall. *From Arrest to Release*. New York: Cowan McCann, Inc., N.D.

—*Courtroom Medicine Trauma*. New York: Cowan McCann, Inc.,

—*From Guns to Gavel*. New York: Cowan McCann, Inc., N.D.

—*From Evidence to Proof*. New York: Cowan McCann, Inc.,

—*Rules of Evidence*. New York: Cowan McCann, Inc., N.D.

—*Where Death Delights*. New York: Cowan McCann, Inc., N.D.

Hendrickson, Robert. *Ripoffs*. New York: Viking Press, 1976.

Hilton, O. *Scientific Examination of Questioned Documents*. New York: Elsevier Science Publishing, 1984.

Kahaner, Larry. *Cults that Kill*. New York: Warner Books, 1988.

Kotter, J.C. *Criminal Evidence*. Cincinnati, OH: Anderson
Publishing, 1980.

Norris, Joel. *Serial Killers*. New York: Anchor Books, 1988.

O'Hara, Charles. *Fundamentals of Investigation*. Springfield, IL:
Chas. C. Thomas Publishing, 1973.

Reinhardt, J. *The Psychology of Strange Killers*. Springfield, OH:
Chas. Thomas Publishing, N.D.

Roland & Bailey. *The Law Enforcement Handbook*. New York:
Facts on File Publications/Metheun Publishing, 1936.

Rubenstein, *City Police*. New York: Farrar, Straus, Giroux, 1973.

Saperstein, R. *Forensic Science Handbook, Vol. 11*. Englewood
Cliffs, NJ: Prentice Hall, 1988.

Forensic Science Handbook, Vol. 1. Englewood Cliffs, NJ: Prentice
Hall, 1982.

Thorwald, J. *Crime and Science*. New York: Harcourt, Brace and
World, Inc., 1967.

16

Espionage

FOR YOUR SPIES ONLY!

Espionage is one of the most romantic action adventure arenas. Such successful characters as Ian Fleming's James Bond, Edward Aarons's Sam Durell and Elleston Trevor, Adam Hall's Quiller, John Gardner's continuation of the James Bond stories, and the works of Donald Hamilton, John le Carre, Tom Clancy, and many others have fascinated millions.

Like detective fiction, espionage stories are often full of danger and intrigue. At least since the days of Mata Hari, readers and film buffs have fallen in love with spies and the drama, suspense, romance, action, and adventure that spy stories provide.

If there is any arena that is not confined to formula plots, it is espionage. Although intelligence agencies throughout the world have specific duties, chains of command, and operational procedures, the more clandestine the operation, the less those in the intelligence community are apt to go by the book, at least the book that's been approved by the formal government.

The writer writing about secret agents out in the field can take a lot more liberties than the writer who writes about cops who must conform to the letter of the law. However, to take license, it should be based on logic and some factual knowledge of the spy game.

215

In this chapter, you will find enough basic information to develop a good spy story, some of the "tricks of the trade," a glossary of espionage terms, and some recommended reading.

If you're about to write a spy novel or film and it's to take place in a foreign country (as most spy stories seem to do), then I recommend you research your locations by referring to national and local maps, photographs, and books on the customs of the people of that country.

INTELLIGENCE AND COUNTERINTELLIGENCE

Intelligence communities consist of military, central, diplomatic-political, economic and industrial intelligence-gathering agencies, as well as counterintelligence agencies.

Espionage is, in broad terms, the gathering of confidential information, usually by clandestine operations, for the military, industrial, political, diplomatic, or economic benefit of another country or organization.

Intelligence is the overt or covert means of gathering information so that a government or other entity can alter its decisions and further actions based on the information supplied by its intelligence operations. Also, the information gathered by those means.

Counterintelligence is the act of detecting and counteracting opposing intelligence agencies or agents and preventing subversion and sabotage at home. Whereas the CIA is responsible for intelligence and counterintelligence abroad, the FBI is the primary counterintelligence agency inside the U.S.

Military intelligence and counterintelligence deals with matters affecting the military, with each branch of service maintaining its own agencies or departments. Tactical intelligence is concerned with knowledge of enemy positions, whereas operational intelligence concerns future plans of the enemy. Strategic intelligence is involved with long-range planning in the event of a war and with the capabilities of enemy forces and weapons.

Although the branches of the military maintain their own intelligence and counterintelligence services, the United States, like most foreign governments, maintains a number of other independent intelligence-gathering agencies and services.

Government agencies responsible for gathering industrial, political, diplomatic, economic and military intelligence, both here and abroad, include the U.S. State Department, the United States Customs Service, the Central Intelligence Agency, U.S. Postal Intelligence, and various organizations that specialize in signal, communications, and electronic eavesdropping, the latter of which, in essence, tap and record suspect telephone, radio, television, satellite, and microwave signals.

U.S. CENTRAL INTELLIGENCE AGENCY

The Central Intelligence Agency (CIA), like most intelligence agencies, maintains an assortment of "desks," e.g., the Soviet Desk, the French Desk, the Polish Desk, etc. Each "desk" is responsible for intelligence on that country and running the case officers, agents, and agents of influence (terms defined in "Spy Speak Glossary" later).

The Agency has stations around the globe, each station headed by a chief of station. (Some countries have bases and base chiefs, to whom station chiefs report.) Under station chiefs are case officers who are nationals of their own country, and agents in place, who have specific jobs in specially target-designated countries.

The CIA is under the Director of Central Intelligence who works hand-in-hand with the National Intelligence Council and the National Security Advisors to the President. Under the National Intelligence Council is its General Counsel, the Inspector General, and the Office of Legislative Liaison.

Reporting directly to the Director of Central Intelligence is his Deputy Director, his Executive Director, and the Director of Intelligence Community Staff.

Reporting to the Executive Director of the Agency are the Public Affairs Office, Office of Equal Opportunity, Bureau of Personnel, and the Comptroller.

Also reporting to the Executive Director are: the Deputy Director of Operations, The Deputy Director for Science and Technology (who is responsible for the Office of Research and Development), the Office of Development and Engineering, Foreign Broadcast Information Service, Office of SIGINT (Signal Intelligence) Operations, the Office of Technical Services, and National Photographic Interpretation.

Under the Deputy Director for Intelligence are African/Latin American Analysis, Analytic Support, Current Production and Central Reference, European Analysis, Global Issues, Imagery Analysis, Near Eastern and South Asian/East Asian Analysis, Research, Scientific, and Weapons Analysis, Soviet Analysis.

Reporting to the Deputy Director of Administration are the offices of Communications, Data Processing, Finance, Information Services, Logistics, Medical Services, Security, Training and Education.

TRAINING OF INTELLIGENCE PERSONNEL

Members of the intelligence communities here and abroad are trained in the use of weapons, demolitions, sabotage, radio codes, secret writing, one-time codes, dissolving paper, microdots, surveillance and countersurveillance, escape and evasion methods, communications with agents and spies, recruitment of agents, possible defectors, drops, scramblers, covert operations, disguises, interrogation and debriefing methods, hand-to-hand combat, and martial arts. Some personnel are required to attend foreign language schools. Many agents, case officers, and spies already speak two or more languages.

RECRUITMENT AND TURNING OF AGENTS AND SPIES

In many instances, U.S. and foreign case officers are placed as diplomats in their embassies or consular offices around the world, using their positions as cover. From there, they attempt to recruit people who will work for them as agents, assets, or spies, attempt to turn enemy agents into double agents, and attempt to get high civilian and military officers to defect. To gain these advantages, the intelligence communities will often lure agents to their side by offers of financial rewards, sexual favors, or out-and-out blackmail.

INTELLIGENCE AGENCIES
AROUND THE WORLD, PAST AND PRESENT

ABWEHR: German Secret Service.

BND: Bundesnachrichtendienst, the Secret Service of the Federal Republic of Germany.

BOSS: South African Bureau of State Security.

CIA: U.S. Central Intelligence Agency.

DS: Drzaven Sigournost. State Security for Bulgaria.

EIS: Egyptian Secret Service.

FBI: U.S. Federal Bureau of Investigation. Responsible for counterintelligence within the U.S.

GRU: Soviet Military Intelligence. Reports to KGB.

HBA: Hauptverwaltung für Aufklarung. East Germany's external intelligence service.

KGB: Soviet espionage agency. Once known as CHEKA, GPU, OGPU, NKVD.

KEMPEI TAI: Japanese Military Police and internal security force.

M15: counterintelligence within Great Britain, akin to U.S. FBI. "MI" stands for Military Intelligence. Now called DI5.

M16: responsible for espionage outside Great Britain, Now DI6.

MOSSAD: short for Mossad Letafkidim Meyouchadim. Israeli external intelligence.

NSA: U.S. National Security Agency. Responsible for monitoring communications, code breaking, and interpreting.

OO: Osobye Otdel. Special Section, Soviet Military Intelligence, also known as SMERSH, a branch of the KGB responsible for kidnapping, terrorism, and assassination.

PIDE: Policia Internacional e de Defense de Estato. Portugese Security Service.

SB: Sluzba Bezpieczenstwa. Polish Intelligence Service.

SDECE: French Secret Service Department of Foreign Information and Counterespionage.

SECOND BUREAU: French, akin to FBI in counter-espionage within France.

SESID: Spanish Secret Service.

SHIN BETH: Israeli Internal Security Force.

SIS (British): British Secret Intelligence Service (MI6).

SIS (Canadian): Replacing the Royal Canadian Mounted Police. Now responsible for Canadian internal security.

SPECIAL BRANCH: Scotland Yard. Makes arrests for MI5 in England.

SSD: Staatssicherheitsdienst. East German Counterintelligence.

STB: Statni Tajna Bezpecnost. Czechoslovakian Intelligence.

ZE-2: Polish Military Intelligence.

GADGETS, DEVICES, AND TOOLS OF THE SPY TRADE

James Bond is probably the most gadget-laden of the fictional spies. Although gadgets don't usually come off as well in narratives as on the screen, a spy without some sort of gadgetry often isn't as intriguing as one that has some devices to use.

One quite deadly little item is a small T-shaped push knife about 3" x 1.75" made of stainless steel, held between the two first fingers for hand-to-hand combat.

The lockpick set is something no self-respecting spy would be without. Some come inside a case resembling a fountain pen.

Then there are the old standbys, sword canes, sword umbrellas, and the Clipitt folding knife, much like a switchblade, that can be clipped to almost any article of clothing.

Sap gloves replace the old burglar's sap by sewing small weights into the lower finger areas.

The "blossom" is like the Ninja throwing knife. It's a folding fourpointed throwing star that can be carried in a belt or pocket, then opened and thrown in one motion.

The fuse igniter that can be improvised from a paper matchbook, some adhesive, a commercial or improvised fuse cord, and a small pin or nail. Instructions on how to put it together are in the U.S. Army Manual TM-31-210, the improvised munitions handbook. This manual also contains other neat tricks, like a delay igniter from a cigarette, a clothespin time delay switch, a dried-seed timer for explosives, and lots of other items a spy might use when his professional gear isn't available.

What's a spy without some bugs? I don't mean the insect variety. There's the old-fashioned telephone watchman that's installed in a telephone system at a surveillance site. Other bugs can be hidden inside a phone or around a room.

Of course, a good spy should also have some bug detection devices and bug locators. To beat a phone bug, a spy might use a code-phone scrambler, an encryption unit, a voice changer, or a voiceless telephone that uses a keyboard to transmit digital impulses. Worried about the voice at the other end? Try using a voice stress analyzer.

Miniaturized radio transmitters are excellent tools if your spy has to stay in touch, and they come in all sizes and shapes, such as a fountain pen and, shades of Dick Tracy, even a wristwatch.

One essential in the espionage game is a good tracking system. Attache cases can be rigged with almost anything from poison gas to a sharp blade to a gun to a hidden camera. Photography and optics miniature cameras and night-vision glasses are frequent elements of espionage stories.

Most spies, believe it or not, don't carry guns, but that's hardly the case for the fictional spy. If your spy is armed, he or she would probably carry a Colt Agent Revolver, an ASP SIMM revolver, a Burger Speed Six, or a Sokolovsky .45 automatic. It's hardly likely he or she would use a submachine gun, but if he or she did, it would probably be an Ingram or a Heckler & Koch P7. And don't forget silencers, even though a silencer isn't really silent. It just keeps the noise level to a minimum.

SPY STORY PREMISES

Spy stories, like crime stories, can begin either with deliberate or nondeliberate involvement. For example, in Ernest Lehman's *North By Northwest*, the story begins with nondeliberate involvement brought about by a man's mistaken identity. In a number of Robert Ludlum's novels, his principal character is drawn into the story rather than plunging into it as Fleming's *James Bond* usually does. Let's take a look at some nondeliberate springboards.

Possible Nondeliberate Involvements

A person taking a trip is asked to deliver an envelope or package for an acquaintance or even for a stranger.

A microdot or other piece of intelligence information is hidden in something belonging to an innocent traveler.

A tourist accidentally witnesses a killing or an event that involves espionage agents.

A tourist or traveler unwittingly becomes romantically involved with a person who is a spy.

An innocent traveler or tourist is mistaken for a spy by another intelligence agency.

An innocent person purchases an item, unaware that the item contains intelligence information that was intended for someone else.

An innocent person is sent on a business mission, and in carrying out the mission, suddenly is given some information and a name but doesn't know what it means or who it's meant for.

An innocent person finds himself or herself being blackmailed into spying or acting as a courier.

A spy carrying certain information and trying to escape pursuers, mails the packet to an innocent friend.

A retired spy or agent becomes the target of opposing agents and doesn't know why.

Possible Deliberate Involvements

A business person who often travels abroad is recruited to do some spying, the agency unaware he or she is an enemy spy.

The mysterious death or disappearance of an agent or calls for an immediate replacement to carry on and to find the reason for the death or disappearance.

A search is instituted for a mole, an agent inserted into an intelligence or security service who passes information to the other side.

An agent sent to bring back a defecting agent or a political asset.

A "sleeper" is activated to perform a special mission.

A non-agent, but one associated with the service, suspects something and begins to investigate on his or her own.

A former safecracker or thief is enlisted to break in and steal secret documents.

An agent supposedly "turns" in order to plant misinformation.

An agent using a cover goes to work on the enemy's secret project.

A person who worked in a "targeted" country is asked to return there to gain delicate information.

Once again, I remind you the premises are nothing more than that. For example, the idea of hiding a microdot on someone otherwise uninvolved with the story has been used countless times, but writers still manage to come up with interesting new plots based on that premise.

What if the microdot was placed in a child's toy so that the child is in danger? What if the traveler in question is an actor or actress who is abroad to film a movie? Or what if the microdot is re-hidden on the spy who is trying to capture it?

What if, as in another premise for nondeliberate involvement, the retired spy calls on a network of other former spies to aid him in ferreting out the assassin, and the network learns they were all slated to be terminated?

What if a replacement agent discovers the missing agent is still alive but suffering amnesia? Or suppose the replacement agent learns the missing agent was terminated by some group within his own agency?

What if a mole turns out to be the one who instituted the search? What if a "sleeper" is the spouse of a CIA agent? What if a defector is responsible for the death of someone close to the agent sent to aid him or her in crossing over?

Your Silent Partner can't create all of the possible alternatives to the basic premises, but perhaps these examples will get the wheels turning.

SPY SPEAK GLOSSARY

Abort: to terminate a mission abruptly.

Agency: term used by outsiders for the CIA.

ALF: Arab Liberation Front.

Agent: a spy.

Agent-in-place: a spy already located in a country.

Agent of influence: a spy who can influence the policy of a host country or who is in an advantageous position to obtain information on a policy level.

Agent potential: requirement for specific assignment.

Agent provocateur: an agent or counterintelligence agent who incites the opposition to action in the best interest to the side of the instigator.

Analysis: what is done to turn raw data into useful intelligence.

Alimony: compensation received by long-term undercover agent coming out from an unfriendly country or assignment.

Apparat: Soviet-bloc intelligence network.

Asset: an agent or recruited spy.

Astorg: cover name for intelligence-gathering Soviet trade agency.

Bag job: breaking and entering to steal or photograph intelligence material.

Base: separate section under a base chief.

Big Daddy: National Security Agency.

Biographic leverage: CIA term for blackmail.

Black: term used to signify a covert operation.

Black box: known as ELINT, an electronic intelligence collecting device.

Black chamber: any room used to code or decode messages.

Black propaganda: propaganda disguised to look like it came from the opposing side. (See "white" propaganda and "gray" propaganda.)

Blown: as in "cover is blown", discovery of a spy or network of spies.

Burn: to reveal the true identity of a spy.

Case officer: officer controlling an agent, assets, or operation for the agency.

Centre: KGB headquarters in Moscow.

Cheng Pao K'o: Chinese counterintelligence.

Cipher: numerical or alphabetical method of concealing a message using either substitution or transposition.

Circus: British intelligence HQ.

Classified: material deemed sensitive, shown only on need-to-know basis to those with clearance. Classifications include confidential, secret, and top secret.

Clearance: authorization to read or handle classified material.

Clean: that which is considered safe after being checked for listening and transmitting devices.

Clear text: message not in or no longer in code.

Cobbler: individual who creates forged passports.

Code: text transformed systematically into unreadable or unclear message so that no one without the code can read the message.

Commint: communications intelligence, i.e., phone, radio transmissions, etc.

The Company: what the CIA calls itself.

Comsec: communications security.

Consumer: the final user of intelligence.

Control: case officer in charge of agent or operation.

Control questions: KGB system of using questions and answers known only to Centre, director, and agent to determine true identity.

The Corporation: term used by KGB for the Communist party in another country.

Cover: a credible fake identity given or assumed by an agent to hide identity as an intelligence agent. Used to infiltrate opposing side. Deep cover is more complex and usually is over a protracted period of time.

Covert: clandestine operation.

Cryptography: study of codes and ciphers. A cryptologist attempts to break codes and ciphers, develop new codes, and encodes and decodes messages.

CSPU: Communist party of the former Soviet Union.

Customer: person or department receiving intelligence material.

Cutout: person setting up meeting, or communicates while separating case officer from agent or agent from agent.

Dead drop: can be city drop, country drop, mobile drop (moving conveyance), or any secret place where an agent can safely leave a message, material or supplies to be picked up later.

Dead letter box: same as dead drop.

Debriefing: method of questioning an agent.

Desk: section of agency devoted to a specific country or operational areas.

Destruct unit: a device that automatically destroys whatever it was attached to in event of unexpected or unwanted interference.

Dirty: disloyal agent. Also, a room containing listening or transmittal devices.

Dirty tricks: an operation designed to embarrass another country. Also, upsetting another agent, agency or person by embarrassment, blackmail, etc.

Dog and pony show: meeting of intelligence officials, often using charts, maps, graphs and audiovisual equipment for presentations.

Double agent: spy openly working for one country while covertly working for another.

Dying of measles: CIA term for eliminating an agent and making it appear as a natural death. (See "terminating with extreme prejudice.")

ECM: electronic countermeasures.

Economic intel: to do with economic planning and/or capabilities in a foreign country.

Elsur: electronic surveillance using wiretaps, hidden transmittal devices and radio transmission intercepts.

Encode: to code a message.

Eyes only: written information to be learned only through reading. FYEO means "for your eyes only" (only for the eyes of the receiver).

The Farm: CIA training facility, Langley and Camp Perry, Virginia.

Field: spy working in target country or outside own country.

Fumigate: to check for bugs.

G-2: Army Intelligence.

The Game: employed in intelligence work.

GCI: Ground Controlled Intercept.

Going bad: agent no longer of value and possibly endangering other lives and mission.

Go over: to change loyalties.

Going private: to leave the agency or service.

Gone to ground: to hide.

Gray propaganda: between black and white. Source not evident.

Letter box: a human cutout that receives and passes on information and messages.

Load: the placing of an item in a drop.

Microdot: photograph reduced to a tiny spot.

Mobile agent: one not restricted to one area.

Mole: an agent working in another country's intelligence agency.

Need to know: when a person requires classified information to do his or her job.

NSA: the National Security Agency, the top U.S. agency for electronic intelligence and security.

Overt: intelligence openly gathered.

Peeps: blackmail photographs.

Photint: photographic intelligence.

Playback: giving false information in return for valid information from opposition by pretense of being one of their agents.

Principal agent: one who places self between other agents and case officer. See "cutouts."

Raw data: unanalyzed intelligence data.

Safe house: location that involves a low risk of discovery.

Salesman: agent.

Shoe: false passport.

Sleeper: agent placed in target country who does nothing beyond his or her cover until activated.

Spook: spy.

Target: operation's objective.

Terminate with extreme prejudice: to order the assassination of an agent, operative, etc.

White propaganda: that which is openly from the country or organization sending out the propaganda.

SUGGESTED READING

Knightley, Phillip. *The Second Oldest Profession*. New York: Norton, 1986.

Knudson, Richard L. *The Whole Spy Catalogue*. New York: St. Martin's Press, 1986.

Kurland, Michael. *The Spy Master's Handbook*. New York: Facts on File, 1988.

Rowan, Richard Wilmer. *Secret Service: Thirty-three Centuries of Espionage*. New York: Hawthorn, 1967.

Wise, David and Ross, Thomas B. *The Espionage Establishment*. New York: Random House, 1967.

17

The Military

Writing about the military, warriors (male and female), and the men and women who love them is fraught with drama, romance, excitement, and suspense and touches upon almost every human emotion.

Military writing demands a thorough knowledge of the armed services, battles, tactics, and personnel if the story and characters are to be credible, whether the story is historical or contemporary.

Although this chapter provides you with basic information about the military and the branches of service, additional research is paramount.

Life in the military is unique, the military being governed by its own laws, relationships, and code of honor. The technical aspects of the military (special units, equipment, armaments, planes, ships, locations of units and forces) are constantly changing.

Research on personnel, ranks, branches of service, armaments, and equipment depends on the period you are writing about and the type of battle and warfare conducted at that time.

The four branches of the United States armed forces are the Army, the Navy, the Marine Corps, and the Air Force. The Marine Corps is a unit of the U.S. Navy. During peacetime, the Coast Guard is administered by the Transportation Department, but during war it also is run by the Navy.

UNITED STATES ARMY

Command Personnel

Secretary of the Army
Under Secretary of the Army
Assistant Secretaries:
Civil Works
Installation and Logistics
Financial Management
Research, Development and Acquisitions
Manpower and Reserve Affairs
Chief of Public Affairs
Chief of Staff (Gen.)
General of the Army
Inspector General (Lt. Gen.)
Deputy Chiefs of Staff:
Logistics (Lt. Gen.)
Operations and Plans (Lt. Gen.)
Personnel (Lt. Gen.)
Army Material Command (Gen.)
Army Forces Command (Gen.)
Army Training and Doctrine Command (Gen.)
First Army (Lt. Gen.)
Second Army (Lt. Gen.)
Third Army (Lt. Gen.)
Fourth Army (Lt. Gen.)
Fifth Army (Lt. Gen.)
Sixth Army (Lt. Gen.)
U.S. Army Europe and Seventh Army (Gen.)
U.S. Forces Korea and Eighth Army (Gen.)
U.S. Army, South (Maj. Gen.)
U.S. Army, Pacific Command (Gen.)

Commissioned Officers and Insignia

General of the Army (five stars)
General (four stars)
Lieutenant General (three stars)
Major General (two stars)
Brigadier General (one star)
Colonel (silver eagle)
Lieutenant Colonel (silver leaf)
Major (gold leaf)
Captain (two silver bars)
1st Lieutenant (one silver bar)
2nd Lieutenant (one gold bar)

Warrant Officer Grades and Insignia

Chief Warrant Officer, Grade 4 (silver bar/four enamel
black squares)
Warrant Officer, Grade 3 (silver bar and three enamel
black squares)
Warrant Officer, Grade 2 (silver bar and two enamel black squares)
Warrant Officer, Grade 1 (silver bar and one enamel black square)

Noncommissioned Officers and Insignia

Sergeant Major of the Army (E-9) (same as Command Sgt. Major
but with two stars, red and white shield on lapel)
Command Sergeant Major (E-9) (three chevrons above three arcs,
wreath between chevrons and arcs with five-pointed star
in center)
Sergeant Major (E-9) (same as above but without wreath encircling
five-pointed star)
First Sergeant (E-8) (three chevrons above three arcs with diamond
between arcs and chevrons)
Master Sergeant (E-8) (three chevrons above three arcs)
Platoon or Sgt. 1st Class (E-7) (three chevrons above two arcs)
Staff Sergeant (E-6) (three chevrons above one arc)
Sergeant (E-5) (three chevrons)
Corporal (E-4) (two chevrons)
Specialist 6 (E-6) (two arcs above eagle device) Eliminated 1985
Specialist 5 (E-5) (one arc above eagle device) Eliminated 1985
Specialist 4 (E-4) (eagle device)
Specialist (E-4) after 1985

U.S. Army Units

Field army: headquarters and two or more corps.
General commanding.
Army corps: two or more divisions. Lt. General commanding.
Division: headquarters and three brigades including artillery,
combat units, combat service support.
Major general commanding.
Battalion: headquarters and four or more companies. (Battalion in
Cavalry = Squadron.) Lt. Colonel commanding.
Company: headquarters section and four platoons. (Company in
Cavalry = Troop, Company in Artillery = Battery.)
Captain commanding.
Platoon: four infantry squads. Lieutenant commanding.
Squad: infantry, ten men. Sergeant leading.

Major Army Commands

Name	**Location of HQ**
Forces Command	Fort McPherson, GA

Training and Doctrine Command	Fort Monroe, VA
U.S. Army Materiel Command	Alexandria, VA
Information Systems Command	Fort Huachuca, AZ
Military Traffic Mgmt Command	Washington, DC
Criminal Investigation Command	Falls Church, VA
Health Services Command	Fort Sam Houston, TX
Corps of Engineers	Washington, DC
Intelligence and Security Command	Arlington, VA
Military District of Washington	Fort Lesley McNair, DC
U.S. Army Strategic Defense Command	Huntsville, AL
U.S. Army Europe	Heidelberg, Germany
Eighth U.S. Army	Seoul, Korea
U.S. Army Japan	Camp Zama, Japan
U.S. Army Western Command	Fort Shafter, Hawaii
U.S. Army South	Fort Clayton, Panama

U.S. Army Unit Organizational List

Units of U.S. Army forces are organized by branches representing each unit's specialty and then grouped in "arms," representing those units whose mission is to fight or directly support the fighting, and "services," representing those units whose main mission is combat support and administration.

The Vietnam War brought some changes because missions in Vietnam were unique.

Combat Arms
    Armor/Cavalry
    Artillery
    Aviation
    Infantry
Combat Support Arms
    Corps of Engineers
    Military Intelligence
    Military Police Corps
    Signal Corps
Combat Service Support Services
    Adjutant General's Corps
    Chemical Corps
    Corps of Engineers*
    Finance Corps
    Judge Advocate General's Corps
    Medical Department
    Military Police Corps*
    Military Intelligence Corps*
    Ordnance Corps
    Quartermasters Corps

Signal Corps*
Transportation Corps
Special Warfare
Military Intelligence
Special Operations
* *Units considered combat as well as service units.*

Combat Units

Armor
Army Security
Aviation
Assignments: Tactical combat assaults, aerial reconnaissance, direct
fire assault, medical evacuation, troop lift, cargo hauling,
evacuation, relocation.
Aviation (fixed wing, attack, cargo, observation utility helicopters)
Cavalry
Air Cavalry
Air Cushion Vehicle
Airmobile Infantry
Armored
Reconnaissance (Air)
Reconnaissance (Ground)
Civil Affairs and Psychological Operations
Classification and Salvage
Engineers
Airborne Brigade Support
Combat
Construction
Land Clearing
Field Artillery
Infantry
Airborne Infantry
Airmobile Infantry
Combat Tracker Platoons
Light Infantry
Long Range Reconnaissance Patrol
Mechanized
Ranger
Rifle Security
Scout Dog
Maintenance
Medical
Ambulance Services
Dental Corps
Evacuation Hospitals
Field Hospitals

Nurses Corps
Prisoner-of-War Hospitals
Surgical Hospitals
Veterinary Corps
Military Intelligence
Military Police
Criminal Investigation (CID)
Police
Ordnance
Ammunition
Maintenance and Supply
Quartermaster
Supplies
Petrol
Signal Corps
Combat Area
Command Radio and Cable
Communications
Construction
Long Lines
Support
Special Forces
Delta Forces
Support Units
Supply and Service
Transportation
Aircraft Maintenance
Boat Transport
Motor Transport
Terminal
Traffic Management
Transport Aircraft

Army Weapons Used in Vietnam

Infantry Weapons
.45 caliber semiautomatic pistol
.45 caliber submachinegun M3-A1
.30 caliber rifle M1
.30 caliber carbine M2
7.62mm rifle M14
5.56mm rifle M16A1
M203 40mm grenade launcher on M16 rifle
40mm grenade launcher
.50-caliber machine gun
7.62mm machine gun
Flame thrower, portable

M16A1 with starlight scope
Recoilless rifle with spotting .50-caliber machine gun
66mm light antitank weapon (LAW)
60mm mortar
81mm mortar
4.2 inch mortar
Claymore antipersonnel mine
Incendiary burster
Hand grenade (delay fragmentation)
Hand grenade (impact fragmentation)
Hand grenade (riot)
Hand grenade (smoke)
AN/PRS metallic mine detector
35mm sixteen tube CS (tear gas) expendable launcher
Armed jeep with M134 7.62mm minigun
3.5 inch rocket launcher
Artillery Weapons
105mm howitzer (towed)
105mm howitzer (sp)
155mm howitzer (towed)
155mm howitzer (sp)
8 inch howitzer (sp)
175mm gun
40mm gun
4.2 inch M30 mortar

Infantry Radios

URC-10 aviation radio
AN/PRRs helmet-mounted receiver with AN/PRT 4 band
    transmitter
AN/PRC25 FM transistorized transmitter/receiver
PRC-77

Combat Vehicles

M113 APC tank, land, water, firefighter. This tank model had many
    modifications and was adapted for a variety of
    special uses.
M42 tank
M48A3 tank
XM 163 Vulcan tank
ZM706 security vehicle, revolving turret
M88 armored recovery vehicle
557A1 command post carrier
M551 Sheridan armored reconnaissance and airborne
    assault vehicle
M578 light armored recovery vehicle

M132 flamethrower
M125A1 self propelled 81mm mortar
Armored personnel carriers
Armed three quarter-ton truck

Cargo and Transportation Vehicles

One-and-one-half-ton cargo truck
Two-and-one-half-ton cargo truck
Three-quarter-ton truck
Electronic container truck
Water distributor truck
Five-ton wrecker
Semi-trailer van supply truck
Two-and-one-half-ton shop van truck
Fuel tank truck (1,200 gal., 2,500 gal., 5,000 gal.)
Five-ton semi
Gamma Goat cargo truck
Two-and-one-half-ton expandable van truck
Convoy security utility truck
Tractor with lowboy trailer
Caterpillar tractor with trailer
Rough terrain forklift
Forklift
Sixteen-ton Conex transporter
Radio vehicle (ambulance conversion)
Ammunition carrier
Flamethrower servicing unit truck
Light weapons carrier mechanical mule
Refrigerated trailer
Liquid transporter
Military police utility truck
Illumination vehicle with twenty-three-inch xenon searchlight
Stake bed truck
Tunnel clearing truck
Recon one-quarter-ton truck
Utility one-quarter-ton truck

Engineer Vehicles

Asphalt spreader
Caterpillar dozer
Cement mixer
Crane carrier
Ditching machine
Dump truck
Front-end loader

Hanson crane
Heavy duty crane
Rock crusher
Rome plow
Rough terrain crane
Scoop loader
Tree crusher

U.S. Army Vessels

Three-man rubber boat
Air cushion ACV
Airboat
Aircraft repair ship (helicopters)
Armored troop carrier ATC
BARC (amphibious resupply cargo)
Barge crane
Barracks Ship
Beach discharge lighter (LTC)
Landing craft (LCM)
Landing craft (LCU)
LARC (five-ton amphibious resupply cargo)
Motorized rubber boat (fifteen men)
River patrol boat
Ski boat

ASSOCIATED WITH MILITARY LIFE

Locations

Air base
Air field
Barracks
Base exchange (BX)
Base Ops (base operations)
Battlefield
Beach head
Bivouac
Bunker
Camp hospital
Chapel
Combat zone
Command post
Control tower
Convoy
Field hospital
Fort
Foxhole
Guard house
Gun emplacement
Hangars
Headquarters
Latrine
Maneuvers

Mess hall, Mess hall kitchen
Military academy
Motor pool
Naval Academy
Noncommissioned officer's
  (NCO) club
Observation post
Obstacle course
Officer's club
Officer's quarters (BOQ)
Officer's school
Outpost
Parade ground
Permanent party housing
Pistol range
Post
Post exchange (PX)
Post office (APO)
Rifle range
Stockade
Supply room
Trench
War college
War games

Uniforms and Equipment

Ammo belt
Backpack
Blanket
Canteen
Combat boots
Combat uniforms
Division or army patch
Dog tags
Dress uniforms
Dufflebag
Field ration
First aid kit
Flight suit

Footlocker
Helmet
Insignia (type of service, company, etc.)
Mess kit
Noncom stripes
Officer's insignia
Service stripes
Sidearm
Special equipment
Toilet articles
Weapon

Associated with Combat

Advance
Air cover
Air raid
Air strike
Air support
Ambush
Ammo
Antiaircraft
Articles of war
Artillery battery
Assault troops
BAR (Browning automatic rifle)
Barrage
Barricade
Battalion
Battle orders
Battles
Bazooka
Blitzkrieg
Blockade
Body counts
Bomb crater
Bombardment
Boobytraps
Breach
Briefing
Buffer zone
Buildup

Camouflage
Casualties
Cease-fire
Choppers
Code
Column
Combat team
Company
Convoy
Counterattack
Debarkation
Debriefing
Decorations (medals, campaign ribbons, battle stars)
Deployment
Deterrent
Diversion
Division
Draft
Drop zone
Dugout
Embarkation
Encirclement
Enemy lines
Engage the enemy
Escape
Evacuation
Expeditionary force

Field telephone
Fighters
Firefight
Firepower
Flak
Flank
Flares
Forced marches
Frag
Gas masks
Grenades
Hostage
Incoming (shells, mortar)
Indian-file
Infiltration
Intelligence
Interrogation
Invasion
Island-hopping
Kamikaze
Landing craft
Landings
Liberty
LRRP (long-range recon
    patrols)
Machine guns
Missing in action (MIA)
Mission
Mobilize
Naval support
Objective
Offensive
Operation
Orders
Overrun
Paratroops
Patrol
Patrols
Pincer movement
Platoon
Pocket
Poison gas

Position
Prisoner of war (POW)
Prisoners
Propaganda
PT (patrol torpedo) boats
Radar
Radio
Raid
Rank
Rations
Reconnaissance
Regroup
Reinforcements
Replacements
Reserve troops
Retreat
Rocket
Scouting party
Shell
Siege
Situation
Skirmishes
Slit trench
Small arms fire
Sneak attack
Snipers
Special forces
Spotter
Strafing
Supply line
Surrender
Tactics
Tanks
Task force
Tracers
Treaty
Troop carriers
Troop movements
Under fire
Volunteer
Withdraw

Associated with the Military

Articles of war
AWOL (absent without
    leave)
Basic training
Bed check
Brass
Bucking for stripes
Chief
Discipline
Drill sergeant
Duty rosters
Flight training
Furlough
Inspection
KP (kitchen police)
Latrine duty
Leave
Liberty
Maggie's drawers (miss on
    rifle range)
Mail call
March in cadence
Military tradition
O.D. (officer of the day)
On report

Over the hill
Parades
Pass
Pipe aboard
Promotions
RA (regular army)
Reassigned
Recruit
Regulations
Reserve
Restricted to post
Reveille
S.O.S.
Saluting
Sentry duty
Serial number
Service record
Ship out
Snafu (situation normal, all
    fouled up)
Swabby
Taps
The Old Man
    (the commander)
Transfer

Military Law and Law Enforcement

Courts Martial (all branches of the Military Justice System)
Military Police (Army and Air Force)
Shore Patrol (Navy and Marine Corps)
CID (Criminal Investigation Department—Army)
NIS (Naval Investigative Service—Navy, Marine Corps)
SID (Special Investigative Department—Air Force)

Means of Attack

Army	Navy	Air Force	Coast Guard
Missiles	Missiles	Missiles	Rockets
Antiaircraft	Torpedoes	Bombers	Light naval
guns	Fighter planes	Fighter planes	cannon
Assault teams	Depth charges	Reconnaissance	Machine
Patrols	Naval shelling	planes	guns
	Bombers	Star wars	

Means of Defense

Armor
Barbed wire
Battle helmets
Bomb shelters
Bunkers
Civil defense
Dug-outs
Early warning system (DEW)
Forts
Foxholes
Gas masks
Glider assault troops
Harbor nets
Intelligence
Land mines

Naval mines
Naval vessels
Outposts
Pillboxes
Poison gas
Radar detection
Reconnaissance planes
Satellites
Shields
Smoke screens
Sonar detection
Spies
Submarines
Trenches

UNITED STATES NAVY

Officers Descending in Rank

Secretary of the Navy
Under Secretary of the Navy
Assistant Secretaries of the Navy
Chief of Naval Operations
Fleet Admiral
Admiral
Vice Admiral
Rear Admiral
Captain
Commander
Lieutenant Commander
Lieutenant
Lieutenant Junior Grade (Lt. J.G. or LTJG)
Ensign
Commissioned Warrant Officer:
Chief Warrant Officer (CWO2, CWO3, CWO4)

Enlisted Ranks

Master Chief Petty Officer
Senior Chief Petty Officer
Chief Petty Officer
Petty Officer 1st, 2nd, 3rd (PO1, PO2, PO3)
Seaman (SN)
Apprentice (SA)
Recruit (SR)

U.S. Navy Insignia

Fleet Admiral: five silver stars (collar), one two-inch gold, four one half-inch stripes (none in peacetime).

Admiral: four silver stars (collar), one two-inch, three half-inch stripes (cuffs/shoulder boards).

Vice Admiral: three silver stars, one two-inch, two one-half-inch stripes.

Rear Admiral (upper half): two silver stars, one two-inch, one one half-inch stripe.

Rear Admiral (lower half): one silver star, one two-inch stripe.

Captain: silver eagle, four one-half-inch stripes.

Commander: silver oak leaf, three one-half-inch stripes.

Lieutenant Commander: Gold oak leaf, two one-half-inch stripes with one-quarter-inch between.

Lieutenant: two silver bars, two one-half-inch stripes.

Lieutenant, Junior Grade: one silver bar, one one-half-inch stripe with one-quarter-inch above.

Ensign: one gold bar, one one-half-inch stripe.

Warrant Officer: one one-half-inch stripe broken with half-inch intervals of blue as follows: Warrant Officer W-4: one break; Warrant Officer W-3: two breaks, two inches apart; Warrant Officer W-2: three breaks, two inches apart.

Enlisted Personnel (noncommissioned officers): A rating badge worn on upper left arm, spread eagle, proper number of chevrons and specialty mark.

Sections of the Navy

Assistant Secretaries for:
    Material
    Personnel and Reserve Forces
Bureaus:
    Military Sea Transportation Service
    Naval Commands
    Naval War College
    U.S. Naval Academy
    Naval Air Training
    Naval Districts
    U.S. Marine Corps
Washington D.C. Bureaus:
    Naval Sea Systems Command (ships)
    Naval Air Systems Command (aircraft)
    Naval Space Warfare Command
    Naval Supply Systems Command
    Naval Facilities Engineering Command
    Naval Medical Command

Office of Naval Research
National Capital Regional Medical Command (Bethesda)
Naval Military Personnel Command
Naval Recruiting Command

Naval Aircraft

Torpedo bombers (WWII)
Reconnaissance planes
Refueling tankers (K-A-6D)
Fighter planes (F-14)
Fighter/bombers
    Medium attack (A-6)
    Light attack (A-7, F/A-18)
Anti-submarine planes
Helicopters
Attack bombers
Folding-wing craft (carrier-based)
Trainers
Electronic warfare (EA-6B)
Airborne early warning aircraft (E-2C)

Naval Vessels and Warships

Aircraft carrier
Battleship
Corvette (WWII)
Cruiser
Destroyer
Destroyer escort
Frigate (no missiles)
Frigate (guided missiles)
Gunboat
Hospital ship
Landing craft
Minelayer (WWII; now delivered by subs/air)
Minesweeper (reserve only; also by MH53 hero's)
Nuclear attack submarine
Diesel attack submarine
Trident or Poseidon missile submarine
Oiler or ammo-oiler or stores ship
Supply ship
Torpedo boat (WWII)
Torpedo boat tender
Troop carrier
Tenders for subs and surface ships

United States Marine Corps
Commissioned Officers:
Commandant—General
Chief of Staff—Lt. General
Officers' ranks same as U.S. Army
Commissioned Warrant Officers (CWO 1-5)
Noncommissioned Officers:
Sergeant Major of Marine Corps
Sergeant Major/Master Gunnery Sergeant
First Sergeant/Master Sergeant
Gunnery Sergeant
Staff Sergeant
Sergeant
Enlisted men:
Corporal
Lance Corporal
Private First Class
Private

THE UNITED STATES AIR FORCE

Its Heritage

The United States Air Force was established as a separate service by Congress in 1947. The history of airpower in support of our national defense, however, dates to 1907 when the War Department created the aeronautical division of the Office of the Chief Signal Officer of the Army.

The division was charged with overseeing matters pertaining to ballooning, air machines, and "all kindred subjects."

Experience in two world wars finally convinced military leaders, the American people, Congress, and the administration that a separate organization should be established to specialize in air operations.

Mission

Aerospace doctrine—the fundamental beliefs that guide the use of our forces in military action—has evolved from the first use of the airplane in World War I to anticipate the most recent influences and developments of the space age.

When the United States Air Force was established as a separate service, it was given primary responsibility for providing this country with the airpower needed to defend it at home and meet its commitments abroad.

Execution of this responsibility requires that the Air Force be able to deny control of the air to enemy air forces and to provide air support and protection to ground and naval forces necessary for them to perform their mission. From the beginning, that mission has recognized the unique speed, range, and flexibility of aircraft and missiles that can be used in defense of the nation's interests.

The President has a full range of defense options. These include small-scale, tactical operations; conventional or nuclear warfare in a large geographic area; and strategic nuclear warfare against another nuclear power. But central to the defense of the United States is the concept of nuclear deterrence: the belief that only if we maintain credible strategic forces will our adversaries be convinced they cannot achieve their aims through armed conflict.

The Air Force is responsible for two elements of the triad of strategic nuclear deterrence: manned bombers and intercontinental ballistic missiles. These, in combination with the third element of the triad, the Navy's sea-launched ballistic missiles, are vital to the free world's defense against strategic nuclear attack.

Organization

Depending on the nation's state of readiness, the Air Force has had up to 1.1 million members, both uniformed and civilian personnel. It consists of the Regular Air Force, the Air National Guard, and the Air Force Reserve working together to carry out the mission of the Air Force.

The United States Air Force organizes its people and other resources into major air commands, separate operating agencies or direct reporting units. Each of its thirteen major commands has a specific role in support of national defense objectives.

Strategic Air Command

The Strategic Air Command (SAC), headquartered at Offutt Air Force Base near Omaha, Nebraska, has the fundamental responsibility of providing the United States with a nuclear capability strong enough to deter an attack on this nation and our allies.

SAC also maintains a long-range bomber force capable of supporting worldwide conventional power projection operations at any level of conflict. Complementing both the nuclear and conventional missions are SAC's airborne reconnaissance, refueling and worldwide command and control systems.

SAC has had as many as 121,000 active duty military and civilian personnel, plus an additional 15,000 reservists. Its weapon systems include B-52, BIB and FB-111 bombers; a tanker force of KC-135s and KC-10s for airborne refueling and U-2, TR-1, SR-71 and RC-135 reconnaissance aircraft.

Air Training Command

Air Training Command (ATC), headquartered at Randolph Air Force Base in San Antonio, Texas, ensures that Air Force people are sufficient in numbers, quality, and expertise are recruited and trained.

Virtually all enlisted members and nearly ninety percent of officers receive their introduction to the Air Force through ATC. Basic training for enlisted members is conducted at the command's Military Training Center at Lackland Air Force Base, Texas. The command has two commissioning programs for officers: the Officer Training School at Lackland and the Air Force Reserve Officer Training Corps at colleges and universities throughout the nation.

Beyond the initial training of enlisted members and officers, ATC directs a network of continuing career training opportunities crucial in an era of rapidly changing technology. A total of 6,300 courses in 350 different career specialties makes ATC the largest education and training system in the free world.

Serving the command have been nearly 77,000 uniformed and civilian personnel.

Air Force Systems Command

The primary mission of Air Force Systems Command (AFSC) is to advance aerospace technology, to incorporate those advances in the development and improvement of aerospace systems and to acquire superior, cost-effective aerospace systems and equipment that can be supported logistically.

Air Force Communications Command

At Scott Air Force Base, Illinois, Air Force Communications Command provides communications, automatic data processing and air traffic control services vital to Air Force operations.

Air University

Headquartered at Maxwell Air Force Base, Alabama, Air University provides professional military education, degree-granting and professional continuing education for officers, noncommissioned officers and civilians.

Alaskan Air Command

With headquarters at Elmendorf Air Force Base near Anchorage, Alaskan Air Command serves as the first line of defense on the shortest air route from Siberia to the heartland of the United States.

The command's F-15 Eagles are on constant alert to provide both air defense and tactical strike capabilities.

Electronic Security Command

Headquartered at Kelly Air Force Base, Texas, Electronic Security Command has an all-source intelligence function. It provides electronic support to the combat mission, operations security, communications and computer systems security, and communications support to Air Force units and unified and specified commands.

Pacific Air Forces

With headquarters at Hickam Air Force Base, Hawaii, Pacific Air Forces is the principal air arm of the United States Pacific Command. Its primary mission is to plan, conduct and coordinate offensive and defensive air operations in an area extending from the west coast of the Americas to the east coast of Africa and from the Arctic to the Antarctic. It has tactical fighter wings in Korea, Japan, the Philippines and Hawaii.

United States Air Forces in Europe

The major air component of the United States European Command. USAFE is headquartered at Ramstein Air Base in Germany. USAFE was dedicated to deterring Soviet aggression.

Air Force Organizational Units

Flight: lowest level unit. Primarily used for small mission.

Squadron: basic unit in the Air Force. Used to designate mission units in operational commands.

Group: flexible unit usually composed of two or more squadrons, tactical, support, or administrative.

Wing: usually composed of two or more squadrons.

Air Division: organization similar to a numbered Air Force but on a smaller scale. Ordinarily limited to operations or logistics.

Numbered Air Force: designed for the control of two or more air divisions but is flexible and can be of any size.

Major command: a major subdivision of the Air Force as assigned to a major or priority mission.

Commissioned Officers

General
Lieutenant General
Major General
Brigadier General
Colonel
Lieutenant Colonel
Major
Captain
First Lieutenant
Second Lieutenant

Noncommissioned Officers
Chief Master Sergeant
Senior Master Sergeant
Master Sergeant
Technical Sergeant
Staff Sergeant
Sergeant/Senior Airman

Enlisted Personnel
Airman First Class
Airman
Airman Basic

U.S. Air Force—Major Air Commands

Name	Location
Air Force Communications Command	Scott AFB, Illinois
Air Force Logistics Command	Wright-Patterson AFB, Ohio
Air Force Space Command	Colorado Springs, Colorado
Air Force Systems Command	Andrews AFB, Maryland
Air Training Command	Randolph AFB, Texas
Alaskan Air Command	Elmendorf AFB, Alaska
Electronic Security Command	San Antonio, Texas
Military Airlift Command	Scott AFB, Illinois
Pacific Air Forces	Hickam AFB, Hawaii
Strategic Air Command	Offutt AFB, Nebraska
Tactical Air Command	Langley AFB, Virginia
U.S. Air Forces Europe	Ramstein AFB, Germany
Air University	Maxwell AFB, Alabama

Major Air Force Squadrons
Aeromed Evacuation
Air Rescue and Recovery
Bomarc
Bomber
Command Control
    and Surveillance
ECM/Reconnaissance
Fighter
Intelligence
Interceptor
IRBM/CBM
Mace/Matador

Mapping
Special Missions
Special Operations Force
Strategic Airlift
Tactical Air Control Systems
Tactical Airborne Command
    Control System
Tactical Airlift
Tactical Bomber
Tanker
Tanker/Cargo Weather

Types of Aircraft

Attack	Interceptor
Bomber, long range	Observation
Bomber, medium range	Reconnaissance
Bomber, strategic	Search and Rescue
Cargo	Special research
Electronic warfare	Tanker
Fighter	Trainer
Helicopter (attack)	Transport
Helicopter (rescue)	Utility

Air Force Programs

Airlift and sealift
Central maintenance and supply
General personnel activities
General purpose forces
Guard and reserve forces
Intelligence and communications
Medical
Research and development
Strategic forces
Support of other nations
Training

Fixed Wing Aircraft in Vietnam

CV-2 Caribou (utility transport)
U-8F Seminole (personnel transport)
U-1 Otter (utility, light cargo, passenger transport)
OV-18 Mohawk (electronic surveillance)
U-21 UTE (twin turbo-prop, command purposes)
0-1 Bird Dog (Recon, observation)
OV-1A (Recon, rocket-firing craft)
U-6 Beaver (utility)

Helicopters

Airmobile surgical center pod (sling loaded under CH54 and
    transported to forward battle zones)
AH-1G Huey Cobra (escort, recon, and direct fire)
CH-21C Shawnee (transport equipment, personnel, equipment)
CH-34C Choctaw (transport cargo and personnel)
CH-37B Mohave (utility)
CM-47A Chinook (cargo, equipment, artillery, troops, carried
    rocket pods, grenade systems, machine guns)
CH-54 Sky Crane (designed to carry exterior payload)
OH-23 Raven (observation, recon and medivac)
OH-13S Sioux (scout, observation, target acquisition)
OH-61 Cayuse (light observation)

UH-1A Huey (personnel transport, supplies, equipment)
UH-1B Huey (transport and aerial weapons platform)
UH-1D Huey (tactical transport and support)
UH-19D Chickasaw (utility, transport cargo and troops)
UH-1E Huey (Marine rescue and assault ship)

Abbreviations and Acronyms

AAC: Alaskan Air Command
AAVS: Aerospace Audio Visual Service
AFAA: Air Force Audit Agency
AFCC: Air Force Communications Command
AFISC: Air Force Inspection and Safety Center
AFLC: Air Force Logistics Command
AFOPA-WR: Air Force Office of Public Affairs-Western Region
AFRES: Air Force Reserves
AFSC: Air Force Systems Command
AFSPACECOM: Air Force Space Command
AMARC: Aerospace Maintenance and Regeneration Center
ANG: Air National Guard (sometimes preceded by state abbrev)
ANGB: Air National Guard Base
ATC: Air Training Command
BSD: Ballistic Systems Division
BW: Bombardment Wing
DoD: Department of Defense
FIG: Fighter Interceptor Group
ICBM: Intercontinental Ballistic Missile
MAC: Military Airlift Command
MAST: Military Assistance to Safety and Travel
MAW: Military Airlift Wing
NAS: Naval Air Station
NORAD: North American Aerospace Defense Command
PA: Public Affairs
PACAF: Pacific Air Forces
PAO: Public Affairs Officer
SAC: Strategic Air Command
SMW: Strategic Missile Wing
SPACECOM: Space Command
TAC: Tactical Air Command
TCG: Tactical Control Group
TFTS: Tactical Fighter Training Squadron
TFW: Tactical Fighter Wing
USA: U.S. Army
USAFA: U.S. Air Force Academy
USAFRSQ: U.S. Air Force Recruiting Squadron
USMC: U.S. Marine Corps
USN: U.S. Navy

Air Force Academy

The Air Force Academy is a unique college. Cadets experience a different lifestyle, including airmanship training, an outstanding academic environment, superb athletic facilities, and the Jack's Valley summer encampment for the incoming freshman class.

> Location: Ten miles north of Colorado Springs in the Rampart Range foothills of the Rocky Mountains.
>
> Public affairs office telephone: (719) 472-2990 or 472-4050; afterduty hours call 472-4050. Fax: (719) 472-3494.
>
> Mission statement: To instruct cadets so that they graduate with the knowledge and character essential for leadership and the motivation to become career officers in the U.S. Air force.
>
> Host unit and major command: U.S. Air Force Academy.
>
> Primary aircraft: T-41, W-18, TG-7, and sailplanes.
>
> Address: U.S. Air Force Academy
> Colorado Springs, CO 80840-5151

THEMES FOR MILITARY STORIES

War or military stories often encompass almost every aspect of drama and human emotions. Although most military stories are quite broad and are filled with action, life and death situations, and suspense, they usually feature personal and romantic relationships as well.

Occasionally, some military stories will focus more tightly on one person or a few select individuals or deal with one specific incident. War stories or those with a military background offer a wide variety of themes:

Account of a special battle	Military discipline
Bigotry in the service	Military justice
Cowardice	Patriotism
Face of the enemy	Problems of recruits
Futility of war	Ravages of war
Heroism	Relationships
Horrors of war	Rescue of prisoners of war
Leadership	Segregation
Life or career of an	Service traditions
outstanding soldier	Training
Lives and experiences of	Veteran issues
prisoners of war	War orphans
Loyalty	War and politics
Man's breaking point	Wartime romance
Medicine in war	Women in uniform

MILITARY STORY PREMISES

Like all other stories, military/war story premises are quite basic. The difference comes in the ingredients. Oliver Stone didn't write the first story built around the men of one *Platoon*, nor was his story the first about the futility of taking and trying to hold one position that would hardly be decisive in the winning of a war. Nor was Tom Clancy's *The Hunt for Red October* the first book about submarine warfare or the conflict between two opposing submarines and their skippers.

What made Stone's *Platoon* and Clancy's *The Hunt for Red October* stand out was the insight into the characters and the research that made both stories as credible and as riveting as they were. Much the same were the reasons for the success of the classic play (and later a film) *Brother Rat*, and *An Officer and a Gentleman*, both of which dealt with the trials and tribulations of academy training in becoming a career military officer.

If you've already chosen a premise, then the lists in this chapter can help you find the story element you need. Ask yourself these questions:

Which branch of service is your story about? The Army? The Navy? The Marines? The Air Force?

Does it take place in the past? In the present? In the future? During war or peace time?

Does your story deal with one or more war concepts such as a particular battle or a relationship between two soldiers, or a soldier and an officer, or two officers? Might the soldiers be members of opposing forces?

Is your story a character study of one individual's personal and military life, or of a select group of individuals?

Is it about the exploits of a special squad, team, unit, or crew on a particular mission?

Is it the retelling of an historical battle or an overview of a war or battle and its effect upon a number of lives?

Does the story examine the role of opposing forces and give insight into characters on both sides?

Does the story deal with women in war as nurses, doctors, soldiers or officers?

Is it about a military hospital or MASH unit in a battle zone?

Is your story about an heroic sacrifice by an individual or a group of individuals?

Is it about espionage or intelligence gathering? A spy? A traitor?

Is it about a conflict within a squad, platoon, or company, between the troops or between the troops and an officer? Does the conflict result in a court martial?

Is it about the testing of new equipment, a plane, or a vessel?

Is it about being trapped or caught behind enemy lines? Being a prisoner of war? Life in a POW camp?

Is it about making command decisions? Courage? Cowardice?
The effect war has on an individual or a group? The change in
  character brought about by war?
Does your story deal with tradition in a military academy? Rigidity
  of rules? Conflict with classmates? A romance?
Are the characters on special assignment? In conflict with
  other personnel?
Is it about dereliction of duty, espionage, a military base crime?
Is the story about a veteran who is bitter or cannot adjust to civilian
  life or has been crippled? Is it about life in a veteran's hospital?
Is it about troops on patrol, keeping an eye on a potential enemy, or
  a provocative incident during a cold war that could lead to a
  real war?
Is it about serving during a "police action" or as a military advisor to
  another army at war, or defending against a terrorist attack?

Each of the questions above could give you an idea for a story.
Combinations of these questions and ideas from the section below on
problems and conflicts can help you develop a story premise.

For example, a special squad or unit is on a particular mission. Two
principal characters could be either two soldiers or a soldier and an
officer. What happens then? Well, suppose they find themselves trapped
behind enemy lines and are taken prisoner. Next, they might discover a
traitor and hold their own kangaroo court, or they might defy their
interrogators. They might learn of a major plan of the enemy and
attempt to escape to warn their own troops. How you choose the
elements to develop these characters, their relationships and the courses
of action they take is up to you. Check the chapters in this book that
deal with character development, vehicles, obstacles, secondary actions,
and locations to help you develop your plot.

In writing stories about the military at war or in peacetime, remember
that most stories dealing with the military deal with a number of
characters who have been thrown together. In the military, people from
different walks of life, with different values, prejudices, ethnic, religious
and financial backgrounds, live, work, and fight together. The
dissimilarity of these characters, the way each thinks, acts and reacts to
one another has a tremendous impact upon their relationships and the
way your story will develop.

PROBLEMS AND CONFLICTS
RELATING TO THE MILITARY

The following list contains some problems, conflicts and resolutions
that might be incorporated into your story.

Two men become sworn enemies and seize each opportunity to bring about the other's downfall. One tries to steal the other's girlfriend. One accuses the other of cowardice or a crime.

A noncommissioned officer takes over command from a superior who is wounded or killed, or no longer fit to command or with whom he or she disagrees.

Two members of opposing forces attempt to hunt each other down, or they come to understand and respect one another as human beings. Perhaps they must learn to work together to survive.

An officer is obsessed with the notion that his or her subordinates plan a mutiny or that one of those subordinates plans to kill him or her. Maybe the officer fears that the subordinates will take no prisoners even if one wishes to surrender.

A unit on an urgent mission is pinned down by enemy fire and seeks either to escape unscathed or to attack and complete the mission. Or perhaps their aim is to divide, some getting the wounded out while others attempt to complete the mission. Maybe one or more of them is taken prisoner and can reveal their mission, or bad weather socks them in and time is of the essence.

A unit told to hold their position comes under heavy fire while waiting for reinforcements or an air strike. Then they learn the help they're waiting for is not coming. Some of the soldiers are ready to turn tail and run because a by-the-book officer is courting disaster.

A person believed cowardly surrenders to the enemy, does something heroic, discovers inner courage, or inherits the responsibility of command.

Two men in the same outfit learn or know they are both in love with the same woman, or two women, with the same man.

A sole surviving soldier in a skirmish switches dog tags with a dead comrade.

A cadet is harassed by or in trouble with an older cadet or a group of fellow cadets.

A cadet is accused of breaking traditions, rules or regulations, of wrongful conduct, or of a crime.

A cadet falls in love and considers leaving the academy, or may even be dismissed.

A cadet has a difficult time juggling classes and athletic activities.

A cadet gets in trouble while helping a fellow cadet.

A recruit gets off to a bad start, either with fellow recruits the sergeant, or with an officer.

An MP or SP (Military Police or Shore Patrol) is assigned to escort or bring back a prisoner.

A POW returns after the war to find he was believed to have been killed in action. His girlfriend has married another, or his wife has remarried. All that he once owned is now gone. Perhaps he becomes a mercenary. Or, what if the POW were a woman?

An incident, if allowed to occur or be discovered, could turn a cold war hot.

A veteran becomes a mercenary.

A soldier stationed in a foreign land becomes involved with a beautiful woman or handsome man of that country, who may either be a spy or a drug trafficker.

A veteran learns that he fathered a child during the war and returns to get it. He brings the child home to live with his family.

If you did not already have a premise for a story with a military background, you should be able to put one together from the various sections in this chapter. Combine the premise with the characters you develop and a full story can be put together from beginning to end.

18

Vehicles

For listings of military ground, air, and sea vehicles, see Chapter 17: The Military.

STREET VEHICLES

Ambulance
Bicycle
Bus
Cement truck
Convertible
Coupe
Dump truck
Fire engine
Garbage truck
Jeep
Mobile home
Motor scooter/moped
Motorcycle

Oil tanker
Pickup truck
Police car
Recreational vehicle or
    camper
Sedan
Sports car
Station wagon
Taxicab
Tractor trailer
Truck
Van

OFF-ROAD

All terrain vehicle (ATV)
Dirt bike
Dune buggy

Humvees
Jeep
Land Rover

ON TRACKS

Cable car
Handcar
Monorail

Subway car
Train (steam, electric)
Trolley car

AIR VEHICLES

Balloon
Biplane
Crop duster
Dirigible
Flying boat
Glider
Hang glider
Helicopter
Hovercraft
Jetliner
Kite

Parachute
Rocketship
Rotor harness
Seaplane
Single-engine
Spaceship
Tow plane
Transport
Trimotor
Turboprop
Twin engine

SNOW AND ICE VEHICLES

Bobsled
Dog sled
Flexible Flyer (sled)
Ice boat
Skates

Skis
Sleigh
Snowmobile
Snowplow
Zamboni

COUNTRY VEHICLES

Buggy
Combine
Donkey cart
Harvester
Horse-drawn cart
Lawnmower

Mule-drawn cart
Plow
Thresher
Tractor
Wagon

SEA VEHICLES

Barge
Bathysphere
Canoe
Catamaran
Cruise ship
Ferry

Fireboat
Fishing boat
Freighter
Houseboat
Hovercraft
Hydrofoil

Hydroplane
Kayak
Powerboat
Racing sloop
Raft
Rowboat
Sailboat
Sea sled
Submarine

Submersible
Surfboard
Swamp buggy
Tanker
Trawler
TriCat
Tugboat
Water skis
Yacht

HEAVY EQUIPMENT

Asphalt spreader
Caterpillar tractor
Crane carrier and crane
Ditching machine
Dump truck
Earth mover
Flatbed truck
Front-end loader

Heavy truck and low boy
    trailer
Heavy bulldozer
Rock crusher
Rome plow
Scoop loader
Skip loader
Tree crusher

19

The Old West

One of the richest and most exciting periods of American history was that of the Old West, and it has long been an integral part of American literature, film, and television.

Although its popularity appears to have lessened over the years, the Western is still standard fare for writers and devotees of that genre both here and abroad.

What was once the West would today be called the Midwest of the United States. But back in 1876, everything west of the ninety-eighth meridian, which included seven states and the territories of Dakota, Wyoming, New Mexico, Utah, Montana, Washington, Idaho, Arizona, and Indian territory (now eastern Oklahoma), was considered the West. Dodge City, of course, is smack in the middle of Kansas. Although the story of the American Indian goes much further back than when the pioneer wagons first rolled west, the days of the American cowboy barely lasted a generation, from the end of the Civil War until the late 1880s.

Nevertheless, it was an era of violence, of fortunes made and lost, and an important part of American history.

It was an era that produced many outlaws and an equal number of famous and infamous lawmen.

It was an era of wars between Indians and whites, of bank and train robberies, of cattle barons and cattle rustlers, of horse thieves and scoundrels, of the coming of the railroad, and of gold and land rushes.

It was rough, rugged, and romantic.

On the following pages you will find lists of some of the heroes of the Old West, famous outlaws, modes of travel, battles and gunfights, weapons, slang of the era, cowboy gear, and other information.

However, it would take volumes dedicated to the period to give you a comprehensive view of the Old West. I therefore suggest you take advantage of the list of suggested reading material at the end of this chapter.

THE CODE OF THE WEST

As there was little if any law in the Old West, those who lived there made up their own rules of conduct. The code was unwritten but observed by most. Those who didn't obey the code were severely punished by their peers, or by sheriffs, deputies, posses, U.S. marshals and, in Texas, the Texas Rangers. When writing about the Old West, one should research the code of the West. The code would undoubtedly play a major part in your story.

LIFE OUT WEST

Life in the Old West was far from easy and vastly different from the life left behind by those who traveled west seeking fortune, new opportunities, and adventure. The very nature of the new territory altered the lives of those traveling west from the civilized cities of the East, and there was almost a daily battle against the elements, the terrain and the Indians. Lawless conflict was everywhere, and conflict is what makes for good drama.

If the Old West is to be the arena for your story, novel or script, you couldn't have chosen a richer one. The Western offers romance, action, suspense, and colorful characters, either original or historical. Depending on the period you choose, the Western offers a multitude of subjects to choose from, such as the law and the lawless, the coming of the railroads, the land and gold rushes, Indian Wars, the cavalry, fur traders, Indian trading post operators, buffalo hunters, homesteaders and farmers, the Pony Express, the discovery of oil, the coming of the telegraph and the telephone, wagon trains, and cattle drives. These are just a sampling of possible subjects for Western stories. Remember, the West was constantly changing and growing, so it is essential that you research the locale and period of time in which you place your story. The West of the early 1800s was vastly different from the West following the Civil War. And as the face of the Old West changed, so did the faces of those who came West.

On the following pages, you will find lists dealing with the Old West from which you can draw ideas for stories, characters, and locations, but I remind you once again, when dealing with history—and the Old West is history—check the facts on the period and locale of your story.

CHARACTERS OF THE OLD WEST

Although the Old West had its share of housewives, doctors, lawyers, tailors, and storekeepers, there were those who were distinctive to the Old West. The following list is a sampling of them.

Blacksmith	Missionary
Buffalo hunter	Mountain man
Bull whacker	Mule skinner
Cattleman	Oil man
Cook	Outlaw
Cowboy	Pony Express rider
Dancehall girl	Preacher
Gambler	Railroad worker
Gold miner	Rancher
Granger (farmer)	Rustler
Gunfighter	Sheepherder
Homesteader	Sheriff
Horse soldier	Shotgun rider
Indian brave	Stagecoach driver
Indian chief	Trail boss
Indian medicine man	Trail driver
Indian scout	Trapper
Indian squaw	Traveling judge
Indian trading post operator	Wagon master
Marshal	Wrangler
Midwife	

NAMES ASSOCIATED WITH THE OLD WEST

I have selected a representative list of names associated with the Old West, some of which are quite well known while others may not be familiar to you. Nonetheless, all of them (and many more) played interesting, dramatic roles in this period of history.

Further research is recommended as each of the people named has a number of stories to tell. *The Hook of the American West,* published by Bonanza Books in New York, might be an excellent place to start. See other suggested readings at the end of this chapter.

Black Bart	General Otis Howard
Sam Bass	Frank James
Charlie Bassett	Jesse James
Judge Roy Bean	Chief Joseph
Billy the Kid	Lillie Langtry
Pawnee Bill	General Robert E. Lee
Jim Bowie	Bill Longley
Matthew Brady	Nat Love (Black cowboy)

Neal Brown
Seth Bullock
Ned Buntline
Calamity Jane
Kit Carson
Butch Cassidy
Nate Champion
Badger Clark
Red Cloud
Crazy Horse
Cochise
Buffalo Bill Cody
Samuel Colt
"Long Haired" Jim Courtright
General George Armstrong
Custer
Wyatt Earp
Jack Garner
Pat Garrett
Geronimo
Wild Bill Hickock
Doc Holliday
Emerson Hough

Chris Madsen
Bat Masterson
Joaquin Murieta
Annie Oakley
Sheriff Commodore P. Owens
Hanging Judge Charles Parker
Henry Plummer
William Clarke Quantrill
Frederic Remington
Santana
General Phil Sheridan
Chief Sitting Bull
Tom Smith
Belle Starr
General Jack Stillwell
John Sutter
Spotted Tail
Jim Taylor
Zach Taylor
Ben Thompson
Jack Thorp
Bill Tilghman
John Wesley Hardin

PLACES ASSOCIATED WITH THE OLD WEST

Interior

Bank
Blacksmith's shop
Bordello
Bunkhouse
General store
Harvey House

House
Saloon
Sheriff's office and jail
Stables
Stagecoach office

Exterior

Campsite
Corral
Fort
Indian camps
Military post

Railroad station
Ranch/Range
Stockyard
Town streets
Trails

MODES OF TRANSPORTATION IN THE OLD WEST

Buckboard
Buggy
Conestoga wagon

Family wagonette
Four-passenger surrey
Horse team

Horse-drawn ambulance
Horses
Jump seat wagon
Mule
Platform spring wagon
Prairie schooner

Six-passenger rockaway
Stagecoach
Steam locomotive
Sulky
Wagon train

ASSOCIATED WITH THE OLD WEST

Bank robberies
Barroom brawls
Bucking broncs
Buffalo hunting
Cattle barons
Cattle drives
Cattle rustling
Feuds
Gambling
Gunfights
Horse thieves
Indian raids
Mining
Mountain men

Necktie parties
Oil fields
Pack mules
Railroad train holdups
Range wars
Roping
Roundups
Santa Fe wagons
The Overland Mail Coach
The Pony Express
Trapping
U.S. Cavalry
Wells Fargo
Wild horses

ASSOCIATED WITH COWBOYS

Bedroll
Boots
Branding iron
Bullwhip
Busting broncs
Cattle drive
Chaps
Chuck wagon
Cow horse
Cowboy hat
Cutting horse
Holster
Lasso
Mavericks
Mustangs
Neckerchief
Night horse
Plug horse

Plug of tobacco
Riding the range
Rifle
Rolling cigarettes
Rope
Roping horse
Saddle
Six-shooter
Slicker
Spurs
Stampede
Stetson
Swimming horses
Ten-gallon hat
Tending the herd
Vest
Work horse
Wrangler

WEAPONS OF THE OLD WEST

.30-40 Krag
Buntline Special

Colt Double Action
Colt Dragoon

Colt Peacemaker
Colt Six-Shooter
Derringer
Dueling pistols
Gatling gun
Hall rifle
Henry rifle
Patterson Colt .34
Patterson Colt Revolver .40

Pepper Box
Remington
Sharps buffalo rifle
Smith & Wesson
Spencer repeating rifle
Springfield Carbine
Trade rifle
Winchester carbine
Winchester rifle

AMERICAN INDIAN TRIBES OF THE OLD WEST

Most tales dealing with the American Indian during the time of the pioneers and the westward expansion took place on the Plains and in what later became known as the West. Indian communities included nations, tribes, and smaller bands that split off from tribes.

Indian groups living in what are now the northern and central plains states included those listed below:

Iowa: Winnebago, Omaha, Sauk, Fox
Kansas: Iowa, Potawatomi, Kickapoo, Wyandotte, Shawnee, Peoria, Seneca, Cayuga, Ottawa
Minnesota: Chippewa, Sioux
Missouri: Potawatomi, Kickapoo, Sauk, Fox
Nebraska: Sioux, Ponca
North Dakota: Chippewa, Sioux, Arikra
Oklahoma: Osage, Pawnee, Cherokee, Creek, Seminole, Kiowa, Apache, Comanche, Chickasaw, Choctaw, Arapaho
South Dakota: Sioux
Wisconsin: Chippewa, Oneida, Menominee, Munsee

Indian tribes west of the Plains included:

Arizona: Apache, Papago, Cocopah, Yavapai, Hopi, Navaho
California: Paiute, Pit River, Hoopa Yurok, Pomo, Maidu, Washoe, Mono, Tule River, Wailaki, Maidu, Mohave, Mission, Yuma, Chukchansi, Chemehuevi
Colorado: Ute
Idaho: Kalispel, Coeur D'Alene, Nez Perce, Shoshone, Bannock, Paiute
Montana: Cheyenne, Crow, Astina, Chippewa, Cree, Sioux, Assiniboine, Blackfoot, Salish, Flathead, Kootenai
New Mexico: Apache, Pueblo, Navaho
Oregon: Walla Walla, Paiute, Wasco, Modoc, Cayuse, Klamath, Havasupai, Hualapai, Mohave, Pima, Maricopa, Snake
Nevada: Shoshone, Paiute
Utah: Shoshone, Ute, Paiute, Gosiute

Washington: Spokane, Yakima, Chehalis, Colville, Swinomish,
Shoalwater
Wyoming: Arapaho, Shoshone

Customs, dress, and relations with white settlers varied greatly, so it
is strongly recommended that you research the period, location, tribes,
and customs of any Indian group you include in your story.

INDIAN WARRIORS AND MEDICINE MEN

Cochise (Chiricahua Apache)
Crazy Horse (Ogalala Sioux)
Four Bears (Mandans)
Chief Joseph (Nez Perce)
Kicking Bear (Sioux)
Kishkekosh (Fox)
Lawyer (Nez Perce)
Little Wolf (Cheyenne)
Low Dog (Sioux)
Owhi (Yakima)
Powder Face (Arapaho)

Quanah Parker (Comanche)
Rain in the Face (Sioux)
Red Cloud (Ogalala Sioux)
Sharp Nose (Arapaho)
Short Bull (Sioux)
Sitting Bull (Hunkpapa
Sioux)
Wolf Robe (Cheyenne)
Young Man Afraid of Horses
(Sioux)

Suggested Reading

Alvin Josephy, ed. *The American Heritage Book of Indians*. New
York: Bonanza Books, 1961, 1982.
Jay Monaghan, ed. *The Book of the American West*. New York:
Bonanza Books, 1963.
The American Indians. New York: Time/Life Books, N.D.
Paul Wellman, *The Indian Wars of the West*. New York: Doubleday
& Co., 1954.

GLOSSARY OF OLD WEST LINGO

Aired his paunch: vomited.
Artillery: also,"cutter,""hardware,""lead-pusher,""smokewagon,"
"equalizer" (gunslinger's weapon).
Bad horse: horse that "spooked" easily.
Bit: portion of bridle used to control the horse, usually through
pressure on the mouth and jaw rather than inflicting pain.
Blue Whistler: bullet. Also, "lead plum."
Bridle: Horse's headgear composed of "crown-piece" or "brow-
band" and on either side, a "check-piece." Bit and reins
completed the bridle. Also, "headstall."
Bronc buster: one who breaks wild horses. Also, "flash rider,"
"bronc snapper," "bull bat."
Bronco: wild horse.
Bucking: high roller, weaver, sunfisher, pile driver.

Cantle: raised backrest of saddle.

Chaps: chaperreras, leather overalls to protect the cowboy's legs from thorny brush.

Choosin' match: time when horses are selected by cowhands, beginning with the foreman.

Chuck wagon: used for carrying and cooking food on the trail.

Cinch-ring branding iron: type of makeshift branding iron.

Cutting horse: horse skilled in separating cattle from herd.

Drag rider: cowboy at rear of herd looking for stragglers.

Draw: drawing weapon from holster.

Fanning (the hammer): slapping pistol hammer back with palm of gunless hand while trigger is kept pulled.

Fiddle-foot: drifter.

Fuzzies: range horses.

Gullet: curved underside of saddle's fork.

Gun hand: hired gun.

Hackmore: used in horsebreaking in place of a bridle.

Heisting: robbing.

Horn: raised knob on saddle.

Hull: (saddle.) Also, "kak," "tree," "wood," "gelding-smacker."

Jug head: horse with little intelligence.

Lead: point. Man riding alongside the front of the herd.

Line: cowboy rope. Also, "string," "whaleline," "twine," "hemp," "lariat."

Lobos: hired guns. Literally, wolves.

Loops: that part of rope used to lasso horses, cattle, etc. Different types include dog loop, blocker loop, and hondo.

Manada: band of mares with a stallion.

Mockey: wild mare.

Night horse: horse skilled in cutting, roping in the dark.

Peaceful as a church: calm.

Pinto: horse of patched color, usually bay/white or black/white.

Plug: broken-down horse.

Puncher: cowboy.

Remuda: pronounced "remootha." Cowboy's string of horses.

Rotgut: hard liquor.

Running iron: type of makeshift branding iron, often used in illegally altering brands.

Sacked the saddle: died.

Sawbones: doctor.

Slicker: also known as "wampus." Yellow oilskin worn to protect against rain.

Sombrero: cowboy's hat. Often called "hair-case," "conk-cover," "lid" or "war bonnet."

Soogans: quilts; part of cowboy's bedroll.

Spoiled horse: outlaw horse, spoiled in breaking.

Spurs: worn on cowboy's boots to initiate horse's action.
Stamp brand: set brand; branding iron used to brand stock.
Swing rider: cowboy riding the flanks of the herd.
Tetchy as a teased snake: edgy.
Top horse: one skilled at cutting and roping.
Trail boss: top man on the trail.
Vaquero: Mexican cowboy. Also, "caballero."

BASIC PREMISES FOR OLD WEST STORIES

Some of the following premises are tried and true, but a twist here and there and some unique characters can make them brand new. Let's take *High Noon,* for example. A man waits for a train that is bringing men who are out to kill him. Suppose it was changed to a man wanted by the Indians and they threaten to burn the town down unless the town hands him over to them by a specific time. It becomes a whole new plot. Use your imagination and see what you can do with the following:

A bounty hunter catches his quarry but then comes to believe that person is innocent of the crime he or she is wanted for.
A feud between two ranchers provokes a range war.
A gunslinger hangs up his guns but is provoked into another gunfight.
A rancher leaves his ranch to hunt down those responsible for killing his wife and family.
Members of a wagon train fight off an Indian attack.
A crooked sheriff leads a posse after an innocent man.
A marshal hunts down an outlaw who he comes to learn is his own brother.
A drifter comes across what's left of a family after an Indian raid and reluctantly takes them under his wing.
A man considered a coward is the only one who stands up to a gang of outlaws that terrorize a town.
A bigoted commander of a fort insists on attacking a peaceful Indian camp on a trumped-up charge.
A lone marshal sets out to track a killer.
A band of outlaws masquerade as Indians to rob stagecoaches, a train, or a wagon train.
An Indian and a white man must depend upon each other to survive and change from enemies to friends.
A westerner splits with the townspeople when he returns with an Indian bride.
A lone surviving woman is taken prisoner by raiding Indians and finds herself soon to be the bride of a warrior brave.
A town hires a former outlaw or gunslinger to be their new sheriff.
A family defends its farm against cattlemen who claim it as grazing land for their herds.

A mysterious loner agrees to work for an attractive widow who is
    struggling to hang on to her ranch.
An undermanned army fort expects a major Indian attack.
A white lieutenant commands an all-black cavalry unit.
A wounded bounty hunter is cared for by the man he came
    to bring in.
The real killer must be found before a necktie party claims the life
    of an innocent man.
A man discovers the brother he thought was killcd in an Indian
    attack is now an Indian brave, the adopted son of the chief of
    the tribe.
A bumbler becomes the town hero and its new sheriff when he
    accidentally kills an outlaw.
The fastest gun in the west wants to retire but is challenged
    to another fight.

GETTING A FRESH START

Okay, let's see what twists we can give some of these basic premises.
Let's try the premise in which a town hires a former outlaw or
gunslinger as sheriff. What if the "former outlaw" isn't really reformed
but came to town to rob the bank? What if the "former outlaw" is an
impostor, and the real outlaw is headed for town?

Now let's try the premise in which two ranchers conduct a range war.
What if we borrow from *Romeo and Juliet* and have the son of one
rancher in love with the daughter of the other? Or let's suppose Indians
attack both ranches, and the two feuding ranchers have to become allies
to survive.

The undermanned fort about to be attacked is pretty standard stuff,
but what if an Indian tribe befriended by the commander of the fort
comes to the rescue? What if some members of the fort take uniforms to
a nearby town and convince people to dress as cavalry so the Indians
believe that reinforcements have arrived?

Look for a twist or change in character. In one premise, a rancher sets
out to find those who killed his wife and family. What if the husband
was killed and his wife sets out to find the killer(s)? What if all the men
in a wagon train are killed and the only ones left to fight off the attack
are women and children? What if after the Civil War a former slave
becomes a bounty hunter, and the man he is after is his former owner?
Check the character lists, involvements and secondary actions to see
what twists can be given to other premises.

SUGGESTED READING

Andy Adams. *The Log of a Cowboy. Boston:* Houghton Mifflin, 1927.

Ramon F. Adams. *Western Words.* Norman, OK: University of Oklahoma Press, 1968.

Dane Coolidge. *Texas Cowboys.* New York: Dutton, 1937.

The Cowboys, New York: Time-Life Books, 1973.

J. Frank Dobie. *The Longhorns.* New York: Bramhall House, 1982.

The Mustangs. Boston: Little, Brown, 1952.

Robert R. Dykstra. *The Cattle Towns.* New York: Alfred Knopf, 1968.

William Foster Harris. *The Look of the Old West.* New York: Bonanza Books, 1965.

Emerson Hough, *The Story of the Cowboy.* Gregg Press, 1970.

Wm MacLeod Raine. *Famous Sheriffs and Western Outlaws.* New York: Doubleday, Doran and Co., 1929.

Mari Sandoz. *The Cattleman.* New York: Hastings House, 1958.

Fay E. Ward. *The Cowboy at Work.* Norman, OK: University of Oklahoma Press, 1987

20

Religion

Although religion seldom plays a prominent role in film and television dramas or in contemporary literature, nevertheless it still is a subject that a writer has to deal with at one time or another.

On the other hand, a writer might, on occasion, see fit to make religion a factor in a plot or in a characterization. Then again, depending upon the locale a writer may be using, religion may become an important element, as in the film *Witness,* which took place in Amish country.

By no means, however, can this book attempt to delve deeply into the world's many religions. It would take volumes to explore any religion, its varieties and manifestations.

The Writer's Partner can make you aware of many of the world's organized religions by the subsequent list along with brief explanations of some selected religions and a bibliography that might help in further research.

In all the major religious traditions, there is a wide range of belief and practice. It will take careful research to determine exactly how to write about the religion of particular individuals or groups.

TERMS ASSOCIATED WITH RELIGIONS AND SECTS

Abecedarianism	Amish
Adventism	Anglo-Catholicism
Agapemonitism	Animism

Arianism
Assemblies of God
Atheism
Baha'i
Baptist
Bhakti
Brahmanism
Buddhism
Calvinism
Catholicism
Christian Science
Church of God
Church of the Nazarene
Confucianism
Congregationalist
Disciples of Christ
Druidism
Dutch Reformed Church
Eastern Orthodox
Episcopalian (Anglicanism,
    Church of England)
Ethical Culture
Ethical Humanism
Evangelicals
Fundamentalists
Greek Orthodox
Hasidism
Hinayana Buddhism
Hinduism
Humanism
Islam
Jainism
Jehovah's Witnesses
Judaism
Karaism
Labadists
Lamaism
Lutheranism
Macmillanites
Mahayana Buddhism
Mahdism
Malikitism
Mandaenism
Mennonites (Plain People)
Methodism

Millennialism
Modernism
Moravian
Mormonism
Mysticism
Paulinism
Pelagianism
Pentecostal (Holy Rollers
    [derogative], Ecstatics)
Pentecostal Assemblies
Pietism
Polish National Catholics
Presbyterianism
Protestantism
Puritanism
Religious Science
Roman Catholicism
Rosicrucianism
Samaritanism
Santeria (Voodoo,
    Expiritismo)
Satanism
Seventh-Day Adventists
Shakers
Shaktism
Shamanism
Shiite Islam
Shinto
Sikhism
Society of Friends
    (Quakerism)
Spiritualism
Sufism
Sunni Islam
Taborites
Taoism
Tibetan Buddhism
Unitarianism
United Brethren
Vajrayana Buddhism
Yoga
Zen Buddhism

Hinduism

Hinduism is one of the oldest living religions, dating back to somewhere between 1500 B.C.E. and 2500 B.C.E. An extremely complicated religion, it boasts many forms, sects, and manifestations. The following is a sampling of some of its elements and offshoots.

Brahmanism

More philosophical than theocentric or God-centered, Brahmanism is a system of rites and beliefs originated by the highest caste among East Indians. Caste rules are very strict about contact with low caste persons, unclean things, alcoholic beverages, and the flesh of a cow, considered a sacred animal.

Yoga

A school of Hindu philosophy with regulated postures, meditation, and disciplined spiritual development leading to enlightenment reached by severing all earthly passions and bringing one's mind under complete control so that the soul is at one with the Absolute.

Bhakti

A movement in later Hinduism expressing the feelings of the more common people rather than the higher caste, which led to the creation of devotional literature to Krishna, considered to be the incarnation of Vishnu, and to Amida, the Buddha, viewed as the incarnation of Compassion.

Popular Hinduism

The worship of the gods Brahma, the Creator; Vishnu, the Preserver; and Shiva, the Destroyer. In Hinduism, the temple is not a place of worship but rather the celestial dwelling place of the gods. Popular Hinduism is more devotional than intellectual. The sacred water of the Ganges River draws millions who seek to bathe in its waters or to die at its banks.

Suggested Reading

Bouguet, C.C. *Hinduism.* London: Hutchinson, N.D.

Godman, David. *The Teachings of Sri Ramana Maharishi.* Boston: Arkana, 1985.

Griswold, H.D. *Insights into Modern Hinduism.* New York: Henry Holt, N.D.

Morgan, K.W. *The Religions of the Hindus.* Ronald Press, N.D.

Pratt, J.B. *India and Its Faiths.* New York: Macmillan, N.D.

Ramakrishna, Sri. *The Gospel of Sri Ramakrishna,* abridged edition. New York: Ramakrishna-Vivekananda Center, 1942.

Buddhism

Buddhism was born in India around 500 B.C.E. It is the religion of Sri Lanka, Burma, Thailand, Cambodia, Vietnam, Tibet, much of Japan, and China. In Buddhism, the formula taught is basically, "I take refuge in Buddha, I take refuge in Dharma (Teaching), I take refuge in Sangha (Community)." Major traditions within Buddhism include Theravada, Vajrayana, and Zen.

Zen

A Chinese and Japanese development of Buddhism. In common with Taoism, Zen Buddhism calls for greater dependence on one's inner nature. Enlightenment is discovered by going from common consciousness to an intuitive way of seeing the truth. In Zen, ritual and scripture are often aspects of practice, but are regarded as representations of truth rather than the truth itself.

Suggested Reading

Anderson, Walt. *Open Secrets: A Western Guide to Tibetan Buddhism.* New York: Viking, 1979.

de Bary, W.T. *The Buddhist Tradition in India, China, and Japan.* New York: Modern Library, 1969.

Humphreys, Christmas. *Buddhism.* New York: Penguin, 1962.

Kapleau, Philip. *The Three Pillars of Zen.* New York: Doubleday, 1989.

Levine, Stephen. *A Gradual Awakening.* New York: Doubleday, 1989.

Reps, Paul, ed. *Zen Flesh, Zen Bones.* New York: Doubleday, N.D.

Suzuki, D.T. *An Introduction to Zen Buddhism.* New York: Grove Press, 1964.

Suzuki, Shunryu. *Zen Mind, Beginner's Mind.* New York: Weatherhill, 1970.

Taoism

A Chinese philosophy and religion founded in the sixth century B.C.E. Some later Taoists practiced alchemy, divination, and exorcism of ghosts and spirits.

Suggested Reading

Chang, Wing-Tsit. *Religious Trends in Modern China.* New York: Columbia University Press, N.D.

Cleary, Thomas, trans. *The Taoist I Ching.* Boston: Shambhala, 1986.

Mitchell, Stephon, trans. *Tao Te Ching.* New York: Harper & Row, 1988.

Yutang, Lin. *The Wisdom of Laotse.* New York: Modern
Library, 1948.
Wei, Francis. *The Spirit of Chinese Culture.* New York:
Scribners, N.D.

Confucianism

Confucianism is a code of conduct set down in Confucius' teachings.
In a Confucian home, the family worships at a home altar where
morning and evening candles are lit, food offered, paper money and
incense burned. At death, rites are supplemented by Buddhist prayers
for the dead and Taoist exorcisms.

Suggested Reading

Confucius. *The Analects.* Translated by D.C. Lau. New York:
Dorset, 1986.
Creel, H.G. *Confucius and the Chinese Way.* New York: Harper,
1960.
Eber, Irene, ed. *Confucianism: The Dynamics of Tradition.* New
York: Macmillan, 1986.
Taylor, Rodney. *The Confucian Way of Contemplation.* Columbia,
SC: University of South Carolina Press, 1988.
Wilhelm, Richard. *Confucius and Confucianism.* New York:
Harcourt, Brace, N.D.
Yutang, Lin, trans. and ed. *The Wisdom of Confucius.* New York:
Modern Library, 1943.

Shintoism

Shinto was the national religion of Japan until 1945. State Shintoism
was an organized means of promoting loyalty, patriotism, and reverence
for the gods of Japan. The Shinto religion has an organized priesthood
with many elaborate rituals, although there is little moral teaching
associated with this religion. The worship of Kami, the word for gods, is
centered in shrines, always approached through the tori), a wooden
gateway made of two vertical posts joined overhead by cross beams that
extend on either side.

Suggested Reading

Holtom, D.C. *Modern Japan and Shinto Nationalism.* New York:
Paragon, 1963.
Kageyama, Haruki. *The Arts of Shinto.* Translated by Christine
Guth. New York: Weatherhill, 1973.
Kato, Genchi. *A Study of Shinto, the Religion of the Japanese
Nation.* New York: Barnes & Noble, 1971.
Ono, Motonori. *The Kami Way: An Introduction to Shrine Shinto.*
Rutland, VT: Bridgeway Press, 1961.

Islam

As seen in today's news headlines, Islam is not only a religious belief but a powerful political force in the Middle East. Founded by the prophet Mohammed, Islam is based on *The Koran,* which is the Moslem's book of religious, legal, social, commercial, and military codes.

Islam's two major sects are the Shiite and the Sunni. This division resulted from disputes over succession to the Caliphate in the decades following Mohammed's death in 632 C.E.

Suggested Reading

al Faruqi, Ismail and Lois Lamya al Faruqi. *The Cultural Atlas of Islam.* New York: Macmillan, 1986.

Farah, Caesar. Islam: *Beliefs and Observances.* New York: Barron's, 1987.

The Koran. translated by N.J. Dawood. New York: Viking Penguin, 1990.

Nasr, Hossein. *Traditional Islam in the Modern World.* New York: Methuen Routledge & Kegan Paul, 1987.

Judaism

Judaism began in the Middle East among wandering Semitic tribes. The patriarch and first prophet of Judaism was Abraham. Moses led the Jews out of Egypt and received God's commandments on Mount Sinai. The reigns of Kings David and Solomon were the pinnacle of power and influence for the ancient Jewish nation.

Today, Judaism has three major divisions. Orthodox Judaism is the most conservative and teaches strict observance of the religious and ethical teachings of the *Torah* and *Talmud.* Reformed Judaism emphasizes following the spirit rather than the letter of Jewish tradition. Conservative Judaism seeks a middle ground, observing many of the ancient rites while accommodating to contemporary conditions.

Suggested Reading

Baeck, Leo. *The Essence of Judaism.* New York: Schocken, N.D.

Baron, Salo W. *A Social and Religious History of the Jews.* New York: Columbia University Press, N.D.

Buber, Martin. *Hasidism and Modern Man.* New York: Harper & Row, 1958.

Strassfeld, Michael. *The Jewish Holidays: A Guide and Commentary.* New York: Harper & Row, 1985.

Wigoder, Geoffrey, ed. *The Encyclopedia of Judaism.* New York: Macmillan, 1989.

Christianity

It would be impossible to comprehend the diversity and influence of Christianity. Almost every aspect of the Western world has been affected by Christianity, which has profoundly influenced social, economic, and political conditions.

During the first centuries after the death of Jesus around 30 C.E., Christianity spread throughout the Mediterranean world and later to northern and central Europe. The early history of Christianity saw persecution and internal strife, particularly over doctrine. The first formal schism occurred in 1054 when the Eastern (Orthodox) and Western (Roman) churches split. In the 1500s a number of groups, known collectively as Protestants, left the Roman church, and new denominations have continued to form.

The diversity of belief and practice in contemporary Christianity could hardly be more complete. The Roman Catholic church has a highly centralized structure, while many Protestant churches are organized at the congregational level. Some Christians believe the Bible is the inerrant Word of God, while others believe the teachings of the Bible must be adapted to modern life. In the Orthodox and Roman Catholic traditions, the liturgy is traceable to the earliest days of Christianity; other churches find the historic liturgies stifling.

Suggested Reading

Barnes, E.W. *The Rise of Christianity.* London: Longmans, N.D.
Case, S.J. *The Evolution of Early Christianity.* Chicago: University of Chicago Press, N.D.
Dodd, C.H. *The Founder of Christianity.* New York: Macmillan, 1970.
McManners, John, ed. *The Oxford Illustrated History of Christianity.* New York: Oxford University Press, 1990.
Tillich, Paul. *A History of Christian Thought.* New York: Harper & Row, 1968.

Mysticism

Mysticism is an aspect of most religions, but in many ways is independent of them. Mysticism has more to do with experience than with doctrine. Nevertheless, mystics usually practice one of the major religions, so you see references to Hindu mysticism, or Jewish, or Christian. Mysticism is also part of many preliterate cultures.

Mysticism tends to cut across doctrinal and sectarian lines. The dialogue between Christian and Buddhist mystics over the last few years has been particularly extensive.

Suggested Reading

'Altar, Farid al-Din. *Muslim Saints and Mystics: Episodes from the Tadhkirat al-Auliya.* Translated by A.J. Arberry. London: Arkana/Penguin, 1990.

Bowman, Mary Ann. *Western Mysticism: A Guide to the Basic Works.* Chicago: American Library Association, 1978.

Cox, Michael. *Handbook of Christian Spirituality.* San Francisco: Harper & Row, 1985.

Johnson, William. *The Still Point: Reflections on Zen and Christian Mysticism.* New York: Fordham University Press, 1970.

Underhill, Evelyn. *Mysticism.* New York: Doubleday, 1990.

Walker, Susan. *Speaking of Silence: Christians and Buddhists on the Contemplative Way.* Mahwah, NJ: Paulist Press, 1987.

Zum Brunn, Emile, and Georgette Epiney-Burgard. *Women Mystics in Medieval Europe.* Translated by Sheila Hughes. New York: Paragon House, 1989.

RELIGIOUS LEADERS

Archbishops
Ayatollahs
Bishops
Cardinals
Chaplains
Deacons
Elders
Evangelists
Lamas
Lay ministers
Lay readers
Ministers
Monks
Monseignors
Mother superiors
Pastors
Popes
Preachers
Priests
Prophets
Rabbis
Rectors
Reformers
Sunday school teachers

OTHERS ASSOCIATED WITH RELIGION

Altar boys
Cantors
Choirboys
Friars
Monks
Muezzin
Nuns
Prophets
Saints
Shamans

RELIGIOUS ARTICLES, RITUALS, AND FACILITIES

Alb
Alms basin
Altar cloths
Amice
Ampulla
Apostles' creed
Archepiscopal cross
Aspergillum
Assumption
Ave Maria

Baptism
Baptismal fonts
Baptistery
Bar Mitzvah
Basins
Bell tolling
Benedictus
Bibles
Blessings
Breastplates
Brith Milah
Call to prayer
Candlemas
Candles
Canon
Catafalques
Catechism
Cathedrals
Censers
Chalices
Chapel
Chapel caps
Chasuble
Cherubim
Choir robes
Christening
Church
Ciborium
Circumcision
Clapper
Communion
Communion veils
Confession
Confessional
Confirmation
Corona
Cotta Cowl
Credence table
Crosses
Crucifixes
Dalmatic
Doxology
Epiphany
Eucharist
Eucharistic cruet
Extreme unction

Faldstools
Figurines
Font
Funeral
Geneva bands
Geneva gowns
Gregorian chant
Hearse
Holy water
Hymnals
Icons
Incense burners
Kaaba
Kaddish
Kamelaukion
Koran
Lavabo
Lectern
Litany
Liturgy
Lord's prayer
Manse
Mantle
Mass book
Menorah
Minbar
Missal stand
Missals
Monstrance
Mourner's Kaddish
Namaz
Nicene creed
Nun's habit
Offering plates
Ordinal
Pallium
Penance
Pendants
Pentateuch
Pentecost
Pews
Phylacteries
Pilgrimages
Poor box
Prayer
Prayer books

Prayer shawl
Prayer wheels
Priest's robes
Processional cross
Psalter
Pulpit
Purgatory
Purificaton
Relics
Reliquary
Reliquary stand
Requiem
Reredos
Rochet
Rosaries
Sacerdotal rites
Sacrament
Sacramental wine
Sacrarium
Sacred vessels
Saint medals
Sanctus
Sanctus bell
Sepher Torah

Seraphs
Sermons
Seven-branched candlesticks
Shofar
Shrines
Sistrum
Stabat Mater
Stained glass windows
Star of David
Statues
Stole
Stoup
Surplice
Tallith
Talmud
Tiara
Tonsure
Torah
Vespers
Vestments
Votive lights
Wedding
Yarmulke

21

Language

Earlier I had said that the writer is God. You create the characters in your story and the situations you place them in and the conflicts they resolve. Early in the story you must describe them, and it is important to use the right descriptive words in doing so.

Describing a character in a novel is usually more detailed and intricate than describing a character in a teleplay or a film script. Whereas the novelist may take paragraphs, if not pages, to describe characters down to the minutest detail, the television- or screenwriter must be more concise. Nevertheless, providing a good physical and emotional description of your characters is essential. For the reader, it paints a clean, vivid picture of the character.

Conjuring up vivid images for producers, casting directors, makeup and wardrobe people, should your story be headed for the big or the small screen, is important if you want your characters to come alive on the screen just as you picture them.

In Chapter Two I included lists of descriptive words as food for thought. One of the best ways to develop the physical descriptions of characters is to use photographs you've taken or magazine clippings as models.

One major difference between the television and screenwriter and the novelist is that often directors and actors seem to resent the writer describing their attitude in a scene or piece of dialogue, feeling that they already know the attitude of the character. Unfortunately, when I didn't offer a description of the character's attitude, the dialogue that reached the screen didn't always come out as I had envisioned it. So, like it or not, if I want a specific attitude, I state it in my script. Actors or directors can always take it out of the script, but like a jury told to ignore a statement made by a witness, the impression's been made.

ACTION VERBS

Abandon	Choke	Drain
Abduct	Clap	Drape
Abolish	Clash	Draw
Abscond	Climb	Dress
Abuse	Clip	Drill
Accelerate	Clutch	Drink
Accuse	Collapse	Drip
Acquire	Collar	Drop
Act	Collide	Drown
Add	Command	Drug
Adjust	Commandeer	Dry
Advance	Count	Duel
Advise	Cram	Dunk
Aim	Crash	Ease
Answer	Crawl	Edge
Apprehend	Creep	Eject
Approach	Cripple	Elevate
Appropriate	Crouch	Elope
Arrest	Cut	Elude
Assault	Dance	Emerge
Attack	Dart	Endure
Avert	Dash	Engage
Bang	Deal	Enjoin
Bar	Deck	Ensnare
Beat	Deduct	Enter
Berate	Descend	Equip
Bite	Describe	Erupt
Blast	Dictate	Escape
Block	Dig	Evacuate
Blow	Discard	Evade
Brighten	Ditch	Evict
Broke	Dive	Examine
Buck	Do	Exert
Bump	Dodge	Exhale
Bury	Dominate	Exit
Bushwhack	Dope	Expel
Catch	Douse	Explode
Charge	Draft	Expose
Chase	Drag	Extend

Extirpate	Gouge	Invade
Extract	Grab	Investigate
Extricate	Grapple	Isolate
Fade	Grasp	Jab
Fake	Greet	Jam
Fall	Grind	Jar
Falter	Grip	Jeer
Fan	Gripe	Jerk
Fast	Grope	Jimmy
Fear	Grow	Jingle
Feed	Growl	Jolt
Feel	Grunt	Jump
Fend	Gyrate	Keel
Fight	Hack	Kibitz
Fill	Hail	Kick
Find	Hammer	Kidnap
Finger	Handle	Kill
Fix	Hang	Kneel
Flag	Harass	Knife
Flap	Haul	Lash
Flash	Hesitate	Launch
Flatten	Hide	Lean
Flaunt	Hijack	Leap
Flay	Hit	Left
Flee	Hitch	Level
Flick	Hobble	Lick
Flinch	Hoist	Limp
Fling	Hold	Listen
Flip	Hover	Lunge
Flit	Hug	Lurch
Float	Hurl	Maim
Flog	Hurtle	Make
Flounder	Identify	Mangle
Flout	Ignore	March
Flush	Illustrate	Mark
Fly	Imitate	Massage
Fondle	Improvise	Maul
Force	Inch	Measure
Fornicate	Indict	Meddle
Fumble	Induce	Meet
Furnish	Inflict	Mimic
Gallop	Inject	Mingle
Gesture	Injure	Mobilize
Give	Insert	Mock
Gnaw	Inspect	Model
Gossip	Interchange	Molest

Mourn	Plod	Regain
Move	Plow	Rejoin
Mumble	Plunge	Relax
Murder	Pocket	Relent
Muster	Poke	Repel
Mutilate	Polish	Repulse
Nab	Pore	Resign
Nag	Pose	Resist
Nail	Pounce	Retaliate
Needle	Pout	Retreat
Nick	Pray	Reveal
Nip	Preen	Ride
Observe	Prepare	Rip
Occupy	Present	Rise
Officiate	Preside	Rob
Operate	Primp	Rock
Pack	Prod	Roll
Paddle	Produce	Rub
Page	Prompt	Run
Pander	Propel	Rush
Panic	Protect	Sail
Parachute	Provoke	Salute
Parade	Pry	Sap
Paralyze	Pull	Save
Park	Pummel	Saw
Parry	Pump	Scale
Party	Punch	Scamper
Pass	Pursue	Scan
Pat	Push	Scare
Patrol	Quit	Scatter
Pause	Race	Scavenge
Paw	Raid	Scold
Peel	Rally	Scoop
Peep	Ram	Scoot
Penetrate	Ransack	Score
Perform	Rape	Scour
Persuade	Rattle	Scout
Pick	Ravage	Scrape
Picket	Rave	Scrawl
Pile	Read	Scream
Pin	Recline	Screw
Pinch	Reconnoiter	Scrub
Pirate	Recoup	Scruff
Pitch	Redeem	Scuffle
Placate	Reel	Sculpt
Play	Refer	Scuttle

Seal	Smell	Stop
Search	Smuggle	Strangle
Seduce	Snap	Strap
Seize	Snare	Strike
Sell	Snarl	Strip
Set	Snatch	Stroke
Sever	Snicker	Struck
Sew	Sniff	Stub
Shake	Snitch	Study
Shanghai ·	Snoop	Stuff
Shape	Snub	Stumble
Sharpen	Snuff	Stun
Shave	Snuggle	Subdue
Shear	Soak	Submerge
Shell	Sock	Submit
Shield	Soil	Suck
Shift	Spear	Summon
Shiver	Spell	Support
Shock	Spike	Surrender
Shoot	Spin	Suspend
Shorten	Splatter	Swagger
Shout	Splice	Swallow
Shove	Split	Swap
Shovel	Spot	Sway
Show	Spray	Swear
Shun	Spread	Swerve
Shut	Spring	Swim
Sidestep	Sprint	Swing
Sigh	Spurn	Swipe
Signal	Spy	Switch
Sip	Squeak	Tackle
Sit	Squeal	Take
Size	Squeeze	Tap
Skid	Stack	Taste
Skim	Stagger	Taunt
Skip	Stamp	Tear
Skirt	Stand	Tease
Slacken	Start	Telephone
Slam	Startle	Terrorize
Slap	Steal	Thrash
Slash	Steer	Thread
Slay	Step	Threaten
Slide	Stick	Throw
Slug	Stiffen	Tickle
Smack	Stifle	Tie
Smear	Stomp	Tilt

Tip	Undress	Weed
Toss	Unfold	Whack
Touch	Untangle	Whip
Tout	Unwind	Whirl
Track	Usher	Whistle
Trap	Vacate	Wield
Tread	Vanish	Wiggle
Trip	Vault	Withdraw
Trot	Vent	Work
Trounce	Violate	Wreck
Try	Wade	Wrench
Tuck	Walk	Wrestle
Tug	Wander	Yank
Tumble	Ward	Yell
Turn	Watch	Yelp
Twist	Wave	Yield
Undo	Wedge	

ONE FROM COLUMN A, ONE FROM COLUMN B

He or she—	How?
Accused	accusingly
Advised	adding
Announced	angrily
Answered	approvingly
Asked	assuringly
Asked (him or her) self	awkwardly
Assured	bluntly
Blurted	breathing hard
Brooded	breathlessly
Chirped	calculatingly
Commanded	chuckling
Cried	compassionately
Demanded	contemptuously
Exclaimed	continuing
Exhaled	crying out
Frowned	defensively
Gasped	devoid of emotion
Gloated	dispassionately
Grinned	effortlessly
Growled	exhaling a sigh
Hesitated	expressionlessly
Inquired	gently
Instructed	glancing off
Jeered	glaring
Lamented	gratefully
Laughed	gravely

Leered	guardedly
Lied	happily
Moaned	hastily
Mocked	hoarsely
Mumbled	in a whisper
Murmured	inquiringly
Muttered	knowingly
Objected	lazily
Panted	leeringly
Prompted	listlessly
Quarreled	looking away
Questioned	loudly
Replied	lying through the teeth
Responded	remembering
Roared	sadly
Said	sleepily
Sang out	sluggishly
Scoffed	snarling
Scowled	sobbing
Screamed	softly
Shouted	spitefully
Shrugged	stifling a yawn
Sighed	stifling a laugh
Smiled	suspiciously
Snapped	taking a deep breath
Snarled	tearfully
Sneared	tenderly
Sobbed	thoughtfully
Spat	tolerantly
Speculated	tonelessly
Stammered	unconsciously
Stared	vengefully
Stated	warily
Stuttered	wearily
Thought	with a smile
Uttered	with a chuckle
Wept	with a yawn
Whined	with assurance
Whispered	with remorse
Wondered aloud	with contempt
Yelled	with a laugh

AMERICANISMS

All-fired: excessive.
All-in: fatigued.

All over: finished.
Allow: agree, admit.
Almighty: powerful.
Almighty dollar: U.S. currency.
Apron strings: control by a woman.
Backwater: insignificant.
Baggage: luggage.
Baggage-smasher: luggage handler.
Bandwagon, on the: following the crowd.
Bar keeper: bartender.
Beat all **hollow:** excel other by far.
Beat it: run away, or instruct to depart.
Beaut: something excellent.
Bedrock: solid or fixed, as price.
Belly-whopper: dive, landing on stomach.
Big head: conceit.
Big mouth: braggart.
Big shot: important man.
Bimbo: girl.
Blackjack: card game; weapon.
Bleachers: arena seats in the sun.
Blowhard: braggart.
Blow-in: spend.
Blowout: tire flat; or, wild party.
Blue chips: best rated stocks.
Bluss: deceive.
Bogus: counterfeit.
Bolt: east fast; or, run fast.
Bonanza: profitable find.
Bone: study hard.
Boom: prosperous period.
Boost: promote.
Bossy: cow.
Bottom dollar: last resources.
Boxcar: pair of sixes in dice.
Bracer: stiff drink.
Brace up: reinvigorate.
Brass: effrontery; or management.
Break: special opportunity.
Breakdown: nervous collapse.
Broad: woman.
Bromide: repetition of common knowledge.
Bronco-buster: horsetrainer.
Buck: dollar.
Bug: annoy.
Bulldoze: overpower.

Bulldozer: front-bladed tractor-demolisher.
Budd-luck: unearned good fortune.
Bum: tramp.
Bum steer: misleading recommendation.
Buncombe: humbug, insincerity.
Bunk: rustic type of bed; untruth.
Bunkie: bedmate or roommate.
Bushwhacker: woods ranger, ambusher.
Bust: to hit; a failure.
Caboose: jail; freight train's last car.
Cain, to raise: make trouble.
Canuck: French Canadian.
Carpetbagger: Northerner seeking personal gain in the South.
Catch on: understand.
Cayuse: Indian pony.
Chestnut: old item.
Chesty: self-important.
Chipper: cheerful. Cinch: easy task.
Clambake: party.
Claw-hammer: coat with tail.
Clearing: man-made open space in woods.
Cobbler: shoe repairman.
Cocktail: mixed alcoholic drink.
Cold feet: timidity.
Commuter: city worker from suburbs.
Con man: deception artist.
Contraption: impractical contrivance.
Coffee break: work intermission.
Cookie: small, thin cake; girl.
Corduroy road: continuously bumpy road.
Corral: enclosure for horses, cattle.
Cowboy: ranch hand.
Cowcatcher: V-shaped guard on locomotive front.
Crackerjack: popcorn confection; item of excellence.
Crawfish: back out from agreement. Crook: Criminal.
Cuss word: swear word.
Cut out: stop or leave.
Cut up: prankster.
Firewater: whiskey.
Fizzle: fail.
Flat: deflated; moneyless.
Flies on, no: smart.
Floorwalker: store usher. Flop: go to bed.
Flophouse: cheap hotel.
Four-time-loser: getting mandatory life sentence under Baume's law.

Flunk: fail.
Four-flusher: braggart.
Four hundred: top society.
Frazzled: nerve weary.
Frenzied finance: excited monetary maneuvering.
Frill: superfluous.
Front: facade or pretense.
Full blast: top speed.
Gall: effrontery.
Galley west: knocked to pieces.
Gerrymander: tricky rearrangement of election districts.
Get the hand of: understand.
Gingersnap: ginger cookie.
Gingerbread: rococo adornment; a form of cookie or cake.
Gin mill: drinking place.
Glad-hand: pretentious welcome.
Go back on: slide out of agreement.
Gold brick: loaf (idle).
Goner: loser.
G.O.P.: Grand Old Party, Republicans.
Graft: illegal bribe money.
Grandstand: playing to audience for personal glory; stadium seating.
Greenback: dollar bill.
Grind: hard studier.
Grip: good hold on situation.
Gripe: complain.
Grist: harvest essence.
Grit: courage.
Grouch: malcontent.
Grub-stake: wherewithal to start an operation.
Gumshoe: detective.
Gusher: strong-flowing oil well.
Guy: fellow.
Hack: taxicab.
Halfbreed: mixture of two races.
Half-cock, go off at: premature action.
Handout: gratuity.
Hatchet, bury the: resolve differences.
Hayseed: unpolished person.
Haze: harass, as an undergraduate.
Heeled, well: well-to-do.
Heeler: servile political operator.
Heft: weight.
Heist: robbery.
Highbinder: ruffian.

High-falutin': pretentious.
High-stepper: high liver.
Hike: walk.
Hired girl: servant.
Hobo: tramp.
Hoe, a long row to: big task ahead.
Hoe-cake: corn meal cake.
Hog: take an excessive portion.
Hoodlum: gangster.
Horse sense: sound judgment.
Howdy: greeting, "How are you?"
Hunk: much.
Husking bee: corn husking party.
Hustle: hurry; deceive.
I.O.U.: note acknowledging debt.
Jag: drunken condition.
Jamboree: carousel.
Jay: simple-minded person.
Jayhawker: plunderer.
Jaywalker: careless pedestrian.
Jerked beef (beef jerky): dried beef.
Jersey lightning: strong drink.
Jibe: agree; or, sarcastic comment.
Jim Crow: discrimination against blacks.
Jim dandy: excellent.
Johnnycake: cornbread.
Joint: cheap place for drinking, dancing.
Joker: hidden deception.
Josh: tease.
Joyride: reckless auto ride.
Jump one's claim: seize another's property.
Kingpin: head of an organization.
Lariat: noosed rope for horse or cattle capture.
Lasso: noosed rope for horse or cattle capture.
Let 'er rip: exclamation of abandonment.
Levee: embankment to prevent river overflow.
Lickety-cut or **lickety-split:** at top speed.
Lightweight: not up to responsibilities.
Limelight: in public eye.
Lineup: arrangement for detective inspection.
Lobby: entrance hall, as in theater.
Log rolling: jockeying for political gain.
Lobby: sluggish.
Long green: U.S. currency.
Loud mouth: obstreperous.
Low down: inside information.

Lumber: walk ponderously.
Lunkhead: stupid person.
Make, on the: looking for a victim.
Mason-Dixon Line: demarcation between Northern and Southern U.S.
Maverick: unbranded or separated calf.
Medicine man: healer in primitive cultures.
Monkey with: interfere.
Moonshine: illicit liquor.
Mosey: shuffle along.
Mossback: ultraconservative person.
Muckrake: dig out the worst information.
Mug: one's face; or, throttling attack from rear.
Mush: one's face; or, drive ahead in snow sled.
Muss: untidy.
Mustang: western horse.
Nary: none.
Nerve: effrontery.
Nifty: stylish.
Notion: whim.
Nubbin: small piece.
Oil, to strike: find oil.
O.K. or **okay:** all right.
One horse: very small, as town.
One ear, **to knock on:** strike down.
Ornery: contrary.
Paleface: white man.
Panhandle: beg.
Pan out: develop satisfactorily.
Papoose: Indian baby (derogatory).
Pardner: working companion.
Pass out: faint; or, die.
Pass the buck: shift responsibility.
Pat, to stand: take unchangeable position.
Pay dirt: reward long worked for.
PDQ: pretty damned quick.
Peaked: ill.
Pesky: annoying.
Picayune: insignificant.
Pickaninny: black baby (derogatory).
Pick-up: casual acquaintance.
Piker: small-time operator.
Pile, make a: build a fortune.
Pinch: an arrest.
Pipe, it's a: easy task ("it's a lead pipe cinch").
Pipe down: keep quiet.

Pipe dream: imaginary good luck.
Plank down: pay.
Plug: promote.
Plug-ugly: a tough.
Possum, play: feign sleep or ignorance.
Post: inform.
PowWow: Indian conference.
Prairie schooner: covered wagon.
Prince Albert: long frocked coat.
Private eye: privately engaged detective.
Pronto: immediately.
Pull, to have: possess influence.
Pull one's leg: deceive, often in fun.
Pull up stakes: leave.
Quitter: unpersevering person.
Ragtime: effervescent music.
Railroad: push through with undue speed.
Raise the ante: increase the bet.
Rake-off: portion of profit, or graft.
Razzle-Dazzle: commotion to distract.
Red: Russian; communist.
Redskin: Indian (derogatory).
Rig: conveyance; or, arrange to win unfairly.
Right off: at once.
Rile: disturb.
Rook: cheat.
Roost: stay in one place, as overnight.
Rope in: persuade for improper advantage.
Rounder: No-good playboy.
Roundup: gather cattle into a herd.
Roustabout: intermittent worker.
Rowdy: rough individual.
Rubber: to gawk.
Rubberneck: sightsee.
Sachem: head man.
Sand: courage.
Sandhog: caisson worker.
Savvy: appropriate knowledge.
Scads: much.
Scalawag: crook.
Scalp: overcharge.
Scarehead: big headline.
Schooner: tall glass for beer or ale.
Scofflaw: disregarder of traffic tickets.
Scoop: get a news story ahead of the competition.
Scram: go away quickly.

Scratch, start from: begin with nothing.
Settle: quiet a person; or, pay a debt.
Shack: shanty.
Shake-down: extortion.
Shakes, no great: not so good as claimed.
Shakes, the: nervous condition.
Shanghai: drug and impress into ship service.
Shank: latter part of something.
Shebang: affair or company.
Shiner: black eye.
Shingle: sign of a doctor or lawyer.
Showdown: final determination.
Shucks: exclamation or regret.
Sinker: doughnut.
Six-shooter: revolver.
Skeddaddle: run away.
Skin: outdo in a deal.
Skunk: low person; defeat totally.
Skyscraper: extra tall building.
Slated: nominated for election.
Sleeper: Pullman car or train.
Slick: tricky.
Slingshot: forked stick-and-rubber-band stone hurling device.
Slob: slovenly person.
Slouch: shiftless posture.
Slowdown: union technique of less work.
Slug: portion of drink; physical punch.
Slush fund: secret political money.
Snag, strike a: come up against an obstacle.
Sneakers: canvas rubber-soled slippers.
Snitch: tattle.
Sockdolager: exceptionally big item.
Sob stuff: lushly sentimental.
Soft snap: easy job.
Spat: disagreement, usually in family.
Speakeasy: unlicensed drinking spot.
Spike a rumor: correct misinformation.
Spill the news: reveal previously undisclosed information.
Spondulics: money.
Spotlight: focused public attention.
Spread eagle: cover the entire field; bombastic patriotism.
Spread oneself: spend excessively.
Speed over: hurry to the place.
Square: a non-up-to-date person.
Square oneself: make restitution.
Squatter: occupier of land who has no title to the property.

Squeal: inform on criminal.
Stag party: male celebration.
Stampede: sudden excited flight.
Stand-in: substitute.
Standoff: evade.
Stoop: porch.
Straddle: appear to favor both sides.
Straight: honest.
Strap-hanger: subway or bus rider.
Straw boss: secondary foreman.
Streak: run or drive fast; appear deliberately unclothed in public
    while moving fast.
Stump the country: speechmaking around.
Stung: deceived or cheated.
Succotash: corn and beans, mixed.
Sulky: two wheeled racing vehicle.
Surprise party: affair to honor unsuspecting person.
Swan, wal I: exclamation of surprise.
Switch: change.
Take for a ride: gangster death ride.
Tanglefoot: cheap whiskey.
Thank-you-ma'am: pothole in road.
Third degree: heavy pressure for confession.
Thumper: big fellow.
Tickler: follow-up system.
Tidy: orderly.
Tiger: emphatic yell at end of college cheer.
Toot: drinking orgy.
Tote: carry away or steal.
Touch: borrow money.
Tracks, make: run away.
Truck farmer: vegetable farmer.
Tuckered out: fatigued.
Tuxedo: tailless dress coat.
Up to you: the decision is yours.
Vamoose: decamp hurriedly or secretly.
Wad: a lot of money.
Wampum: money.
Washout: dull, unexciting person or affair.
Whale: strike a person repeatedly.
Wet blanket: depressing person.
Wheelhorse: hard worker.
Whitecap: white crested wave.
Whitewing: street cleaner.
Whole kit and kaboodle: everything.
Whodunit: murder mystery.

Whoop it up: celebrate.
Wire-puller: maneuverer.
Yegg: safeblower.
Yellow dog: coward.
You bet: "You're right" (also "You betcha").

BRITICISMS

Bag: grip or luggage.
Bag-man: traveling salesman.
Beet-roots: beets.
Berth: dock.
Big shop: department store.
Bill: check.
Biscuit: cracker or cookie.
Blind: shade.
Board-residence: board and lodging.
Bonnet: hood of car.
Booking agent: ticket agent.
Booking clerk: ticket seller.
Booking office: ticket office.
Bookstall: bookstore.
Boot: shoe, trunk of car.
Boots: shoeblack.
Box: trunk.
Braces: suspenders.
Carriage: passenger car.
Chemist's shop: drugstore.
Counter-jumper or **counterman**: sales clerk.
Cupboard: closet.
Draper: dry goods merchant.
Drapery: dry goods.
Draughts: checkers.
Driver: locomotive engineer.
Egg flip: milk punch.
Flat: apartment.
Footpath: sidewalk.
Frock: dress.
Frock coat: Prince Albert coat.
Galoshes: overshoes, rubbers.
Garden: front yard.
Gnat: mosquito.
Goods shed: warehouse.
Goods trains: freight train.
Goods truck, van, wagon: freight car.
Gradient: grade.

Grangerize: supplement book with extra material.
Guard: conductor.
Guard's van: caboose.
Gum: mucilage.
Haberdashery: men's furnishings store.
Hall porter: doorman.
Innkeeper: tavern or hotel keeper.
Ironmonger: hardware seller.
Jolly: uncommonly, very.
Jug: pitcher.
Ladder: run (in stocking).
Leader: editorial.
Leaderette: editorial paragraph.
Lift: elevator.
Lift man: elevator operator.
Lorry: truck.
Luggage van: baggage car.
Mess about: to disorder.
Metals: railroad rails.
Motor: automobile.
Omnibus: bus.
Oxford ties: shoes.
Pail (for coal): scuttle.
Pair of horses: team.
Petrol: gasoline.
Pillar-box (or post): mailbox.
Points: switches.
Points man: switchman.
Porridge: oatmeal.
Post: mail.
Post bag: mailbag.
Pressman: journalist.
Publican: saloon keeper.
Public house: saloon.
Rates: local property taxes.
Reel of cotton: spool of thread.
Ripping: enjoyable.
Roll: biscuit.
Saloon carriage: parlor car.
Satchel: lunch box.
Scullery: pantry.
Shunt: switch.
Shunter: switchman.
Spanner: wrench.
Stairs: stepladder.
Stall: orchestra seat.

Stoker: fireman.
Stop: stay.
Store magazine: factory.
Storey (of building): story.
Subscription ticket: commutation ticket.
Suspenders: garters.
Sweets: candy.
Take silk: become a judge.
Tariff: scale of charges, bill of fare.
Ticket: check.
Tidy: good; pretty.
Tinned: canned.
Torch: flashlight.
Tram: streetcar.
Tramway: streetcar line.
Tub (verb): bathe.
Tub (noun): bath.
Tyre: tire.
Waistcoat: vest.
Walking stick: cane.
Wireless: radio.

COMMON EXPRESSIONS

Ace in the hole.
At sixes and sevens.
Ax to grind.
Backseat driver.
Baker's dozen.
Bats in his belfry.
Bear by the tail.
Beat around the bush.
Bell the cat.
Between the devil and the
     deep blue sea.
Between a rock and a
     hard spot.
Bit off more than he
     could chew.
Blow hot and cold.
Bone to pick with you.
Break the ice.
Break a leg.
Bring home the bacon.
Brought down the house.
Bunch of baloney.

Burn the candle at
     both ends.
Bury the hatchet.
Calm before the storm.
Can't take it with you.
Chicken feed.
Chip on his shoulder.
Chip off the old block.
Clean as a whistle.
Crocodile tears.
Dark horse.
Dirty work at the crossroads.
Doing a land-office business.
Do it up brown.
Don't look a gift horse in the
     mouth.
Don't call us, we'll call you.
Don't take any wooden
     nickels.
Drinks like a fish.
Drugstore cowboy.
Dutch treat.
Feather in his cap.

Feed the kitty.
Feeling his oats.
Fly in the ointment.
First hundred years are
    the hardest.
Fly off the handle.
Get down to brass tacks.
Gets in my hair.
Give him the raspberry.
Give the little girl a
    big hand.
Go fly a kite.
Got cold feet.
Got up on the wrong side of
    the bed.
Have a heart.
He's a four-flusher.
Hitting on all fours.
I'll bite.
I'm from Missouri.
In on the ground floor.
In the pink.
In the red.
It's a dog's life.
It's for the birds.
It's in the bag.
It's in the cards.
It's old hat.
Keeping up with the Joneses.
Keep your shirt on.
Key to the city.
Laid an egg.
Learn the ropes.
Life of Riley.
Never turned a hair.

No love lost between them.
Nose to the grindstone.
Not by a long shot.
Not my dish of tea.
On the ball.
On the spot.
Off his rocker.
Paint the town red.
Pass the buck.
Pay through the nose.
Pull the wool over his eyes.
Pull your leg.
Put it on the cuff.
Raining cats and dogs.
Rings a bell.
Rob Peter to pay Paul.
She's just a clothes horse.
Shotgun wedding.
Skeleton in the closet.
Smell a rat.
Sock it to me.
Tail between his legs.
Take it or leave it.
Take it with a grain of salt.
That's banana oil.
Took him for a ride.
Took him for all he
    was worth.
Too many irons in the fire.
Under the weather.
What's the dope?
When in Rome do as the
    Romans do.
Wine, women and song.
You're the doctor.

PHRASES, IDIOMS, AND COLLOQUIALISMS

A chip off the old block.
A promise made is a debt unpaid.
As alike as two peas.
Ball and chain.
Better half.
Bitter with the sweet.
By the skin of the teeth.
Cross the Rubicon.

Darkest before dawn.
Everybody's doing it.
Feet of clay.
Flag waving.
Four-flusher.
Gold standard.
Gotta see a man about a dog.
Hang your clothes on a hickory limb but don't go near the water.
He's not worth his salt.
Here today, gone tomorrow.
House built on sand.
Hundred percenter.
I'll fight it out on this line if it takes all summer.
If the mountain will not come to Mohammed, Mohammed will go to
    the mountain.
It pays to advertise.
It's bred in the bone.
Keys of the city.
Knocked into a cocked hat.
Life is just a bowl of cherries.
Lot of water over the dam.
Love is blind.
May the best man win.
Mazuma,.
Milk of human kindness.
Mother love.
Never kick a man when he's down.
Out of the frying pan into the fire.
Pot of gold at the end of the rainbow.
Put your shoulder to the wheel.
She's no bargain.
Shines like a good deed in a naughty world.
Something's rotten in Denmark.
Sound in mind and body.
Tempus fugit.
That's a horse of a different color.
The cat's whiskers (or pajamas).
The good die young.
The Judas kiss.
The king is dead, long live the king.
The last, long mile.
The straight and narrow.
The straw that broke the camel's back.
The time, the mood, the place.
The ugly duckling.
Three lights on a match.

Three sheets to the wind.
Time marches on.
Time will tell.
Two-edged sword.
Two bits.
Unpardonable sin.
Vanity, vanity, all is vanity.
Wolf in sheep's clothing.

SHORT-ORDER COOK SLANG

Adam and Eve on a raft: poached eggs on toast.
Adam and Eve on a raft, wreck it: scrambled eggs on toast.
Brown cow: chocolate milk.
Burn one: malted milk with chocolate ice cream.
Cowboy: western omelette.
Cremate: well done.
Draw one: coffee.
Eight-six: no more left.
Grade A, or **Squeeze one**: milk.
Hold the grass: no lettuce.
Lumber: toothpicks.
Schmear: cream cheese.
Short stack: two pancakes.
B.L.T. down: bacon, lettuce and tomato sandwich on white toast.
O.J.: orange juice.
T.J.: tomato juice.
With shoes on: order, to go out.

SLANGUAGE

The purpose of this list of slang words is to add to their literal meanings as found in common dictionaries. For example, the literal meaning of the word "buns" would normally be described in a dictionary as "small rolls," whereas the slang expression "buns" refers to "buttocks."

Slang words often have more than one meaning and the meanings often change. When you're using slang, check if the words are still being used that way (or are contemporaneous with the story) or if they have taken on other meanings as well.

Much slang is profane or obscene. If your characters use such language, consult a contemporary slang dictionary for the more raw sorts of gutter talk.

Bag: to grab; arrest; purse; a form of drug distribution.
Bang: intercourse.
Bazooms: large breasts.

Beat: tired; take away as in "beat him out of it."
Beaut: beautiful, excellent.
Berk: kill.
Bi: bisexual.
Bimbo: girl, slut.
Bird: a girl; obscene, insulting gesture with middle finger.
Bit: your thing, what you do best, as in "did his bit."
Blast: wild party, good time; shoot.
Blow: leave; spend; play an instrument.
Bod: body.
Bombed: intoxicated, under the influence of alcohol or drugs.
Bone: study hard.
Boobs: breasts.
Bottom Line: the last; the way it is.
Boxed: caught in, surrounded.
Boxcars: pair of sixes in dice.
Brass: top management, the bosses.
Broad: female.
Buck: go against; trying to achieve; dollar bill.
Bug: annoy; crazy.
Bum: borrow; hang around; slumming.
Bum steer: mislead.
Burn: steal; got a bad deal; kill; angry facial expression.
Bust: hit; broke; to fail as in "busted out"; police raid, arrest.
Butch: gay man or lesbian who plays masculine role;
    masculine hairstyle.
Buy: to accept or believe something.
Buzz: feeling high, light headed.
Call: confront someone.
Can: fired; the bathroom; jail cell; buttocks.
Cap it: put a lid on it; shut up.
Cat: hip person.
Catch: female part in homosexual relationship.
Chalk: in horse racing, a favorite; cocaine.
Cherry: virgin.
Chick: female.
Chicken: frightened, coward.
Chicken shit: red tape; despicable act.
Clap: venereal disease; gonorrhea.
Closet: in hiding; not revealing other side of person.
Clock: person's brain.
Cool: okay, good.
Cop: steal; plead, as in "cop a plea."
Cop out: beg off; pull out; admit to something.
Cowboy: wild guy.

Crash: go where not invited; fall asleep; use someone's pad (dwelling).
Croaker: unethical doctor.
Cut out: to leave.
Daisy chain: sexual activity between three or more people.
Deal: earning money by selling drugs.
Dig: understand.
Dime: ten dollars.
Dirty: possessing drugs.
Divvy: divide up.
Do: oral copulation; kill, as in "do him."
Doll: a drug in pill form.
Downer: depressant; insult; sad ending.
Drag: puff; bored; unpleasant.
Dump: bowel movement.
Dyke: lesbian.
Far out: out of the ordinary.
Fay: derogatory term for white person.
Finger: point out someone; obscene, insulting gesture with middle finger.
Fink: squealer; creep; informer.
Fink out: to fail to perform.
Flag: stop.
Flake: phony; irresponsible; unbalanced; crazy, cocaine.
Flap: backtalk.
Flick: movie.
Flip: go crazy; change.
Fox: Attractive female.
Foxy: desirable.
Freak out: lose control; go crazy.
Funky: with the times.
Fuzz: police.
Gangbang: more than two males having intercourse with one female.
George: okay: to seduce and have sex with; a bowel movement.
Globes: female breasts.
Gleep: an insult.
Greaser: derogatory description of a Mexican.
Gross: disgusting.
Hack: taxicab; cliche; tolerate; one doing routine work.
Handle: name; cope.
Hang loose: stay relaxed.
Hang tough: stick with it.
Hangup: emotional or psychological problem.
Haggle: argue over.
Hard time: stiff prison term.

Hassle: conflict.
Header: took a fall; went down head first.
Heat: police.
Heavy: bad guy; deep; disturbing.
Heeded: having money.
Heist: robbery.
Hip: aware, with it.
Hit: kill by contract.
Home boy: black male.
Honcho: leader; powerful.
Honky: derogatory name for white person.
Horny: need for sexual release.
Hype: swindle; con; promotion.
Ice: kill.
In: socially acceptable.
Jazz: extraneous talk, "cut the jazz."
Jive: bullshit, lies.
Job: police term for being on the force.
Jugs: female breasts.
Juice: strength; connections.
Kiester: rear end.
Kibitz: watch; partake; clown around.
Kicks: good time.
Kiss ass: play up to someone.
Kite: write bad checks.
Knockers: female breasts.
Kype: steal.
Lace: money.
Later: good-by; "see you later."
Lez: lesbian.
Lift: steal.
Loaded: rich; drunk.
Long: abundance of anything; "long bucks" or "long green" is lots of money; "long on drugs."
Long gone: be gone from here.
Loose: sexually promiscuous.
Make: detect something or someone.
Man: The Man: police.
Mean: good, as in "he plays a mean trumpet."
Mickey Mouse: policeman.
Mister Charlie: white man; boss; the establishment.
Moxie: courage; loudmouth.
Narc: narcotics officer.
Nebbish: helpless, unfortunate person; poor soul.
Nicked: arrested.
Nickel: five dollars; five-year prison term.

Nerd: poor soul; dumb; lacking social graces.
Ofay: derogatory name for white person.
Offed: killed.
On: center of attention, as in "being on."
Originals: Levi's that have never been washed.
Pad: apartment; home.
Picker: peeping tom.
Piece: sexual intercourse; gun.
Pinky: white person.
Pissed: angry, drunk.
Plastic: credit cards.
Po' boy: welfare check.
Rap: talk.
Read: understand, as in "do you read me?"
Ride: annoy, pester.
Rip: as to rip off, steal; get away with.
Sack: bed; fire.
Scabbed: cheated.
Score: make out; obtain.
Scratch: money; delete.
Shack up: move in with; live with; have sex with.
Shades: sunglasses.
Shaft: take advantage of; get rid of; fire.
Shuck: jive; bullshit.
Sickie: someone off balance, mentally ill, deranged.
Silk: white person.
Sister: black woman.
Skin: handshake.
Skinny: truth.
Slide: leave, depart.
Smack: heroin.
Smokey: good.
Snow: fool; lie to.
Snuff: kill.
Space: need of privacy, room to breathe.
Spaced out: high on drugs.
Specs: eyeglasses.
Spill: talk.
Spookey: weird, strange.
Stash: supply of drugs.
Stew: airline stewardess.
Stir: prison.
Stoned: drunk or high on drugs.
Stool, stoolie: informer.
Straight: heterosexual; clean of drugs.
Suede: black person.

Swing: go to parties; have sex.
Switch hitter: bisexual.
Tacky: lack of good taste.
Tapioca: broke.
Tapped: broke.
Ticked off: angry.
Tight: close.
Want: a warrant for arrest.
Wasp: white Anglo-Saxon Protestant.
Waste: kill.
Whacko: nut.
Wheels: car, vehicle.
Wigged: upset, crazy.
White spot: white person who associates with black people.
Whitey: white person.
Wiped: killed.
Wired: high on drugs.
Wiseguy: mobster.
Working girl: prostitute.
Wrinkle room: gay bar.
Zap: exclamation for movement, action.
Zonk: kill.
Zonked: high, out cold.

RECENT COMMON EXPRESSIONS

Beats me.
Bent out of shape.
Bought the farm.
Bug off.
Closet queen.
Cool it.
Cut out.
Deep six him.
Do your thing.
Don't dump on me.
Don't lose your cool.
Don't piss me off.
Don't press my button.
Don't sweat it.
Don't tread on me.
Flesh peddler.
Get lost.
Get off my back.
Get off my case.
Got it made.

Hot to trot.
I'm gone.
I'm outta here.
It's a blast.
It's a cop out.
It's in the bag.
Keep the faith.
Lighten up.
Make my day.
Make tracks.
Make your move.
Nobody's perfect.
Off the wall.
On his uppers.
Out of his gourd.
Out of sight.
Piss off.
Put a lid on it.
Put the make on.
Read my lips.

Right on.
Standup guy.
Stop flappin' your gums.
Straighten up and fly right.
Take a hike.

That's heavy.
They're good people.
To be in deep shit.
We shall overcome.
What's happening.

DOWN-HOME TALK

There's probably a book that captured the colorful and imaginative words of "down-home," country talk. If there isn't one, somebody ought to write a collection of the vivid expressions that folks in rural areas use every day.

Though you're probably acquainted with some of these already, here's some down-homers I managed to pick up over the years.

A piece: some distance away.
Baignet: a French-style doughnut (New Orleans).
Balky: a wino (New England).
Binder: a rubber band (Minnesota).
Boiled dinner: a heated argument (New England).
Boondocks, the boonies: way out in nowhere.
Boondoggle: not doing it well, whatever it is.
Boots: car tires.
Bought the thumb: storekeeper's thumb is added to the scale.
Briarpatch kid: born out of wedlock.
Buckle buster: very funny.
Bumpkin: country person, redneck, hayseed.
Buzz: boozed.
Car bonnet: hood of automobile.
Car shoes: auto brakes.
Cleaned his plow: beat him up.
Cocksure: overconfident.
Coon's age: a long time.
Cooties: lice.
Crank it up: start the car.
Crab thumper: Maryland native.
Deaf as a post: stone deaf.
Don't give a hoot: don't care.
Doozie: real sharp, special, really something.
Dotlin: small child.
Double dyed: very good quality.
Duffer: old fool, awkward.
Fair t' middlin': okay, all right, in between.
Fallin' off: losing weight.
Fetch: bring.
Fiddlesticks: baloney, lot of hot air.

Fit as a fiddle: feeling great, raring to go.
Fixin': preparing to do something.
Fleshened up: put on weight.
Foose: beer foam.
Frog skins: money.
Get born: wake up.
Giggle soup: hard liquor (North Carolina).
Go-to-meetin' clothes: clothes normally worn to church services.
Godfrey mighty: an exclamation (Maine).
Gussied up: fancily dressed.
Heap: lots of.
Hey y'all: hello.
Hobo: sandwich.
Hogwallers: mud holes.
Hornswaggled: bewildered.
Hot ticket: fast girl.
Irish turkey: corned beef and cabbage.
Jawbreakers: hard candy.
Jawin': talking a lot.
Juggin': drinking alcohol.
Lallygag: hang around; lag behind; flirt.
Later: goodbye (Maine).
Liar's bench: bench in front of a country store.
Loose as a goose: feeling no pain.
Mean as a skunk: as nasty as you can get.
Mess: enough fish for a whole meal.
Nary: none.
Nasties: sick, not feeling well.
Nose is outta joint: upset, jealous.
Numbnuts: stupid person.
Old coot: old man.
One in the oven: pregnant.
One-man band: wedding ring.
Plumb: all, as in "plumb tuckered out."
Poh'boy: Texas sandwich.
Poke: bag.
Porch: veranda, stoop.
Privy: outhouse.
Puckered up: angry; ready to be kissed.
Rig: car, truck, vehicle
Right much: large amount (North Carolina).
Right smart: sharp.
Righten up: tidy the room (Maine).
See y'all: see you later, see you around.
Simmer down: quiet.
Sittin'on the nest: pregnant.

Slew: many.
Speck not: probably not.
Specs: eyeglasses.
Sprinklin': tiny amount, equal to a "tad."
Sticks: rural.
Tad: very small amount.
Tan yore hide: give a good spanking, beat up.
Thanks a heap: thanks a lot.
Thigh slapper: real funny.
Toad floater: heavy rain.
Tol'able: fair amount; put up with.
Tongue bangin': a scolding.
Trashy poor: very poor.
Tuckered out: tired.
Turtle: one lacking an education.
Uppity: haughty.
We'uns: us.
Wet boot: very tight.
Yardbirds: chickens.
Yea, bo!: you bet; certainly.
You'uns: you people.
Young 'uns: children.

SOUTHERN WORDS AND SAYINGS

Aim to: plan to do.
Airish: cold.
Backslider: fallen from grace, or left the fold.
Bad to: reputation for liking; "bad to fish."
Biggity: vain, overbearing, haughty.
Bitty Bit: a small amount, term often used by women.
Branch water: usually water from well or water system (may be from stream or "branch," i.e., a creek).
Broomsage: dry wild straw, wrapped and fastened together with twine. Used for house broom.
Brushbroom: yard broom made from branches of dogwood sprouts and other pliable trees. Used to sweep dirt yards. Also makes good switch.
Carry on: to act foolishly.
Carry: to tote.
Chaps: children, usually male.
Chunk: throw, toss.
Clodhopper: field worker or heavy work shoes.
Cowlick: hair standing out on one's head (looks like cow licked it).
Curious: peculiar in habit or action.

Dinner on the ground: covered dish picnic often served at all-day preaching or singing.

Directly: in a little while, or a couple of weeks.

Doo-hicky: substitute name. Same as watcha-ma-call-it or thinga-majig.

Fix: to prepare, as in fix breakfast.

Fixing to: about to, or think about starting.

Hey or Hay: hello.

Much obliged: thank you; hope to return favor.

Piddle: waste time, doing nothing particular.

Reckon: think or suppose so.

HOW TO SPEAK SOUTHERN

Ah: the thing you see with, and the personal pronoun denoting individuality. "Ah think ah've got somethin' in mah ah."

Aig: a breakfast food that may be fried, scrambled, boiled or poached. "Which came first, the chick or the aig?"

Aint: the sister of your mother or father. "Son, go over and give your Aint Bea a big hug."

Arn: an electrical instrument used to remove wrinkles from clothing. "Ah'm not gonna arn today. It's too hot."

Arshtaters: a staple of the Irish diet and the source of french fries. "Ah like arshtaters, but ah hate to peel 'em."

Awf: the opposite of on. "Take your muddy feet awf the table."

Awraht: okay. "If you want to go back home to your mother, the's awraht with me."

Bad off: desperately in need of, also extremely ill. "Jim's in the hospital. He's bad off."

Batry: a boxlike device that produces electricity. "Looks like your car's got a dead batry."

Bidness: the art of selling something. "My cousin Archie is in the real estate bidness."

Bobbycue: a delectable southern sandwich that is, according to North Carolina natives, prepared properly only in certain parts of North Carolina. It consists of chopped pork, cole slaw, and a fiery sauce made of vinegar, red pepper, and ketchup. "Four bobbycues to go, please."

Bound to: certain to. "Too much beer is bound to give you a hangover."

Caint: cannot. "Ah just caint understand why this checkbook won't balance."

Co-cola: the soft drink that started in Atlanta and conquered the world. "Ah hear they even sell Co-cola in Russia."

Cut awf: to switch off. "It's too bright in here, honey. Why don't we cut awf that light bulb?"

Dinner: the meal southerners eat while northerners are eating lunch. When the northerners are eating dinner, southerners are eating supper. "We're just havin' butterbeans and biscuits for dinner, but we'll have a big supper."

Doc: a condition caused by an absence of light. "It's mighty doc in here."

Done: finished; already. "Has the bus done gone?"

Far: a state of combustion that produces heat and light. "Ah reckon it's about time to put out the far and call in the dawgs."

Fayan: an electrical appliance that circulates air. "It's hot in here. Cut on that fayan."

Fixin: preparing to. "Ah'm fixin to dig me some worms and go fishin'."

Fur piece: a considerable distance. "It's a fur piece from here to Jacksonville."

Git: to acquire. "If you're goin' to the store, git me a six-pack of beer."

Heepa: a great deal of. "You in a heepa trouble, boy."

Hep: to aid or benefit. "Ah can't hep it if ah'm still in love with you."

Hern (and **hisn**): feminine (and masculine) possessive, and the opposite of hisn. "Is that blonde hair really hern?"

Libel: likely to, liable. "If your wife finds out you're runnin' around with that go-go dancer, she's libel to kill you."

Light bread: a pre-sliced loaf of soft, white, store-bought bread.

Muchablige: thank you. "Muchablige for the lift, mister."

Nome: a child's negative reply to a female adult's question. "Jimmy, did you pull that cat's tail?" "Nome."

Picayunish: overly fastidious, picky. "That little blood spot won't hurt that egg. Don't be so picayunish."

Play like: to pretend. "You play like you're the nurse and I'll be the doctor."

Rench: to wash off soapy water with clear water. "Ah'll wash the dishes if you'll rench 'em."

Rernt: ruined. "Boy drove that car so rough he's plum rernt it."

Sugar: a kiss. "Come here an give your momma some sugar."

Tacky: an expression used exclusively by southern females and almost always in regard to wearing apparel. Can mean anything from unfashionable to downright ugly. "Did you see that dress she was wearin'? Honey, it was so tacky."

Tar: a round inflatable object that sometimes goes flat. "You shouldn't drive that car without a spare tar."

Warshrag: a cloth used for cleaning people or dishes. "Hang up that warshrag when you're done usin' it."

Wore out: exhausted, used up. "No use tryin' to fix that washing machine. It's plum wore out."

Yankee dime: a kiss. "How 'bout a yankee dime, sugar?"

Yawl: a useful southern word that is consistently misused by northerners when they try to mimic a southern accent, which they do with appalling regularity. Yawl is always plural because it means you-all, or all of you. It is never—repeat—never used in reference to only one person. At least not by southerners. "Where yawl goin'?"

Reference Note: for slanguage related to police and crime, see *The Writer's Complete Crime Reference*, Writer's Digest Books, 1990.

22

Locations

Following are lists of locations associated with the elderly, with youth, and a list of general locations. These location lists are in addition to lists in other chapters tailored to the writing genres covered there.

The list of film commissions can aid you in getting further information on locations in the U.S. and several other countries.

UNUSUAL LOCATIONS

A location is unusual or offbeat depending on what type of scene the writer intends to play there. For example, the following locations would be unusual for a romantic sequence.

A roller rink
A roller derby
Going up or down an escalator
In a fish market
In a graveyard
In a fully occupied elevator
In an auto wrecking yard
Inside a men's or ladles' restroom
Moving through a busy restaurant kitchen
Mud wrestling matches
Right smack in the middle of army or naval maneuvers, etc.

These locations would not give the same effect as the beach scene in *From Here to Eternity,* or the country scene in the classic *Picnic.*

Those are the more traditional locations. If your romantic scene is to have more charm and humor, then try to write the scene in a location that is in high contrast to the mood in which your characters would normally be..

When writing a comedy scene, the more solemn, staid, or stuffy the location, the better. What really made the "woman having an orgasm" scene in the film *When Harry Met Sally,* was playing the scene in the middle of a busy delicatessen while customers around them were eating.

The scene would not have been half as funny had it been played in one of their apartments. If you're going for slapstick, it's better to have those pies flung at a high society affair than in a bakery.

Chase scenes along long stretches of country road or going around a dozen or so curves in the road are boring and have been done to death. Even the chase scene under the elevated train and going against traffic has been way overdone.

What suggestions do I have to make? Well, how about:

Across a golf course
Across a crowded park and along the bridle path
Onto the runways of a major airport during the busiest time
of the day
Onto a crowded beach filled with sun worshippers
Through a zoo or wild animal park

LOCATIONS ASSOCIATED WITH THE ELDERLY

Community center	Park
Convalescent hospital	Park bench
Cruise	Retirement hotel
Home	Retirement resort
Library	Social club
Museum	Tour
Nursing home	Veterans' hospital

LOCATIONS ASSOCIATED WITH YOUTH

Athletic field	Disco
Backyard	Fast food restaurant
Bar	Fraternity house
Beach	Friends' house
Bookstore	Gadget store
Bowling alley	Gym
Bridle path	Hobby shop
Camp ground	Library
Classroom	Movie house
Club house	Neighborhood hangout
College campus	Record store

Room at home
School yard
Ski lodge

Sports facility
Street corner
Swimming hole

FOREIGN BEACHES

CHILE: Vina del Mar
CUBA: Varadero
EGYPT: Alexandria Beaches
ENGLAND: Beachy Head, Bexhill-On-Sea, Bournemouth, Brighton,
Bude, Falmouth, Jersey (Island), Margate, Newquay,
Weymouth
FRANCE: Biarritz, Cabasson, Cannes, Cavaliere, Le Levandou, Le
Touquet-Paris-Plage, Nice, Pompelone, Riviera, Saint Clair,
Salins
GERMANY: Travemünde
GREECE: Glyfadi, Kalamaki, Phaliron
IRELAND: Traymore, Youghal
ISRAEL: Tel Aviv
ITALY: Lido, Liguria, Marina di Ravenna, Nettuno, Osta Mare,
Rapallo, Rimini, San Remo, Viareggio
MEXICO: Acapulco
MONACO: Monte Carlo
POLAND: Sopot
PUERTO RICO: Buck Island, Dorado
SOVIET UNION: Kobuliti (Georgia), Mamaia (Black Sea)
SPAIN: Benidorm, Costa Blanca, Costa de Sol, Deva, La Coucha,
Ondaretta, San Sebastian
TURKEY: Anamur, Antalya
URUGUAY: Montevideo
VIET NAM: Cap St. Jacques
WINDWARD ISLANDS: Vigie, St. Lucia
YUGOSLAVIA: Dalmatia

ARCHAEOLOGICAL AREAS
(representative locations where important findings have occurred)

ANDES MOUNTAINS: ruins of cities
AFRICA: South Rhodesia, Carthage, Zimbabwe Palace
AUSTRIA: Hallstatt
BULGARIA
BURMA: temples, sculpture
CENTRAL AMERICA: Mayan civilization
CRETE: Phaistos Palace, inscribed stone
EAST COAST OF AFRICA
EASTER ISLAND: statues from indigenous rock
EGYPT: Tel-el-Amarna, Oxyrhyneus, Luxor, etc.

ENGLAND: pillars of Stonehenge, Dorsetshire pre-Roman remains, Silchester, etc.
EUROPE: cave paintings
FAR EAST
FRANCE: Lascaux cavern paintings
GREECE: excavated cities, e.g., Olympia and Salonika
INDIA: sculptures, city ruins
IRAQ: Nineveh
ISRAEL: Masada in Judea, the mountain-top fortress
ITALY: Etruscan remains, Pompeii, etc.
JORDAN: Petra ruins, Ruweiha ruins, manuscript finds in Qumran
MEXICO: Mexico City, Mayan and Aztec ruins, Tenochtitlan, Olmec sculptures
MIDDLE EAST: city ruins
NEBRASKA: Lynch
PALESTINE: Megiddo
PERU: Nazca, designes on plain, Cuzco Inca ruins
SPAIN: cave paintings
TURKEY: Gordion
WICKLIFFE, KENTUCKY: Indian city
YUCATAN: Mayan paintings
YUNAN PROVINCE, CHInA: bronze statuary

AREAS, CENTERS, PARKS, AND SUBURBS IN THE U.S.

ATLANTA: Decatur, Marietta, Peachtree Center
BOSTON: Back Bay, Brookline, Cambridge, Newton, Roxbury
CHICAGO: Evanston, "Gold Coast," Lake Forest, The "Loop," Oak Park, Crumb Hill, Stockyards, "Old Town" Triangle
CLEVELAND: Cleveland Heights, Shaker Heights
DALLAS: Fair Park, White Rock Lake Park
DETROIT: Belle Isle, Birmingham, Bloomfield Hills, Grosse Point, Lafayette Square
HARTFORD: Constitution Plaza
HOLLYWOOD, FL: Gold Coast, Millionaire's Row
HOUSTON: Bellaire, River Oaks, West University
JERSEY CITY: Journal Square, Lincoln Park
KANSAS CITY: Swope Park
LOS ANGELES: Bel Air, Beverly Hills, Black Channel, Griffith Park, Downey, Glendale, Hancock Park, Hollywood, Holmby Hills, Pasadena, Pomona, Riverside, San Bernardino, Watts
MIAMI: Coral Gables
NEW HAVEN: Worcester Square
NEW YORK: Chinatown, Bronxville, Easthampton, Financial District, Garment District, Greenwich, Connecticut, Greenwich Village, Harlem, New Rochelle, Rockefeller Center, Rye,

Forest Hills, Sugar Hill, Scarsdale, Times Square, 34th Street, Shopping Districts, Bughouse Square (Union Square), Lincoln Center

NEW ORLEANS: French Quarter (Vieux Carré), Storyville (old bordello section)

PHILADELPHIA: Bala-Cynwyd, Chestnut Hill, Drexel Hill, Germantown ("Main Line"), Upper Darby, West Chester, Independence Mall, Penn Center

PITTSBURGH: Golden Triangle, Sewickley (suburb), Gateway Center

PORTLAND, ME.: Big Eddy (Skid Row)

RALEIGH, N.C.: Capitol Square

SANTA BARBARA: Montecito

SAN DIEGO: Balboa Park, Gaslamp District

SAN FRANCISCO: Berkeley, Chinatown, Latin Quarter, Nob Hill, Telegraph Hill, Oakland, Trocadero, Daly City

SYRACUSE: Bradford Hills

ST. LOUIS: Forest Park, Plaza Redevelopment

WASHINGTON, D.C.: Alexandria, Arlington, Chevy Chase, Foggy Bottom, Georgetown, The Mall, Silver Spring, MD, Somerset

FOREIGN AREAS, CENTERS, PARKS, AND SUBURBS

ALGIERS: Casbah

ANKARA: Youth Park

ATHENS: Praeus

BANGKOK: Thonburi Area

BELGRADE: New Belgrade

BERLIN: Friedrichstadt, Spandau, Europa Center

BOMBAY: The Fort, Malabar Hill

BRUSSELS: Grand Plaza (or Palace)

BUDAPEST: Holy Trinity Square, Kossuth Square, Margaret Island

BUENOS AIRES: Belgrano, Flores, Plaza de Mayo, Ramos Mejia

CAIRO: Heliopolus

CALCUTTA: Chitpur, Cossipore, Manicktala

CAPETOWN: Kirstenbosch, Mowbray, Rondebush

CARACAS: Los Caobos, Plaza Bowar

COPENHAGEN: Raahuspladsen, Tivoli Gardens

DUBLIN: Connaught Place, Merrion Square

DUKERIES, CENTRAL ENGLAND: Fine Estates

FRANKFURT: Palmengarten

GERMANY: Oberammergau (site of annual Passion Play every ten years)

HAMBURG: Reeperbahn, St. Pauli District

HONG KONG: Kowloon, Stanley, Tiger Balm

ISTANBUL: Grand Bazaar, Taksim Circle

ISFAHAN, persia: Great Square

JAKARTA: Chinatown
JERUSALEM: Tophet, The Wailing Wall, The Old City
JOHANNESBURG: Mayfair, Parktown, The Wilds
LENINGRAD: Palace Square, Decembrist Square
LIMA: Plaza de Armas, Plaza de Bolivar
LISBON: Cidade Baiza, Terreiro de Paco
LONDON: Belgravia, Chelsea, Haymarket, Hyde Park, Grosvenor
    Square, Kensington, Limehouse, Mayfair, St. Marylebone,
    Soho, Surrey, Alasatia (former debtor-sanctuary)
MADRID: La Florida, Museo del Prado, Plaza Mayor,
    Puerta de Hierro
MANILA: Dewey Boulevard, Escolta, Chinatown, Ermita,
    Intramuros
MELBOURNE: Exhibition Street, Collins St.
MEXICO CITY: Coyoacan, Plaza de la Constitucion
MILAN: Piazza del Duomo, Piazza della Scalla,
    Piazza del Mercianti
MONTEVIDEO: El Prado, Independence Square, Rodo
MOSCOW: Gorky Park, Gersena St., Tavetnow Boulevard
RIO de JANEIRO: Road of Royal Palms
ROME: Seven Hilled City
SHANGHAI: Bubbling Well Road, Nanking Road, The Bund
SINGAPORE: Raffles Place, Battery Road
SALISBURY PLAIN, ENGLAND: Stonehenge
SOUTH AFRICA: Spanish Main
SYDNEY: Elisabeth St., St. George St.
TOKYO: The Ginza
YOKOHAMA: Chinese Quarter, Motomachi Area, Isezaki Area
VATICAN: Palace of the Pope
VERSAILLES: Palace, The Gardens

AMUSEMENT AREAS

AMERICAN WONDERLAND (Ephrata, PA)
ANIMAL LAND (Lake George, NY)
ANIMAL LAND (Oakland, CA)
AQUALAND (La Plata, MD)
BATTERSEA PARK (London)
BENSON ANIMAL FARM (Nashua, NH)
BIALYSTOK (Poland)
BOARDWALK (Atlantic City, NJ)
CAPRI (Italy)
CARSON CITY (Catskill, NY)
CHILDREN'S FAIRYLAND (Oakland, CA)
CHILDREN'S ZOO (San Diego, CA)

CHRISTMAS VILLAGE (San Diego, CA)
COLUMBIA GARDENS (Butte, MT)
CONEY ISLAND—DREAMLAND (Brooklyn, NY)
CRYSTAL BEACH (Buffalo, NY)
CYPRESS GARDENS (Winter Haven, FL)
DEER FOREST (Benton Harbor, MI)
DISNEYLAND (Anaheim, CA)
DISNEYWORLD (Orlando, FL)
ENCHANTED FOREST (Baltimore, MD)
ENCHANTED FOREST (Old Forge, NY)
FANTASY ISLAND (Buffalo, NY)
FANTASYLAND (Gettysburg, PA)
FREEDOMLAND (Bronx, NY)
FRONTIER CITY (Virginia Beach, VA)
FRONTIER DAYS (Prescott, AZ)
FOX'S WILD ANIMAL FARM (Troy, NY)
GASLIGHT VILLAGE (Lake George, NY)
GHOST TOWN (Lake George, NY)
GLEN ECHO PARK (Washington, DC)
HOME OF 1000 ANIMALS (Lake Placid, NY)
IDLEWILD PARK (Ligonier, PA)
LAND OF MAKE BELIEVE (Wilmington, NY)
LINNANMAKI (Helsinki, Finland)
LUMBERTOWN USA (Brainerd, MN)
MILLION DOLLAR PIER (Atlantic City, NJ)
MOTHER GOOSELAND (Missoula, MN)
NATATORIUM AMUSEMENT PARK (Spokane, WA)
NIBLO'S GARDEN (formerly, New York City)
NORTH POLE (Wilmington, NY)
OPERATION SANTA CLAUS (Redmond, OR)
OSTIA ("Coney Island" of Rome, Italy)
PALISADES AMUSEMENT PARK (NJ)
PAUL BUNYAN CENTER (Brainerd, MN)
PERALTA PLAYLAND (Oakland, CA)
PIXIE WOODS (Stockton, CA)
PRATER (Vienna, Austria)
SAN SEBASTIAN PLAYGROUND CENTER (Spain)
SANTA CLAUS PARK (Santa Claus, IN)
SANTA'S LAND (Putney, NH)
SANTA'S VILLAGE (Jefferson, NH)
SANTA'S VILLAGE (Santa Cruz, CA)
SEA CIRCUS (Asbury Park, NJ)

SEALIGHT PARK (Hawaii)
SIX-GUN CITY (Jefferson City, NH)
SKANSEN (Stockholm, Sweden)
STEEL PIER (Atlantic City, NJ)
STEEPLECHASE PARK (Brooklyn, NY)
STORY BOOK ISLAND (Rapid City, SD)
STORYLAND (Hyannis, MA)
STORYLAND (Pompano Beach, FL)
STORYTOWN, USA (Lake George, NY)
TIVOLI GARDENS (Copenhagen, Denmark)
WALDMEER AMUSEMENT PARK (Erie, PA)
WHITE CITY (Chicago, IL)

LOCATIONS—GENERAL

Airfield
Airport
Amusement park
Apartment
Armory
Auto racing track
Auto wrecking
  yard
Backroad
Backstage
Bank
Barn
Barracks
Baseball field
Basketball court
Battlefield
Beach
Bicycle path
Blacksmith shop
Board room
Boat house
Boat yard
Bridge
Bridle path
Bunkhouse
Bus depot
Cabin
Cage
Campsite
Canal

Cattle country
Cave
Cell
Cellar
Cemetery or
  grave yard
Church
Circus ring
Club
Coastline
Coffee shop
Communications
  center
Concert hall
Condominium
Construction site
Control room
Control tower
Cottage
Crematory
Desert
Deserted road
Dock
Dog racing track
Dressing room
Dry bed
Elevator
Ethnic neighbor-
  hoods
Factory

Factory town
Falls
Farm country
Farmhouse
Film studio
Fire station
Firing range
Fishing pond
Football field
Gambling casino
Garage
Garbage dump
Garden
Gasoline station
Ghost town
Gold mine
Golf club
Guard tower
Handball court
Hangar
Harbor
Headquarters
Helicopter pad
Highway
Hiking trail
Historical site
Hockey rink
Hospital
Hothouse
House

Ice rink
Ice skating rink
Indian country
Jai alai court
Jungle
Junk yard
Lake
Landfill
Launch control
    center
Launching pad
Library
Loading dock
Logging camp
Mailroom
Memorial
Metropolitan area
Military base
Mine
Mine field
Mortuary
Motor pool
Mountain
Movie theatre
Museum
Naval base
Obstacle course
Ocean
Office
Office building
Oil field
Old Spanish
    mission
Park
Parking lot
Pen
Pier
Plains
Planetarium
Playground
Police station
Polo field
Post office
Prison

Prison yard
PX
Race track
Racquetball court
Railroad station
Railroad tracks
Ranch
Ranchhouse
Reception room
Recording studio
Recreatonal
    center
Reservoir
Residence
Resort
Restaurant
Retreat lodge
River
Riverfront
Road
Rodeo
Rooftop
Rugby field
Running track
Runway
Sanctuary
    (wildlife, or
    religious)
Sandbox
Sand dune
Sawmill
School
Shack
Ship yard
Shopping mall
Showroom
Silo
Ski lodge
Ski slope
Slums
Small town
Soccer field
Sound stage

Southern
    plantation
Space launching
    center
Stable
Stadium
Stage
State or
    national park
Store
Subway
Swamp
Swimming pool
Switching station
Synagogue
Temple
Tennis club
Tennis court
Tent
Terminal
Training area
Tomb
Toolshed
Town house
Treehouse
Truck stop
Tunnel
Village
Volcano
Volleyball court
Walk-in freezer
War room
Warehouse
Water tower
Waterfall
Wilderness
Work area
Well
Wine country
White-water
    rapids
Winery
Yard
Zoo

FILM COMMISSIONS

Metropolitan, regional, and state film boards offer invaluable information—often including maps, photos, history, climate, and much else—free for the asking. If you've chosen for your story a locale you can't easily visit in person, a film commission's information packet may be able to supply that telling detail that clinches a dead-on, convincing evocation of place.

You can contact film commissions through local and state chambers of commerce; foreign film commissions can be contacted through their embassies or trade mission headquarters. Your local library's reference section will also provide information on film commissions and boards.

State offices

ALABAMA
Alabama Film Office
340 North Hull Street
Montgomery, AL 36130

ALASKA
Alaska Motion Picture and Television Production
3601 C Street, 722
Anchorage, AK 99503

ARIZONA
Arizona Film Commission
1700 West Washington Avenue, 4th Floor
Phoenix, AZ 85007

ARKANSAS
Arkansas Motion Picture Development Office
1 State Capitol Mall
Room 2C-200
Little Rock, AR 72201

CALIFORNIA
California Film Commission
6922 Hollywood Boulevard
Hollywood, CA 90028

COLORADO
Colorado Motion Picture and Television
1313 Sherman Street, Suite 500
Denver, CO 80203

CONNECTICUT
Connecticut Film Commission
210 Washington Street
Hartford, CT 06106

DELAWARE
Delaware Development Office
99 Kings Highway
Dover, DE 19903

DISTRICT OF COLUMBIA
Mayor's Office of
Motion Picture and Television
1111 E Street Northwest, Suite 700
Washington, D.C. 20004

FLORIDA
Florida Film Bureau
Fletcher Building
107 West Gaines Street
Tallahassee, FL 32399

GEORGIA
Georgia Film and Videotape Office
P.O. Box 1776
Atlanta, GA 30301

HAWAII
Film Industry Branch
P.O. Box 2359
Honolulu, HI 96804

IDAHO
Idaho Film Bureau
700 West State Street
2nd Floor
Boise, ID 83702

ILLINOIS
Illinois Film Office
100 West Randolph, Suite 3-400
Chicago, IL 60601

INDIANA
Indiana Film Commission
Department of Commerce
1 North Capitol
Indianapolis, IN 46204

IOWA
Iowa Film Office
Department of Economic Development
200 East Grand Avenue
Des Moines, IA 50309

KANSAS
Kansas Film Commission
400 West 8th Street, Fifth Floor
Topeka, KS 66603

KENTUCKY
Kentucky Film Office
Berry Hill Mansion on Louisville Road
Frankfort, KY 40601

LOUISIANA
Louisiana Film Commission
P.O. Box 94361
Baton Rouge, LA 70804

MAINE
Maine Film Commission
Office of Tourism & Economic Development
State House Station
Augusta, ME 04333

MARYLAND
Maryland Film Commission
217 East Redwood
9th Floor
Baltimore, MD 21202

MASSACHUSETTS
Massachusetts Film Office
10 Park Plaza Suite 2310
Boston, MA 02116

MICHIGAN
Michigan Film Office
1200 Sixth Street, 19th Floor
Detroit, MI 48226

MINNESOTA
Minnesota Motion Picture and Television Board
401 North 3rd Street
Suite 460
Minneapolis, MN 55401

MISSISSIPPI
Mississippi Film Office
1200 Water Stillers Building
Box 849
Jackson, MS 39205

MISSOURI
Missouri Film Commission
P.O. Box 118
301 West High, #770
Jefferson City, MO 65102

MONTANA
Montana Film Commission
1424 9th Avenue
Helena, MT 59620

NEBRASKA
Nebraska Film Office
301 Centennial Mall South
Lincoln, NE 68509

NEVADA
Motion Picture and Television Development
McCarran International Airport, 2nd Floor
Las Vegas, NV 89158

NEW JERSEY
New Jersey Motion Picture and Television Commission
One Gateway Center, Suite 510
Newark, NJ 07102

NEW MEXICO
New Mexico Film Commission
1050 Pecos Trail
Santa Fe, NM 87501

NEW YORK
New York State Governor's Office for MP/TV Development
1515 Broadway
32nd Floor
New York, NY 10169

NORTH CAROLINA
North Carolina Film Office
430 North Salisbury Street
Raleigh, NC 27611

NORTH DAKOTA
EDC/Tourism Promotion
Division Liberty Memorial Building
Bismark, ND 58505

OHIO
Ohio Film Bureau
77 South High Street, 28th Floor
Columbus, OH 43266

OKLAHOMA
Oklahoma Film Office
P.O. Box 26980
Oklahoma City, OK 72316-0980

OREGON
Oregon Film Office
595 Cottage Street Northeast
Salem, OR 97310

PENNSYLVANIA
Pennsylvania Film Bureau
Forum Building, Room 455
Harrisburg, PA 17120

PUERTO RICO
Puerto Rico Film Institute
P.O. Box 2350
San Juan, PR 00936

RHODE ISLAND
Rhode Island Film Commission
150 Benefit Street
Providence, RI 02903

SOUTH CAROLINA
South Carolina Film Office
P.O. Box 927
Columbia, SC 29202

SOUTH DAKOTA
South Dakota Tourism
Capital Lake Plaza
Pierre, SD 57501

TENNESSEE
Tennessee Film Entertainment
Music Commission
320 6th Avenue North, 7th Floor
Nashville, TN 37219

TEXAS
Texas Film/Music Office
P.O. Box 12728
Austin, TX 78711

UTAH
Utah Film Commission
6220 State Office Building
Salt Lake City, UT 84114

U.S. VIRGIN ISLANDS
United States Virgin Islands
Film Promotion Office
P.O. Box 640
Saint Thomas, USVI 00804

VERMONT
Vermont Film Bureau
134 State Street
Montpelier, VT 05602

VIRGINIA
Virginia Film Office
P.O. Box 798
Richmond, VA 23219

WASHINGTON
Washington State Film and Video
312 First Avenue
North Seattle, WA 98109

WISCONSIN
Wisconsin Film Office
123 West Washington
P.O. Box 7970
Madison, WI 53707

WYOMING
Wyoming Film Commission
I-25 and College Drive
Cheyenne, WY 82002

Indian

American Indian Registry for the Performing Arts
3330 Barham Blvd., #208
Los Angeles, CA 90042

International

ARGENTINA

Argentine Film Commission
1888 Century Park East, Ste. 1900
Los Angeles, CA 90067

AUSTRALIA
New South Wales:
New South Wales Film and TV Office
45 Macquarie Street, 4th Fl.
Sydney, New South Wales 2000 Australia

Queensland:
Queensland Film Development Office
100 George Street
4th Floor
Brisbane, Queensland 4000
Australia

Victoria/Melbourne:
Melbourne Film Commission Division of Film Victoria
409 King Street
Melbourne, Victoria 3000
Australia

Western Australia:
Western Australian Film Council
336 Churchill Avenue, Suite 8
Subiaco 6008
Western Australia

AUSTRIA
CineAustria
11601 Wilshire Boulevard, Suite 2480
Los Angeles, CA 90025

BAHAMAS
Bahamas Film Promotion Bureau
P.O. Box N 3701
Nassau, Bahamas

Bahamas Film Bureau, Miami
255 Alhambra Circle, Suite 414
Coral Gables, FL 33134

BELIZE
Belize Foreign Film Commission
1769 N. El Cerrito Place
Suite 309
Hollywood, CA 90028

CANADA
Telefilm Canada
144 South Beverly Drive, Suite 400
Beverly Hills, CA 90212

CHILE
Chile Film Commission
734 Suecia Avenue
Providencia Santiago
Chile

COSTA RICA
Costa Rican Film Commission
9000 West Sunset Suite 1000
Los Angeles, CA 90069

GERMANY
Munich Film Information Office
Tuerkenstrasse 93
D-8000 Muenchen 40
Germany

ISRAEL
Government of Israel Economics and Trade
6380 Wilshire Boulevard
Los Angeles, CA 90048

JAMAICA
Jamaica Film Office
35 Trafalgar Road, 3rd Floor
Kingston 10 Jamaica

NEW ZEALAND
New Zealand Tourist and Publicity Office
10960 Wilshire Blvd, Suite 1530
Los Angeles, CA 90024 U.S.A.

PERU
Institute Nacional De Cultura Del Peru
P.O. Box 1878
Hollywood, CA 90028

TAHITI
Tahiti Film Office
12233 West Olympic Boulevard, Suite 100
Los Angeles, CA 90064 U.S.A.

THAILAND
Thailand Film Promotion Center
599 Burnrung Muang Road
Bangkok 10100
Thailand

23

Reference
and Research

If there's one thing fiction writers often despise, it's doing their own research.

Why?

Probably because searching for information and facts is a tedious and time-consuming process and not half as much fun as sitting around and letting the old imagination run rampant. Nevertheless, dramatic license should be based on fact or at least some semblance of fact.

In most cases, if you provide some substantiation of fact or logic that the readers or viewers can buy, they are more likely to go along with whatever license you take thereafter.

Many writers like myself have built up fairly extensive research libraries of our own. Unfortunately, no matter how extensive the library, there's always going to be something to take you in search of more information on your subject.

I would not attempt to cover all the bases in doing research. It would take a separate book to do that. Fortunately, such books exist and are listed in this chapter. I will offer some suggestions as to the types of research you might consider and a sampling of various titles, places, and publications that could be of value to you.

First, let's identify means of researching a person, subject, or period of history. These include:

Biographies and autobiographies
Bookstores
Computer searches
Films, tapes, recordings
General encyclopedias
Law enforcement agencies
Library card catalogs
Local, State, and Federal Government Agencies
Manufacturers and trade associations
Maps
Newspaper morgues, old magazines, out-of-print publications
Newspapers, wire services
Photographs
Public records
Special dictionaries
Subject encyclopedias
Talking to people familiar with the subject
Textbooks
Trade publications and periodicals dealing with specific subjects, individuals, companies, etc.
TV and radio stations
University libraries and departments

There are organizations and associations for most industries, sports, and hobbies, from day-care centers to space centers to travel to earthworms. Most of these can be found in *The Directory of Directories,* an annual published by Information Enterprises in Detroit and distributed by Gale Research. Some other sources for titles and authors dealing with specific subjects are the following:

American Book Publishing Record. New York: R.R. Bowker, annual.

American Reference Books Annual. Littleton, CO: Libraries Unlimited, annual.

Besterman. *World Bibliographies on Bibliographies.*

Gates, Jean Key. *Guide to the Use of Libraries and Information Sources,* 6th Ed. New York: McGraw-Hill, 1989.

Horowitz, Lois. *Knowing Where to Look: The Ultimate Guide to Research,* Rev. Ed. Cincinnati: Writer's Digest Books, 1988.

Katz, Bill and Robin Kinder. *The Publishing and Review of Reference Sources.* New York: Haworth Press, 1987.

Mann, Thomas. *A Guide to Library Research Methods.* New York: Oxford University Press, 1987.

Nelson, *Guide to Published Library Catalogs, Paperbound Books in Print.* New York: R.R. Bowker, annual.

Sheehy, E.P., ed., *Guide to Reference Books.* Chicago: American Library Association, 1986.

Subject Guide to Books in Print. New York: R.R. Bowker, annual.

Taylor, Margaret. *Basic Reference Sources.* Metuchen, NJ: Scarecrow Press, 1985.

Wynar, Bohdan S., ed. *ARBA Guide to Subject Encyclopedias and Dictionaries.* Littleton, CO: Libraries Unlimited, 1986.

The U.S. Government Printing Office in Washington, D.C. also prints many books and pamphlets on specific subjects. They can furnish you with a catalog of subjects available.

Your local librarian may have these books on hand or can direct you to where and how you might secure them.

DICTIONARIES, ENCYCLOPEDIAS, AND GUIDE BOOKS

Here is a brief list of topics for which dictionaries, encyclopedias, and guide books are widely available. Many others can be obtained through the public and university libraries, and new and used bookstores.

American biography
American economic history
American foreign policy
American history
American religions
Animals
Banking and finance
The Bible
Biochemistry
Computer science
Constitutional law
Crafts
Crime and justice
Earth sciences
Education
Electronics
Evolution
Folklore, mythology and legend
Food
Historic places
History of ideas
Human behavior
Islam
Jazz
Mathematics
The Middle Ages
Military history

Mystery and detection
Philosophy
Prehistoric life
Religion and ethics
Scientific biography
Soviet law
World art
World literature

Some useful guide books include the following:

Freidel, Frank. *Harvard Guide to American History.* Cambridge,
MA: Belknap Press, 1974.
Kurland, Michael. *The Spymaster's Handbook.* New York: Facts on
File, 1988.
Poulton, Helen. *The Historian's Handbook.* Norman, OK:
University of Oklahoma Press, 1972.
Pruett, James and Thomas Slavens. *Research Guide to Musicology.*
Chicago: American Library Association, 1985.
Rowland, Desmond and James Bailey. *The Law Enforcement
Handbook.* New York: Facts on File, 1985.
Stanton, Shelby. *Vietnam Order of Battle.* New York: Galahad
Books, 1987.
Wilson, John and Thomas Slavens. *Research Guide to Religious
Studies.* Chicago: American Library Association, 1982.

Another source of information on many subjects is Time/Life Books.
They publish series on subjects ranging from history to the occult.

I hasten to repeat that these are samples of what is available. It pays
to be sure you have adequate sources before beginning the actual
research. Information and technologies change, so make sure you have
the most recent information available.

One of the most comprehensive books on how to do research is *A
Guide to Library Research Methods* by Thomas Mann, published in
1987 by Oxford University Press. This book lists dictionaries,
encyclopedias, guides, and other avenues of research.

Where's What, published in 1976 by Warner Books, helps the writer
get information on subjects including:

Agriculture
Biographic reference books
Court records
Credit resources
Department of Commerce
Department of Defense
Department of Housing and Urban Development
Department of Human Services
Department of Interior

Department of Labor
Department of Justice
Department of Police Records
Department of State
Department of Treasury
Educational records
Insurance records
Library reference books
Motor vehicle records
Neighborhood inquiries
Newspapers and Magazines
Post Office Department
Vital Statistics

CAPITALIZATION

Capitalize common nouns or generic terms when part of a name: Occidental College, Los Angeles County, Union Station Federal Building, Imperial Valley, World War II. Do not capitalize common nouns in plurals: Los Angeles and San Bernardino counties.

Capitalize titles before a name but not after a name or when standing alone: Secretary of State Warren Christopher; Warren Christopher, secretary of state. Exception: the President of the United States and the Pope. Capitalize Presidential and Presidency. Do not capitalize occupational descriptives: laborer Frank Jones, attorney Fred Roberts, singer Patrice Munsel, actor Harrison Ford.

Place such descriptives after the name if they are more than two words long:, not Italian opera star Renata Tebaldi, but Renata Tebaldi, the Italian opera star.

Capitalize principal words in titles. Principal words include nouns, verbs, the first word, and prepositions and adverbs of four or more letters: *The Man Who Came to Dinner, Captain From Castile.*

Capitalize major government organizations: House Committee on Un-American Activities, Police Department, Board of Public Works, House of Commons, Diet, Senate, House, Cabinet. Capitalize Congress when referring to the U.S. Congress (but not congressional), Legislature when referring to a specific state legislature, and City Council when referring to a specific city council. Do not capitalize subdivisions of government organizations: inspection division of the Building and Safety Department, subcommittee of the Senate Banking and Currency Committee, antitrust division of the Justice Department. (Standing legislative committees are capitalized, but not subcommittees.)

Do not capitalize club and business committees or boards: boards of trustees.

Capitalize political parties (Democratic Party, Republican Party, Communist Party) but not the same words when they refer to doctrines or beliefs (democratic, republican, and communist forms of government.)

Do not capitalize nation, administration, state, federal city, county, and government when they stand alone. But capitalize State in such names as State Division of Highways.

Do not capitalize seasons of the year (fall), compass directions (northeast), a.m. and p.m., college classes (sophomore), or school subjects, except names of languages (chemistry, Latin, French).

Capitalize geographic regions: Midwest, South, Far West, Southern California, Northern California, East Side, Bay Area. Do not capitalize regions not regarded as entities: western Missouri, southern Orange County. Capitalize ideological and political areas: East-West, West Germany.

Capitalize names of planets: Venus and Mars. Lower case sun, moon, and earth.

Capitalize nationalities and races: German, Irish, Indian, Black, Nisei, Caucasian.

Capitalize trademark names such as Coke, Dacron, Frigidaire, Jell-O, Laundromat, Levis, Lockheed Constellation, Miltown, Orlon, Photostat, Band-aids, Technicolor, Teletype (but it is better to use a generic term).

Capitalize Social Security when referring to the U.S. system.

Capitalize legislative acts but not bills: Walter-McCarran Immigration Act, Smith bill.

Capitalize U.S. armed forces (Army, Navy, Air Force, Marine Corps, Coast Guard, National Guard, Air Force Reserve), and Marine, but not soldier, sailor, airman, or coast guardsman.

Capitalize holidays, historical events, major special events, and hurricanes: Labor Day, Christmas, New Year's Day, National Safety Week, Hurricane Hazel. Do not capitalize founders' days and homecoming weeks of colleges, schools, and clubs.

Do not capitalize the names of schools or departments of a university or college: University of California law school, USC history department.

Capitalize decorations and awards: Medal of Honor, Nobel Peace Prize, Man of the Year.

Capitalize words referring to the Deity: God, Christ, He, His. Do not capitalize heaven and hell. Use Pope and Pontiff, Mass, Latter-day Saints, Seventh-day Adventists.

Capitalize Flag when referring to the U.S. Flag, but make it "flags were flying."

Capitalize ages, eras, and periods but not centuries: Dark Ages, Jazz Era, Space Age, 20th century.

Capitalize articles, chapters, classes, sections, and pages when followed by figures, Roman numerals, or letters: Page 1, Article A.

Capitalize *The* in *The Times* when referring to *The Los Angeles Times.*

Particles like de, la, von, occurring in foreign names are lower case when preceded by the given name (Charles de Gaulle) but otherwise capitalize (General De Gaulle; La Farge). In general, give names in the forms used by their owners and by which they are generally known: Nelson A. Rockefeller, not N.A. Use forms like M'Namara only in all-cap headlines.

These forms indicate capitalization and lower-case usage not already covered specifically: Boy Scouts (organization), boy scout (person), cold war, Early American (furniture, architecture), Iron Curtain, Latter-day Saints, Mass, Los Angeles County Grand Jury (but grand jury), Pacific fleet, Red (Communist), Seventh-day Adventists, Teamsters Union, United Air Lines, Western Airlines.

ABBREVIATIONS

GENERAL RULE: Abbreviations should have some justification other than the negligible saving in space.Do not use abbreviations that might be confusing to the reader.

Abbreviate months of six or more letters when used with dates: Sept. 21, 1952, April 7, 1962.

Abbreviate states of five or more letters when used with cities or other place names: Norman, OK, Eglin Air Force Base, FL. Do not abbreviate Alaska, Hawaii, Iowa, Ohio, or Utah (except in postal codes). The standard abbreviations are AL, AZ, CA, CO, CN, DE, FL, GA, ID, IL, IN, KA, KY, LA, MD, MA, NC, ND, NH, NJ, NM, NY, OK, OR, PA, RI, SC, TN, TX, VT, VA, WA, WI, WV, WY.

Abbreviate Canadian provinces as follows: Alta., B.C., Man., Nfld., N.W., Ont., Que., Sask.

Abbreviate street (St.), avenue (Ave.), boulevard (Blvd.), terrace (Ter.), court (Ct.), drive (Dr.), road (Rd.) when used in addresses (1042 W. Main St.), but not port, circle, plaza, place, oval, lane.

Abbreviate standard titles when used before names: Mr., Mrs., Ms., Dr., Sen., Rep., Lt. Gov., Gen., Supt., Do not abbreviate attorney when referring to a private attorney. Do not abbreviate Secretary General of the United Nations or Postmaster General of the United States.

Abbreviate company (Co.), corporation (Corp.), association (Assn.), incorporated (Inc.), and brothers (bros.) in commercial names: Johnson, Billings & Co.

Spell out the names of organizations the first time in the story, except the obvious, such as AFL-CIO, FBI, GOP, PTA, UCLA, USC, YMCA, and YWCA. Do not create your own abbreviations.

Spell out United States and United Nations when used as nouns except in direct quotations and headlines. Abbreviate them as adjectives (U.S. policy, U.N. General Assembly).

Do not abbreviate days of the week in stories or headlines.

Do not abbreviate degrees, inches, feet, yards, miles, hours, and minutes except in statistical summaries.

Use these abbreviations before names for military ranks: Army—Gen., Lt. Gen., Maj. Gen., Brig. Gen., Col., Lt. Col., Maj., Capt., 1st Sgt., Staff Sgt., Sgt., Pfc., Pvt., Recruit.

Navy and Coast Guard—Adm., Vice Adm., Rear Adm., Commodore, Capt., Cdr, LCdr, Lt., Lt.(jg), Ens., CWO, CPO, Seaman, Seaman Apprentice, Seaman Recruit.

Marine Corps—Commandant, Lt.Gen, Maj.Gen, B.Gen, Col., Lt.Col, Maj., Capt., 1stLt., 2ndLt., WO (warrant officer).

Air Force—generally same as Army except T. Sgt., Airman 1 C., Airman.

Spell out General of the Army, fleet admiral, and admiral of the fleet (British).

Avoid abbreviation of unfamiliar rates (PO lC.).

NUMBERS

GENERAL RULE: Spell out one through nine and use Arabic numerals for 10 and higher for cardinals and ordinals. Use figures for ages, weights, time, measures, money, dates, scores, temperatures, votes, and percentages.

Contract ordinal numbers for such designations as 6th Fleet, 1st Marine Division, 8th U.S. Circuit Court of Appeals. He fled up 2nd Street.

Do not start a sentence with a number.

Spell out numbers denoting eras: Gay Nineties, Roaring Twenties.

Use Roman numerals for personal sequence: Pope John XXIII, John Smith III. Use Arabic numberals for impersonal sequence: Sputnik 4, Venus 2, Explorer 22.

Treat sums of money this way: 10 cents, $1, $1,327.30, $120,000, $1.25 million, $1,347,372, $3 billion.

Use a comma in numbers of four digits or more: 1,234, 12,134.

Spell out foreign money denominations: 347,000 pounds, 125,000 pesos, 75 marks.

Keep the simplest related forms in series: He had six suits, fourteen pairs of shoes, and one tie.

When another set of figures immediately follows an age figure, insert a word to separate the figures: John Jones, 27, of 1423 W. 7th St., was...

For highways: U.S.99, California 50, Interstate 1.

For percentages: 2%.

For time: 8:20 p.m. PST (if necessary).

For firearms: .45 caliber revolver, 12 Ga shotgun

Spell out and hyphenate fractions except in tabular matter: two-thirds. Generally prefer decimals to fractions: 3.5 million rather than $3^{1/2}$ million.

NAMES AND TITLES

For Protestant clergymen: the Rev. John Jones, therafter Mr. Jones. Jewish clergymen: Rabbi Jacob Wise, Rabbi Wise.

The prince of the church is James Francis Cardinal McIntyre, never Cardinal James Francis McIntyre, but Cardinal McIntyre is correct.

Use Christian names or initials after titles of officials except the President of the United States or a governor: District Atty. Elmer Smith, President Clinton, Governor Brown.

Unwieldy titles should follow names: Frank Smith, assistant vice president of the First National Bank. As a general rule only titles of one to three words should precede names.

Do not use a comma before name affixes: John Roberts Jr.

Use Ms. or Mrs. before names or women of college age or older unless they are entertainers, athletes, or other professional persons: Ms. Mary Jane Reed, Ms. Reed, Doris Day, Ms. Day.

In Chinese names, the element after the hyphen is usually lower case: Chiang Kai-shek, Chou En-lai, Mao Tze-tung. The first name is the family name. Many Koreans follow the Chinese practice of putting the family name first, but the given names are not hyphenated: Yun Po Sun. Many Indonesians, like Sukarno, have only one name. In Latin American names, the second name is usually the main surname (the father's): Ricardo Fuentes Lobo (Fuentes), Juan Duran y Casahonds (Duran), Adolfo Lopez Mateos (Lopez or Lopez Mateos).

In addition, since the "feminist movement" of the seventies, in addition to Mrs. and Miss, the term Ms. has been included with the feminine titles. It eliminates the necessity of classifying the married or unmarried status of a woman.

NEWSMAN'S DICTIONARY

A, AN. A is.used before all consonants except the silent *h:* a history, an hour, an 8-mile hike.

AFFECT, EFFECT. *Affect* is always a verb and means to influence. *Effect* is either a verb or a noun. As a verb *effect* means to bring about or accomplish a major change.

ALUMNUS, ALUMNA, ALUMNI. An *alumnus* is a male college graduate. The plural is *alumni.* An alumna is a female college graduate. The plural is *alumnae. Alumni* is used when referring to a group of men and women college graduates.

ANTICIPATE, EXPECT. *Anticipate* means to expect and prepare for something. *Expect* is usually the word you want.

ASSAULT, BATTERY. *Assault* is a threat. *Battery* is a physical attack.

CHRISTMAS. It's Christmas or Yule but not Xmas.

CLAIM, CONTEND, ASSERT. The use of *claim* in the sense of contend or assert, is considered incorrect by purists, who say claim should be completed with a noun or infinitive: he claimed the championship. But claim has come in so strong that not much can be done about it. *Contend* and *assert* are still good words in reporting trials and other controversies. The old standby, *said,* is the least editorial speech-tag verb.

COLLISION. Both vehicles or other bodies must be in motion to have a collision.

COMPARE WITH, TO. There's a difference of opinion on these terms. Some grammarians say *compare to* should be used to show similarity and *compare with* to show contrast. H.W. Fowler in *Modern English Usage* uses *compare to* to suggest a similarity and *compare with* to set forth the details of a supposed similarity or estimate its degree. Following Fowler, one number would be compared with another.

CONTINUAL, CONTINUOUS. *Continual* means frequently or closely repeated. *Continuous* means without interruption.

COUPLE is plural. Most other collectives are either singular or plural, depending on the way they're used.

EUPHEMISMS. Within good taste, avoid pale substitutes for words. If it's rape, call it rape.

EX-. It's ex-New York governor and not New York ex-governor, since ex- modifies the entire term.

FARTHER, FURTHER. Although the distinction is fading, *farther* should still be used to show distance and *further* to show degree, quantity, or time.

FOLLOWING, AFTER. *Following* is trying hard to become a preposition but hasn't yet won recognition as such in dictionaries. Use *before* and *after,* not *prior to* and *following.*

FORMER, LATTER. Why make the reader go back to try to figure out which is which? Generally avoid *former* and *latter,* and *respectively.*

IMPLY, INFER. A writer or speaker *implies* something in the words he uses. A reader or listener *infers* something from the words he reads or hears.

KNOT. A nautical knot is a unit of speed: 6.080 feet an hour. It's redundant to say "30 knots an hour."

LADY, WOMAN. *Woman* will usually do the job unless it is a title, or a cliché.

LIKE, AS. *As* is losing out in the battle of usage, but normally consider *like* a preposition to be followed by an object: If you are like me, you will do as I do.

MAJORITY, PLURALITY. *Majority* means more than half a certain number. *Plurality* means more than the next highest number. In an election with three candidates and 120,000 votes, if one candidate received 70,000 votes, one 30,000 and one 20,000, the winner would have a plurality of 40,000 votes and a majority of 20,000. If you are not writing about an election, *most* is better than *majority.*

MURDER, HOMICIDE. *Homicide* is the killing of one person by another. It includes murder and manslaughter. *Murder* is malicious homicide. *Slaying* is a general term for homicide.

NEITHER...NOR and EITHER...OR are not compound subjects; they are alternate subjects and require a verb that agrees with the nearer subject. Correct: Neither they nor he is going. Neither he nor they are going.

NONE always takes a singular verb: *None* of the pegs fits.

OBITS. In obituaries a man leaves his *wife,* not his *widow.* Funeral services are *conducted* but a funeral may be *held.* Mass is *celebrated, said,* or *read.* Rosary is *recited* or *said.* The body is *sent* to the former home, not *shipped.*

OBTAIN, GET. *Obtain* implies effort directed toward acquisition of something. *Attain* is to arrive at a goal. *Procure* is to gain possession of something, often temporarily. *Gain* implies getting something that is profitable or advantageous. *Win* is to gain, especially against opposition. *Earn* is to gain by one's own exertion. *Get* means all or these things but is rather listless. *Secure* means to fasten or make safe.

RACIAL IDENTIFICATION. Do not use racial identification unless it is pertinent to the story. But when it is pertinent, do not hesitate to use it.

REALTOR. Reserve the term *realtor* for a real estate person who belongs to a local board affiliated with the National Association of Real Estate Boards.

REDUNDANCIES. Avoid such redundancies as "consensus of opinion," "true facts," "completely destroyed," "in order to," "whether or not," "filled to capacity," "2:30 p.m. this afternoon."

REVOLVER. A "revolver" has a revolving cylinder that carries the bullets to the barrel. An *automatic* is not a revolver, but a *pistol* describes either.

SUPERSTITIONS. The best known grammatical superstition concerns the split infinitive. H.W. Fowler in *Modern English Usage* says the separation of *to* from its infinitive is not in itself desirable, but is preferable to either ambiguity or artificiality. For example: "Our object is to further cement trade relations" is better than "Our object is further to cement trade relations." If it helps the sentence to split an infinitive, do it; if it doesn't, don't. Another superstition of many newspapermen is that a grammatical rule prohibits splitting a compound verb (a verb made up of an auxiliary such as *will* and an infinitive or participle). When an adverb is to be used with such a verb, its normal place is between the auxiliary and the rest. For example: "I have never seen her" and not "I never have seen her." Fowler says, "not only is there no such objection to thus splitting a compound verb, but any other position requires special justification."

VERBAL, ORAL. *Verbal* means in words, either written or oral. *Oral* means by mouth, spoken.

24

Putting It All Together

By now, I'm sure you're aware that *The Writer's Partner* serves a multiplicity of purposes.

If you're stuck for a name or a name in a foreign language, it's here. If you're stuck for an action verb, it's here. If you're fed up with "he said" and "she said," there's a long list of alternatives.

If you're stuck for an idea, there's Chapter Four, Switching, and each subject area has a list of basic premises. If you need aid in creating a character, an obstacle to overcome, a conflict to establish, an action to take, it's here.

Where can you get more information on a subject? Most subject chapters list references, or check Chapter Twenty-two, Reference and Research. If you need help in coming up with a story notion, it's here.

Although *The Writer's Partner* cannot create characters for you or plot or write your story, the information, lists, and examples in this book can aid you in putting together interesting characters, themes and premises upon which to build a story, along with reference and research information, plus suggested problems, conflicts, obstacles, crises, and so forth, to fully develop a story from beginning to end.

The first step in writing a story is to come up with a subject and a premise. If you're searching for a premise, check the subject chapters for basic premises.

But suppose you've already chosen a subject. Let's say the subject is love. Is it to be a straight love story, a comedy, or a romance played against action/adventure, intrigue, or crime? The arena in which you decide to play your love story will help determine the type of characters you will people your story with, the location, and all of the other elements of your story.

The chapter on romance has information, suggestions, and extensive lists that can help you come up with a theme, romantic problems, types of romantic attraction, where and how lovers meet, involvements, and relationships.

Suppose the theme deals with infidelity and a May/December romance. The story could deal with an older married man who falls in love with a young woman, or an older married woman who falls in love with a young man. Whichever, we have star-crossed lovers. If the affair were to continue unhampered, we'd have no major conflict and thus no drama. It would merely be a character study.

To add drama, something must occur that brings about conflict and intensity.

How do we determine what the conflict shall be? First, we must decide who the two lovers are. Who is the married older man or woman? What kind of person is her or she? What is that person's job or profession?

Next, how and where do the two lovers meet? Check Chapter Three on deliberate and non-deliberate involvement and the romance chapter on attractions, where and how lovers meet, and so on.

Once the lovers meet and the relationship begins, determine the goals of the lovers. Do they intend to continue the affair, hoping not to be discovered? Is the older person considering divorce? What direction is the romance taking?

Let's deal with the two lovers by referring to Chapter Two, Characters and Development, and Chapter Ten, on Romance. Who the two people are and what their jobs or professions are will play an important role in developing your story.

For example, let's say the older lover is a politician running for an important office. Discovery and scandal could wreck a political career.

Suppose the older lover is a male police officer. Who is the young woman he falls in love with? Checking the character lists, she could be a policewoman assigned to him as his new partner. Or she could be a witness he is protecting, or a suspect in a case he is investigating.

Suppose the character is a college professor. What if the girl is one of his students or another professor? Here again, the lists can offer a number of suggestions. Then, to develop the plot, all you have to do is ask yourself "What if?"

Now what about the spouse? You could have the spouse remain ignorant of the affair, or the spouse might learn of it. If the latter, what would the spouse do? Would the spouse remain silent? Would the spouse become enraged and consider some violent act? Again, it would depend on the character of the spouse that you developed.

Next are the goals. What are the older man and the younger woman looking for, individually and jointly? Does each have a career, children, and other family to contend with? Is the romance to be merely a warm, wonderful but brief encounter, or is the older character planning to seek a divorce and then marry the younger woman? Where is the romance going, and how will it end? You have two alternatives, a happy ending or a sad one. Does the older person return to the spouse or wind up with the younger lover? The choice is yours.

Finding an ending is now essential, and much will depend on the principal characters and the consequences they face regarding the love affair and possibly their careers.

Once you know your destination, it is a matter of getting there and introducing the conflicts, problems and obstacles that must be overcome, or not overcome, during the story.

Conflict is the essential element of drama. The fact that the older lover is married creates one conflict immediately. The dramatic action that conflict could produce would center on giving up the love affair or getting a divorce. But suppose the spouse sets out to destroy the other spouse's career, or suppose the offended spouse attacks the mate or the lover? The lover might become homicidal, as in the film *Fatal Attraction*.

Let's examine some possibilities that would require another opposing force in addition to the existing conflict.

Who could that opposing force be? The chapters on character and romance could offer some suggestions.

Suppose the older lover is a male politician. The opposing force might be someone who discovers the affair and attempts blackmail, or a political opponent who sees an opportunity to turn it into a scandal, thus wrecking our protagonist's political career.

Perhaps the older lover has a grown son, that son, falls in love with a girl, and then learns that she is having an affair with his father.

The point is, *The Writer's Partner* is not writing the story for you, but is here to make you think WHAT IF?

WHAT IF the lovers were police officers teamed as partners?

WHAT IF the younger woman tries to get rid of the older cop's wife by framing an ex-con for the murder?

WHAT IF?

The Writer's Partner could go on and on giving you examples of how to put a character or a story together, but unfortunately it cannot read your mind. Not knowing the arena or premise you have chosen or how you intend to develop your story and your characters, all your Partner can do is offer suggestions for your consideration. Then, once you have established your premise, your characters, their goals and the way you wish to end your story, *The Writer's Partner* can offer further suggestions on what directions you might take to arrive at the story's eventual destination.

The Writer's Partner is a writer's supermarket. It can't cook your dinner for you, but it can provide all the ingredients. By checking the Table of Contents, you can find lists of conflicts, involvements, problems, subject information, things associated with subjects, secondary actions, obstacles, twists, crises and climaxes to help lead you to that final resolution. Beginnings, middles and endings, reference, research are all here to help you put it all together.

WEB WORDAGE

Language on the World Wide Web is constantly changing. The following information is based on information researched in 1999 and early 2000.

This section is primarily devoted to giving you insight into the most commonly used terms associated with computers and the Internet. Also included are some of the major portals and suggestions and links that are of interest to writers.

MOST COMMONLY USED NETSPEAK & E-MAIL ABBREVIATIONS

ASAP = As soon as possible
BCNU = Be seeing you
BTW = By the way
F2F = Personal meeting, face to face.
FCOL = For Crying out loud
FYEO = For your eyes only
FYI = For your information
FWIW = For what it's worth
GG = Got to go
IMO = In my opinion
LOL = Laugh out loud
PLS = Please
TAFN = That's all for now

INTERNET LINGO & GLOSSARY OF COMPUTER/INTERNET TERMS

Artificial Intelligence: Computer science simulating human intelligence—as in speech recognition, deduction, creative response, etc.

ASCII (pronounced *askee*): Acronym for "American Standard Code for Information Intelligence" assigning numeric values up to 256 characters, including letters, punctuation, etc. Universal format.

Backup: Duplicate copy of a program or data on a disk or saved data.

Baud rate: Speed at which a modem can transmit data.

BBS: Abbreviation for "bulletin board service".

Bit: Binary digit, the smallest unit of information taken by the computer.

Boot: Starting or re-starting the computer.

Bug: Error in logic coding causing a program malfunction.

CD-ROM: Compact disk with read-only memory, material stored using laser optics.

Chat room: Data communication location linking computers for "conversations."

Chip: Integrated circuit.

CPU: Central processing unit.

Crash: Failure of a program or disk drive, resulting in loss of all unsaved data.

Cursor: On-screen indicator marking the place a keystroke will appear when struck.

Cyberspace: The Internet environment as well as e-mail.

Cyberspeak: Jargon or slang related to computers and cyberspace.

Database: File composed of records.

Desktop publishing: Combining text and graphics in order to create printable documents.

Directory service: Service enabling the user to locate a host or services. Also called a Search Engine.

Disk drive: Electromechanical device reading from and to disks.

DOS: Disk operating system.

Encryption: Process of encoding data to prevent unauthorized access, especially during transmission.

FAQ: Abbreviation for "frequently asked questions."

File: Collection of information, program, set of data.

Firewall: Security system to protect against hackers.

Graphical User Interface or GUI (*Gooey*): Represented on the computer screen by icons, files, programs, menus and dialogue boxes—the user can select and activate these items by the click of the mouse and in some instances by using the keyboard.

Hacker: A computerphile well versed in computer technology who most often seeks to gain illicit access to or tamper with other computers and systems without permission.

Hard copy: Printed output.

Hit: Retrieval of information from a website; or, a visitor to a website.

Home page: An entry page for a website.

Host: The main computer in a system of computers connected by communication links.

HTML: Abbreviation used for "hypertext markup language" used to create documents on the World Wide Web.

HTTP: Abbreviation for the "hypertext transfer protocol" that the client/server uses to gain access to a website.

Hyperlink: A portion of a document that permits the user to move to another page or site by clicking on a highlighted linking element.

Icon: The small image displayed on the screen representing an object, file, or program that can be manipulated by the user.

Import: To bring information from one program or system to another.

IP: Stands for the "internet protocol address" that identifies the host (computer).

Log on: The process of identifying oneself in order to connect to a computer or website.

Mainframe computer: A computer designed for major and intensive computational tasks.

Meltdown: The complete collapse of a computer network often caused by an overload of traffic.

Menu: The list of options of programs from which to select.

Modem: The device enabling a computer to receive and transmit over a standard telephone line.

Netiquette: Network and Internet etiquette.

Newbie: Inexperienced user on Internet.

Online: Capable of communicating with another computer.

Operating System: Software controlling usage of hardware resources, such as disk space, memory, and CPU time.

Password: Identification code.

Pixel: Sometimes referred to as pel, the picture element forming an image produced on screen by a computer or on paper by a printer.

Portal: A website that serves as a gateway to the Internet consisting of a variety of links, content, and services to guide the user to other sites.

Search engine: A program on the Internet that searches for keywords in files and documents.

Server: A local network controlling access to the Internet and its resources.

Sleep: A mode that allows your computer to suspend all unnecessary functions to save energy.

Spam: Unsolicited e-mail sent out to numerous recipients at one time.

URL: Abbreviation for "uniform resource locator" or the address of a resource on the Net.

Virus: Infectious intrusion of a computer.

Web browser: An application that provides the means to view HTML documents, go to links to other sites, and transfer files and programs.

Webmaster: Individual responsible for maintaining a site on the Web.

Window: Interfaces for applications on a monitor's screen—containing a document, program, or message.

Word processor: Electronic program for text-based documents.

Zip Drive: Removable disk capable of storing 100 megabytes of data or more.

WEB-REFERENCE LINKS

WRITER'S GUILD OF AMERICA: It's time for you to join!
www.wga.org

WRITE LINKS: Reference/resource sites
www.writelinks.com
www.resourcesforwriters.com

SECURITY: The National Fraud Information Center
www.fraud.org

HIGH-TECH CRIME NETWORK: Computer & high-tech crimes
www.htcn.org

CIA: Publications and handbooks
www.odci.gov/cia/publications/pubs.html

FBI: The Federal Bureau of Investigation
www.fbi.gov

U.S. DEPARTMENT OF JUSTICE: Home page giving you links to
organizations & information, press rooms, Freedom of
Information Act, publications and documents, business with
Department of Justice, Fugitives & Missing Persons and Justice
for Kids and Youth
www.usdoj.gov

ANTI-DEFAMATION LEAGUE: Hate crimes website
www.adl.org

LISTING LINKS TO U.S. AGENCIES & DEPARTMENTS:
Government site listing links to all government agencies both state
and federal, along with a multitude of government sites covering
almost every subject.
www.governmentguide.com

BOOKWIRE: R. R. Bowker's "Inside the Book Business" web page
www.bookwire.com

NATIONAL HOCKEY LEAGUE
(teams and team offices)

NHL League Headquarters
1251 Ave. of the Americas
New York, NY 10020
www.nhl.com

Atlanta Thrashers
1 CNN Ctr. or Box 105583
Atlanta, GA 30348

Boston Bruins
One Fleet Ctr., #250
Boston, MA 02114

Buffalo Sabres
Marine Midland Arena
One Seymour Knix 111 Plaza
Buffalo, NY 14201

Carolina Hurricanes
5000 Aerial Ctr., #100
Morrisville, NC 27560

Mighty Ducks of Anaheim
2695 E. Katella Ave.
Anaheim, CA 92803

Calgary Flames
P.O. Box 1540, Station M
Calgary, Alta T2P 3B9

Chicago Blackhawks
1901 W. Madison St.
Chicago, IL 60612

Colorado Avalanche
1635 Clay St.
Denver, CO 80204

Dallas Stars
211 Cowboys Pkwy
Irving, TX 75063

Detroit Red Wings
600 Civic Ctr. Dr.
Detroit, MI 48226

Edmonton Oilers
11230 110 St.
Edmonton, Alta. T5B 4M9

Florida Panthers
One Panther Pkwy
Sunrise, FL 33323

Los Angeles Kings
555 N. Nash St.
El Segundo, CA 90245

Montreal Canadiens
1260 Rue de La Gauchetiere
Quest, Montreal, Que H3B 5E8

Nashville Predators
501 Broadway
Nashville, TN 37203

New Jersey Devils
50 Rte 120 or P.O. Box 504
E. Rutherford, NJ 07073

New York Islanders
Nassau Veterans Coliseum
Uniondale, NY 11553

New York Rangers
Two Pennsylvania Plaza
New York, NY 10121

Ottawa Senators
1000 Palladium Dr.
Kanata, Ont. K2V 1A5

Philadelphia Flyers
First Union Center
3601 South Broad St.
Philadelphia, PA 19148

Phoenix Coyotes
Cellular One Ice Den

9375 E. Bell Rd.
Scottsdale, AZ 85260

Pittsburgh Penguins
Civic Arena
66 Mario Lemieux Pl.
Pittsburgh, PA 15219

St. Louis Blues
401 Clark
St. Louis, MO 63103

San Jose Sharks
525 W. Santa Clara St.
San Jose, CA 95113

Tampa Bay Lightening
401 Channelside Dr.
Tampa, FL 33602

Toronto Maple Leafs
Air Canada Center, 40 Bay St.
Toronto, Ont. M5J 2X2

Vancouver Canucks
800 Griffiths Way
Vancouver, BC V6B 6G1

Washington Capitols
601 F St. NW   incomplete
address-Washington, D.C. ??

Additonal SPORTS LEAGUE OFFICIAL OFFICES

Amateur Athletics Union Assn.
P.O. Box 10000
Lake Buena Vista, FL 32830
www.aausports.org

Amateur Softball Assn.
2801 NE 50th St.
Oklahoma City, OK 73111
www.softball.org

American Horse Shows Assn.
220 E 42nd St.
New York, NY no zip
www.ahsa.org

American Kennel Club
51 Madison Ave.
New York, NY 10010
www.akc.org

Canadian Football League
110 Eglinton Ave. W
Toronto, Ont M4R 1A3
www.cfl.ca

CART
755 W. Big Beaver Rd.
Troy, MI 48084
www.cart.com

Fish & Game Assn.
1301 E. Atlantic Blvd.
Pompano Beach, FL 33060
www.igfa.org

LPGA
100 International Golf Dr.
Daytona Beach, FL 32124
www.lpga.com

Little League Baseball
P.O. Box 3485
Williamsport, PA 17701
www.littleleague.org

Major League Soccer
110 E 42nd St. #1000
New York, NY 10017
www.misnet.com

NASCAR
1801 Intl.Speedway Blvd.
Daytona Beach, FL 32120
www.ncaa.org

NCAA
6201 College Blvd.
Overland Park, KS 66211
www.ncaa.org

National Rifle Assn.
11250 Waples Mills Rd.
Fairfax, VA 22030
www.nra.org

Pro Bowlers Assn
P.O. Box 5118
Akron, OH 44334
www.pbatour.com

PGA
100 Ave. of Champions
Palm Beach Gardens, FL 33410
www.pgaonline.com

Pro Rodeo Cowboys Assn.
101 Pro Rodeo Dr.
Colorado Springs, CO 80919
www.prorodeo.com

Special Olympics
1325 G St. NW, #500
Washington, DC 20005
www.specialolympics.org

Thoroughbred Racing Assns.
420 Fair Hill Dr.
Elkton, MD 21921
www.traofna.com

USA Track & Field
1 RCA Dome #140
Indianapolis, IN 46225
www.usatf.org

U.S. Auto Club
4910 W 16th St.
Speedway, IN 46224

U.S. Figure Skating Assn
20 First St.
Colorado Springs, CO 80906
www.usfsa.org

U.S. Olympic Committee
One Olympic Plaza
Colorado Springs, CO 80909
www.olympic-usa,org

U.S. Skiing Assn.
P.O. Box 100
Park City, UT 84060
www.usskiteam.com

U.S. Soccer Federation
1801 S Prarie Ave.
Chicago, IL 60616
www.us-soccer.com

USA Swimming
One Olympic Plaza
Colorado Springs, CO 80909
www.usa-swimming.org

U.S. Tennis Assn.
70 W. Red Oak Lane
White Plains, NY 10601
www.usta.com

U.S. Trotting Assn.
750 Michigan Ave.
Columbus, OH 43215
www.ustrotting.com

WNBA
645 5th Ave.
New York, NY 10022
www.wnba.com

Writing the Second Act
Building Conflict and Tension in Your Film Script

Michael Halperin, Ph.D.

WRITING THE SECOND ACT

BUILDING

CONFLICT

AND

TENSION

IN YOUR FILM SCRIPT

MICHAEL HALPERIN

Every screenplay needs an attention-grabbing beginning and a satisfying ending, but those elements are nothing without a strong, well-crafted middle. The second act is where most of the action is: where your characters grow, change, and overcome the obstacles that will bring them to the resolution at the end of the story. Naturally, it's also the hardest act to write, and where most screenplays tend to lose momentum and focus. Author Halperin helps you slay the dragon with *Writing the Second Act*, designed especially for helping screenwriters through that crucial 60-page stretch. Structural elements and plot devices are discussed in detail, as well as how to keep the action moving and the characters evolving while keeping the audience completely absorbed in and entertained by your story.

MICHAEL HALPERIN is a professional writer whose numerous credits include TV shows (*Star Trek: The Next Generation, Quincy*), nonfiction books (*Writing Great Characters*), and interactive media programs (*Voyeur*). He has also worked extensively as a consultant in the television industry, including Executive Story Consultant for 20th Century Fox Television and Creative Consultant on the animated series *Masters of the Universe*. He currently teaches screenwriting at Loyola Marymount University in Los Angeles and is in the process of developing a business-to-business Web site for the entertainment industry.

$19.95, ISBN 0-941188-29-9
240 Pages, 6 x 9
Order # 49RLS

Script Magic
Subconscious Techniques to Conquer Writer's Block

Marisa D'Vari

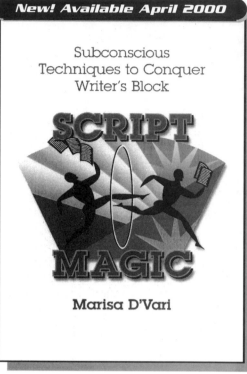

New! Available April 2000

Subconscious Techniques to Conquer Writer's Block

SCRIPT
MAGIC

Marisa D'Vari

Script Magic answers the prayers of every screenwriter who's ever spent time staring down a blank page. Pursuing the dream of landing that big script sale can be stressful, and that stress and pressure can be counter-productive to the writing process. *Script Magic* is a powerful antidote to writer's block that both professional and aspiring creative writers can benefit from, based on a deceptively simple principle: If you're not having fun writing it, your script probably isn't going to be any fun to read, either. And if it's not fun to read, how is it ever going to be sold and made into a movie that people will want to spend their money to see?

Using easy and fun techniques designed to circumvent the practical, critical conscious mind and tap into the rich creative resources of the subconscious mind, readers will learn how to revitalize their writing and improve their productivity. Create engaging characters, dialogue that jumps off the page and screenplays that sell!

MARISA D'VARI has 20 years of hands-on experience working in Hollywood as a studio story analyst, consultant and executive. She currently produces and hosts her own nationally syndicated cable TV show, "Scene Here," and conducts seminars on screenwriting all over the country. Visit her Web site at **www.scriptmagic.com**.

Doubleday Stage & Screen Selection

$18.95, ISBN 0-941188-74-4
250 pages, 6 x 9
Order # 47RLS

Screenwriting 101

The Essential Craft of Feature Film Writing

Neill D. Hicks

Hicks, a successful screenwriter whose credits include *Rumble in the Bronx* and *First Strike*, brings the clarity and practical instruction familiar to his UCLA students to screenwriters everywhere. In his refreshingly straightforward style, Hicks tells the beginning screenwriter how the mechanics of Hollywood storytelling work, and how to use those elements to create a script with blockbuster potential without falling into cliches. Also discussed are the practicalities of the business—securing an agent, pitching your script, protecting your work, and other topics essential to building a career in screenwriting.

"Neill Hicks makes complex writing concepts easy to grasp, in a way that only a master teacher could. And he does so while keeping his book one hell of a fun read."
Eric Edson, Screenwriter and Executive Director of the Hollywood Symposium

NEILL HICKS is a professional screenwriter and a senior instructor at the UCLA Extension Writer's Program, where he has been honored with the Outstanding Instructor Award. He has also taught graduate courses on screenwriting at the University of Denver, presented a seminar on Selling to Hollywood at the Denver International Film Festival, and conducts screenwriting workshops throughout the United States, Canada, and Europe. Visit his Web site at **www.screenwriting101.net**.

Movie Entertainment Book Club Selection
Doubleday Stage and Screen Selection

$16.95, ISBN 0-941188-72-8
220 pages, 6 x 9
Order # 41RLS

The Writer's Journey
—2nd Edition
Mythic Structure for Writers

Christopher Vogler

1st Edition - Over 100,000 Sold!

THE WRITER'S JOURNEY
2ND EDITION
MYTHIC STRUCTURE FOR WRITERS

CHRISTOPHER VOGLER

See why this book has become an international best seller, and a true classic. First published in 1992, *The Writer's Journey* explores the powerful relationship between mythology and storytelling in a clear, concise style that's made it required reading for movie executives, screenwriters, scholars, and lovers of pop culture all over the world.

Writers of both fiction and non-fiction will discover a set of useful myth-inspired storytelling paradigms (i.e. *The Hero's Journey*) and step-by-step guidelines to plot and character development. Based on the work of Joseph Campbell, *The Writer's Journey* is a must for writers of all kinds interested in further developing their craft.

The updated and revised 2nd edition provides new insights and observations from Vogler's ongoing work on mythology's influence on stories, movies, and man himself.

> *"This is a book about the stories we write, and perhaps more importantly, the stories we live. It is the most influential work I have yet encountered on the art, nature, and the very purpose of storytelling."*
> **Bruce Joel Rubin**, Screenwriter, *Ghost, Jacob's Ladder*

Book of the Month Club Selection • Writer's Digest Book Club Selection • Movie Entertainment Book Club Selection • Doubleday Stage and Screen Selection

CHRIS VOGLER has been a top Hollywood story consultant and development executive for over 15 years. He has worked on such top grossing feature films as *The Thin Red Line*, *Fight Club*, *The Lion King*, and *Beauty and the Beast*. His international workshops have taken him to Germany, Italy, United Kingdom and Spain, and his literary consulting service Storytech provides in-depth evaluations for professional writers. To learn more, visit his Web site at **www.thewritersjourney.com**.

$22.95, ISBN 0-941188-70-1
300 pages, 6 x 9
Order # 98RLS

Myth & the Movies

Discovering the Mythic Structure of 50 Unforgettable Films

Stuart Voytilla

Foreword by **CHRISTOPHER VOGLER**, author of "The Writer's Journey"

With this collection of essays exploring the mythic structure of 50 well-loved U.S. and foreign films, Voytilla has created a fun and fascinating book for film fans, screenwriters, and anyone with a love of storytelling and pop culture.

An informal companion piece to the best-selling *The Writer's Journey* by Christopher Vogler, *Myth and the Movies* applies the mythic structure Vogler developed to films as diverse as "Die Hard," "Singin' in the Rain" and "Boyz N the Hood." This comprehensive book offers a greater understanding of why some films continue to touch and connect with audiences generation after generation.

Movies discussed include *Annie Hall, Beauty and the Beast, Chinatown, Citizen Kane, E.T., The Fugitive, The Godfather, The Graduate, La Strada, The Piano, Pulp Fiction, Notorious, Raiders of the Lost Ark, The Searchers, The Silence of the Lambs, T2–Judgment Day, Sleepless in Seattle, Star Wars, Unforgiven,* and many more.

STUART VOYTILLA is a writer, script consultant, and teacher of acting and screenwriting. He has evaluated hundreds of scripts for LA -based talent agencies. His latest screenplay, *The Golem,* is being produced by Baltimore-based Princess Pictures.

Movie Entertainment Book Club Selection

$26.95, ISBN 0-941188-66-3
300 pages, 7 x 10, illustrations throughout
Order # 39RLS

Stealing Fire From the Gods

A Dynamic New Story Model for Writers and Filmmakers

James Bonnet

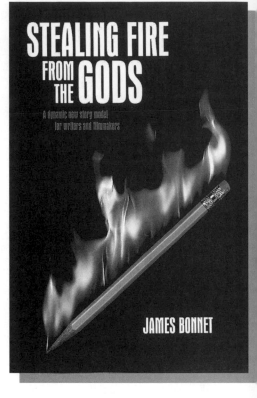

Great stories affect us so much because they teach us about life, and about ourselves. In the tradition of Carl Jung, Joseph Campbell and Christopher Vogler, James Bonnet explores the connection between mythology and personal growth—and the implications that connection has for storytellers in particular.

Unlike films, novels, and other forms of modern storytelling we're accustomed to today, the great myths, legends and fairy tales passed down through the ages were not created by individual authors. They evolved from ancient oral traditions, fueled by forces within the creative unconscious that are still accessible to us today. *Stealing Fire From the Gods* investigates those forces and teaches writers how to use the same elements that make those traditional tales so enduring to make your own stories more powerful, memorable and emotionally resonant. Author James Bonnet takes you on a journey through the creative process of storytelling, uncovering not only what makes a story great but also how the creative process can reconnect us to our lost or forgotten inner selves.

JAMES BONNET, founder of Astoria Filmwrights, is a successful Hollywood screen and television writer. He has acted in or written more than forty television shows and features including *Kojak*, *Barney Miller* and the cult classics *The Blob* and *The Cross and The Switchblade*. Visit his Web site at **www.storymaking.com**.

Movie Entertainment Book Club Selection

$26.95, ISBN: 0-941188-65-5
300 pages, 6 x 9
Order # 38RLS

Fade In: The Screenwriting Process
—2nd Edition

Bob Berman

A classic used by professionals and universities around the world since the first edition debuted in 1988, *Fade In* is a concise, step-by-step road map for developing a story concept into a finished screenplay. In addition to covering the basics of screenwriting—everything from structure and character development to terminology, form and writing revisions, Berman shares his experiences as a screenwriter who got his start relatively late in life. Readers can glean valuable tips and insights on the realities of breaking into the professional screenwriting "biz" and how the whole system works, from getting your script read to getting an agent to making deals.

Also included is the author's original script, *Dead Man's Dance*, complete with an agent's critique of this screenplay.

BOB BERMAN is a screenwriter and a professional nonfiction writer. He currently lives in Westchester County, New York where he has begun work on a new screenplay and conducts private script consultations.

$24.95, ISBN 0-941188-58-2
350 pages, 6 x 8-1/4
Order # 30RLS

MICHAEL WIESE PRODUCTIONS

11288 Ventura Blvd., Suite 821
Studio City, CA 91604
1-818-379-8799
mwpsales@mwp.com
www.mwp.com

Write or Fax
for a
free catalog.

Please send me the following
books:

Title	Order Number (#RLS___)	Amount
_____	_____
_____	_____
_____	_____
_____	_____

SHIPPING _____

California Tax (8.00%) _____

TOTAL ENCLOSED _____

Please make check or money order payable to
Michael Wiese Productions

(Check one) ___ Master Card ___ Visa ___ Amex

Credit Card Number_____

Expiration Date_____

Cardholder's Name_____

Cardholder's Signature_____

SHIP TO:

Name_____

Address_____

City_____State_____Zip_____

Order online for the lowest prices at
www.mwp.com